HAWKERS & WALKERS
in Early America

SECOND EDITION

THE YANKEE PEDDLER

From the drawing by Felix O. C. Darley in Frank Leslie's Weekly

The first Yankee peddlers were young men. able to cope with the dangers of the wilderness through which they had to travel. Subsequently older men took up the peddler's pack

HAWKERS & WALKERS
in Early America

*STROLLING PEDDLERS, PREACHERS
LAWYERS, DOCTORS, PLAYERS, AND
OTHERS, FROM THE BEGINNING TO
THE CIVIL WAR*

By
Richardson Wright
Editor of *House and Garden*

WITH 68 ILLUSTRATIONS
FROM OLD SOURCES

Imprinted and Published by
J. B. LIPPINCOTT COMPANY
in the City of Philadelphia

THIRD IMPRESSION

TO
EVELYN AND FRANCIS L. WURZBURG

FOREWORD

OOK down upon a road and you see people end-
lessly coming and going. Stand a moment and
watch them. Where are they going? Why are
they travelling? What do they carry? Whence
have they come?

Many things may set a man's feet upon the road: love of a
woman; the quest of adventure; the need and desire for money;
the pursuing of pleasure.

To-day the traffic is bent mostly on pleasure and the pursuit
of money. Huge trucks rumbling along with their burdens of merchandise, oil, machinery, food. Obese buses swollen with travellers and their luggage. A doctor's car, the green cross on its
radiator. The mail-truck crammed with bags and packages.
Countless groups of men and women, youths and maidens, speed-
ing for the pleasure of the ride, and to get where pleasure is to be
found. Men darting along to business appointments. Workmen
in luxurious or decrepit cars going to or coming from the fat job
or the lean one. Whole families squeezed into ancient, baggage-
freighted motors. Even Gypsies, gaudy in bright clothes and
spangles, ride proudly by in automobile-caravans gaily bedecked.
Scarce anyone is afoot. Such glimpses as the swift passing
affords bear witness to the great variety of nationalities and races
in the pageant.

And still, through the hastening and obvious tides of to-day's
traffic weave the slower and almost ghostly tides of all the past.
Let the eye pierce this palpable and vivid scene before us to the
more deliberate panorama of a hundred years ago!

The truck fades into a blue and red Conestoga wagon, goods
piled under its canvas-covered top, and horses straining at the
load. The Gargantuan bus shrinks to a stage coach. The doctor's
motor to a doctor's gig. The mail wagon is drawn by horses and
carries a passenger or two. There are fewer men and women
going forth for pleasure, and such as do, ride in a coach and four,
though now and then a farm wagon holds a family going to the

7

fair or market in town. The roads are narrower and wind through the shade of tall trees. Coach and carriage and gig and wagon joggle and sway along the rutted road. The Gypsies travel in a cart with a string of ponies trailing behind. There are peddler's wagons loaded with tinware from Connecticut, pottery from New Jersey, and dress goods from Philadelphia. Bundles of brooms bob at the back like great plumes, and beneath the body of the cart sway balloon-shaped bags of paper rags. A parson passes by on horseback, perhaps a crazy-haired itinerant preacher headed for a protracted meeting; or a colporteur, his saddle-bags stuffed with Bibles and tracts. A farmer herds sheep along the road to town and the slaughter house. Other animals pass—animals in cages gaudy with paint and religious scenes, an elephant padding laboriously in their wake. Occasionally, a theatrical troupe in coaches, their scenery and costumes dragged in a big wagon behind. Now and then a judge passes by in state in a coach, riding his circuit. A clock peddler passes, his clocks stowed in portmanteaus lashed to his horse. Men afoot—men with packs on their backs, trudging from house to house selling Yankee notions. Hawk-nosed New Englanders most of them are, with an occasional Jew and German and Dutchman. Itinerant workmen are here too—journeymen carpenters, and shoemakers, printers, cabinet-makers, tinkers, tailors, painters, and labourers seeking work. Many of them are barefoot.

Once again peer through these tides of traffic—to two hundred years ago.

The Conestoga wagon gives place to a string of pack ponies hauling goods. The horses have bells at their collars which jingle as they pass. The coach has gone. Most of the people are on horseback and afoot, for the road is often too narrow and too rough even for a cart. Peddler and parson, peep-showman and dancing teacher, doctor and worker, all trudge by slowly but no less determinedly. A post-boy joggles along on horseback, tooting his horn. The road is merely a trail. Where trees have fallen across it, the scant traffic turns aside into the wood or meadow. The people all have the same racial look, save where a band of

Indians, their squaws bent beneath loads, trudge toward a settlement or trading post. Scarcely anyone is travelling for pleasure. Most of them are bent on the pursuit of a living. The tide moves haltingly.

Through these mists look back again—three hundred years.

The scene is primitive and primeval. A blazed trail threads its narrow way through forest and over meadow. Indians are evident on all sides. A deer springs across the path and an occasional bear pads along it, snuffing the ground. Suddenly you come to a clearing, the tree stumps still in the field. A log cabin stands there, its windows mere gun slits.....

The great oak slab door pulls back slowly. A man appears on the threshold. Women and children follow him. He is carrying a pack and a gun is in his hand. The women gather about him as if fearful of what may happen. These are times when men go into the forest and never appear again. These are days when, coming back to their homes, they find them in ashes, their women and children slain or carried away.

Finally he bids them adieu, shoulders his pack, takes one last glance at the cabin and the group before it, and turns his face toward the trail. A moment and he is lost in its depths.

The first trader. The first peddler. The first faint movement of commerce.

CONTENTS

ILLUSTRATIONS

13

ILLUSTRATIONS 15

HAWKERS AND WALKERS
in Early America

CHAPTER I

THE YANKEE PEDDLER

 CLOUD hung over the domestic peace of the Bronson Alcott home.

Having educated that embryo Transcendentalist up to the point where he was ready to enter Yale, his parents and other doting relatives sat stiffly in their chairs pondering his future. They were about to state just what it was they wanted him to do and to become, when, speaking his own mind, into this august council, young Bronson tossed a bomb. Yale was a nice place, he said, but he'd much rather take to the road. Perhaps if he wandered down South he might pick up an occasional job teaching. Yankee teachers were in demand down there.

Their fond plans baulked, the family uttered a feeble protest or two, and succumbed to his entreaties. Thereby Yale lost a brilliant son and the ranks of the peddlers gained a picturesque and persistent recruit. For he didn't try very hard to land teaching jobs, and they rarely materialized. When he reached Norfolk, he became a trunk-peddler, hawking tinware and almanacs from door to door. With the money he made on this first trip he went to New York where he plunged to the extent of the best suit of clothes Broadway could provide. And in this sporty raiment he strutted up and down the streets of Wolcott, admired by his friends. So envious of this prosperity was his brother, Chatfield, that Bronson had no difficulty in persuading him to become a peddler. The two of them made anywhere from 33 to 200 per cent profit—sufficient inducement to keep them following the road for several years, not only in the South but in New Jersey as well.

And that was Bronson Alcott's youthful preparation for becoming one of the most brilliant thinkers of his day.

In its beginning his life story differed little from that of hundreds of youths and men who found adventure in peddling and who, as forerunners of our domestic commerce, helped to colour and make amusing and mildly picaresque the itinerant life of early America.

Each generation of young Americans has discovered its own vivid, distinctive, and picturesque variations of adventure. Trading with the savage Indian in the depths of the wilderness furnished enough excitement to satisfy the most lusty of youths. Indian wars and wars with other nations gave abundant outlets for the excess energy of young men who dreamed fierce dreams. Between these military forays, many youths found excitement and, incidentally, their business education, along the easier-going—but none the less adventuresome—paths of peaceful commerce that threaded their way from settlement to settlement and penetrated the awesome, virgin stretches of the frontiers.

For a long time in this country an active form of selling goods was peddling. Most of the peddlers, or chapmen, as they were often called, hailed from New England, Connecticut especially.

Their trade fell into various branches. There were the general peddlers, who hawked an assortment of useful "Yankee notions"—pins, needles, hooks and eyes, scissors, razors, combs, coat and vest buttons, spoons, small hardware, children's books, cotton goods, lace and perfume. Besides there were the specialized itinerant dealers—tin-peddlers, clock-peddlers, chair-peddlers, peddlers of spices, essences, dyes, woodenware, pottery, brooms, books, and a host of other items; and even these specialists, as we shall see, often carried several side lines of goods and did many other things beside selling their wares. Sometimes they vended very cumbersome articles—washing machines, spinning wheels, cabinet organs, and winnowing machines and corn shellers. Even wagon-makers hawked their product and they could be met driving through the country with a train of light carts or carriages; and in winter they had a string of sleighs lashed together. There were, in addition, the peddlers on the canals and rivers, and the wholesale itinerant merchants. A still further distinction can be made between local peddlers with a relatively small route and those who travelled great distances.

The dealer in small wares, essences and such, was called a "trunk-peddler," because he carried his goods in one or two small, oblong, tin trunks slung on his back by a webbing harness or a leather strap.

Although in Colonial times the peddler's stock was limited to a few items, by 1830 it had extended to all sorts of merchandise. Large wagons loaded with drygoods, hats, boots, shoes, clocks, firearms, hardware, and even furniture became a common sight on our country roads.

From house to house the peddler went, from town to town. And quite a flutter he caused when he appeared on the village green and opened his pack. Women dropped their chores and men their work, and gathered about to hear gossip of the neighbourhoods the peddler had recently left, and to see his wares.

A peripatetic merchant, he showed up wherever there was a chance for a sale. Not only did he visit the isolated country homes with his stock of goods, but he managed to be present on market days in town, at vendues or auction sales, on military training days, and at the spring and autumn country fairs.

May and November were the usual months for these fairs, and sometimes they lasted three days. To them farmers brought their horses and cattle for sale and sundry goods of household manufacture. There were sports and bouts of all kinds, accompanied by a noise of blaring trumpets and scratchy fiddles and screeching whistles and of people having a good time.

Training or regimental muster-days, when the local militia paraded, were also exciting events to which peddlers and mountebanks flocked. In Colonial times they were called Train Band Days. For a week prior, the town would be denuded of boards and joists to make booths, and the shops of molasses to make gingerbread and candy. The country people brought in cider and apples and nuts and buns for sale. And everyone felt generous and proud of the militia and all were intent on enjoying themselves. It was the sort of occasion when they didn't mind spending a penny or two on the trinkets the peddlers offered.

THE YOUNG PEDDLERS

The early peddler, if contemporary documents are to be believed, was a lanky and hawk-beaked youth; an adventurous, brave, mercenary fellow, who had a rare understanding of human nature and a ready tongue. His most effective salesmanship was the "soft sawder" of flattery. He was accused of purveying wooden nutmegs and cucumber seeds, oak-leaf cigars, shoe-peg oats, polyglot Bibles (all in English) and realistically painted basswood hams. He was, moreover, a commercial bird of passage. He always left his customers convinced and satisfied with their share of the bargain, but he usually managed to clear out after finishing his deal.

In the social scheme of things his position was that of the mobile jelly between the two substantial layers of a cake. He did not belong to the settled, established and respectable merchant class, although, like the jelly and the layer, he clung to this upper crust and was related to it; nor, on the other hand, was he so totally dishonest and depraved as to belong to the lower layer of persistent rogues.

When Timothy Dwight, the president of Yale, wrote his "Travels in New England and New York" in 1823, he observed that "many of these young men employed in this business, part at an early period with both modesty and principle. Their sobriety is exchanged for cunning, and their **decent** behaviour for coarse impudence." He even went so far as to say that "no course of life tends more rapidly or more effectually to eradicate every moral feeling." The latter statement, however, is characteristic of the Cloth in all ages; whatever exuberant youth does, the clergy consider wrong. And these peddlers were young men.

The fact of youth is important. The first peddlers had to be reckless, bright young fellows with abundant grit and virility, capable of taking care of themselves. They had to cope with the potentialities and dangers of long and solitary stretches of wilderness between towns—the trackless way, the fearsome beasts and the insolent Indian. To venture a peddling journey from Connecticut to Georgia would excite more comment, fear, and local wonder, than a journey to Tibet would to-day. These youths had to supply much of their own food and slept in the open most of the time. Men who could venture this could venture anything. And, when they did encounter a town or a civilized spot, they set out with gusto to paint the place a deep vermilion!

One staid, local New England historian classes peddlers with rum dealers and gamblers, calling them a dissolute lot, because they would show up at regimental musters, and trouble invariably ensued. Always rowdies, these peddlers!

Another observer, writing in a paper that bears the fearsome name of *The Penny Magazine of the Society for the Diffusion of Useful Knowledge* and published in London (an excellent little periodical despite its title) explains to its seekers after useful knowledge that "even the Americans themselves—possessing a respectable share of self-esteem—do not estimate very highly the character of their peddlers; this, no doubt, owing to the many ingenious frauds and deceptions which some of them have, from time to time, been detected in, and yet, while it would be considered a grave misdemeanour in any regular tradesman who would attempt the very same species of knavery, yet when a peddler is detected in having sold you, from the store of his spice-box, wooden nutmegs instead of the true and genuine East Indian article, instead of any particular odium attaching to him for having cheated you, you get heartily laughed at for having suffered yourself to be imposed upon, while he escapes with the fruits of imposition and the general remark, 'I guess it was only a regular Yankee peddler trick.'"

The reputation the early peddler won was enjoyed by chapmen of even so late a date as the Civil War. In fact, it was shrewdly turned to account as a bit of humour in the introductory remarks that preceded the bargaining. A peddler would drive up to a house and blithely address his prospective customer in some such patter as this: "Madam, are you in need of any pocket saw-mills? Horn gun flints? Basswood hams? Wooden nutmegs? White oak cheeses? Tin bung-holes? Or calico hog troughs?" And having gained the smile of the lady of the house, he proceeded to recite what he actually did have in his wagon—tinware, mats, glassware, brooms, washboards, clothes pins, rolling pins, matches, paddy irons, kettles, and pots.

The young peddler of the beginning days rarely kept to the trade all his life; after a time he settled down. His travels afforded him a fairly complete survey of the rural markets; he could judge the best neighbourhoods in which to open a store. Often there was a girl in the case—some country lass in a country town. There the peddler settled, opened up a general store, and passed into the respectability of the merchant class.

PEDDLING AS A START IN LIFE

Edward Ward, who made a trip to New England in 1699 observes of Boston that "in the chief or High Street there are stately Edifices, some of which have cost the owners two or three Thousand Pounds the raising . . . For the Fathers of these Men were Tinkers and Peddlers." Even so early was peddling recognized as the first step in the amassing of a fortune.

Jumping to a later date—1750—we read the story of James Duncan, one of the first settlers of Londonderry, Vermont, who started out in early life "with a small pack of goods as a peddler, and from this small beginning he rose to be quite an extensive merchant."

When he was a young man, Benedict Arnold went among the Dutch at the head of the Hudson and into Canada selling woollen goods—stockings, caps, mittens, etc.,—which his father-in-law obtained from Connecticut in exchange for merchandise that he imported from the West Indies. Arnold also traded in Canadian horses that he brought down to New York, together with poultry, corn, and fish, and then shipped to Jamaica for sale.

Collis P. Huntington, a Connecticut Yankee, laid the foundation of his business career by acquiring a small consignment of goods in New York and travelling for six years through the South and the West peddling and collecting notes for Connecticut clock manufacturers. These travels gave him an idea of the topography of the land that later helped him in his railroad developments. He started this peddling when he was a mere lad. When he was twenty-one he established a general store at Oneonta, New York, the largest of its kind in that section. In '49 he went to the gold fields, trading *en route* and in Sacramento set up a store for miners. The rest of his career is concerned with the Central Pacific and Southern Pacific Railroads. Thus from a peddler's pack started the great fortune that now acquires priceless master paintings and rare books for the public education and delight.

B. T. Babbitt, the soap manufacturer, whose product is known to every housewife, was a razor strop and Yankee notions peddler as a young man. John Boynton, through whose munificence Worcester Polytechnic Institute was founded in 1865, acquired his first money as a maker and peddler of tinware.

These are a mere handful picked at random from the countless stories of the beginnings of successful lives that can be traced to the peddler's pack. For many men, peddling was the first step they took in their commercial careers. Perhaps their descendants to-day may not wish to stress this fact, but their own biographies tell the story, and it is one for which they need have no reason to blush.

THE CHANGE IN PEDDLERS

As the years passed, the type of man who took to peddling changed considerably. From the reckless, young fellows of the beginning, youths capable of finding their own way and taking care of themselves in the wilderness, peddling slipped into the hands of older men, as the roads became safer and the wilderness less fearsome. Many of them were incompetent for any other sort of work—queer characters, born vagabonds, commercial Ishmaelites, for whom the highway held an irresistible fascination. Some of these old men were horse-and-cart peddlers, but not a few of them continued trunk-peddling and went afoot.

Those who can remember these old trunk-peddlers always recall two features about them—that their trunks held an amazing assortment of small wares and that they were packed with a skill only long experience would bring. They came to a house, laid out their stock of goods, perhaps made a ten-cent sale, and then slowly put their goods back again. How did it ever pay them? They evidently lived on hand-outs and slept in barns. No one ever heard of their retiring rich.

Of course, not all the peddlers slept in barns or were obliged to suffer hardships. At the Hartford Atheneum is preserved a quaint document that bears the title: *Arrival and Departure of Pedlars or The Pedlars' and Yankees' Log Book.* It lists the itinerants who put up at the old Wadsworth Tavern on Albany Avenue, Hartford, between August 1, 1820, and March 24 of the following year. In that time 147 of them patronized the inn.

Some taverns, though, were averse to entertaining these

THE PACK PEDDLER

THE BASKET-PEDDLER AND HIS CART

lowly vagrants. Buckthorn Inn, in New York City, for example, displayed, with amazing commercial candor, a sign that read:

> Four pence a night for a bed
> Six pence with supper
> No more than five to sleep in one bed
> No boots to be worn in bed
> Organ grinders to sleep in the wash house
> No dogs allowed upstairs.
> No beer allowed in the kitchen
> No Razor grinders or Tinkers taken in.

PEDDLERS AND THE OPENING OF THE FRONTIERS

Both young and old, these peddlers played an unforgettable rôle in the romance of our early widening frontiers. The first commercial move westward was made by Indian traders —the Dutch of New York and the Pennsylvanian, who carried goods into the territory lying beyond the fringe of the settlements. The Dutch were trading regularly with the Iroquois at Albany by 1700. But these New Yorkers were not very intrepid merchants. When they reached an advantageous point, they built a fort and a trading post, and the Indians were induced to bring in their pelts for exchange. The Pennsylvanians, on the other hand, were a more adventurous, crafty and chivalrous crowd. Their pack trains crossed the Alleghanies and penetrated to the Ohio and the Wabash in the early years of the eighteenth century. They carried a variety of goods which were bartered for pelts. Now and then, when they could escape the eye of the authorities, they sold arms and ammunition to the Indians. The Pennsylvanian traders also had a line of trading cloth called "duffels" and "strouds." As early as 1727 these hardy Pennsylvanian traders with their pack horses were developing commerce along the Ohio with the Mingoes, Delawares and Shawnees.

When emigrants began to filter into these regions, the old Indian traders—usually Irish and Scotch-Irish—often took to peddling and to pack-training.

While this fur trader was the first commercial agent to make a peaceable penetration of the opening western lands, the Yankee notions-peddler from New England followed on the heels of migration. Whether it was the California Trail or the Oregon, we find him quick to take advantage of these new markets. And he had not only the settlers to sell to, but the Indians as well. One expedition to Oregon in 1832 encountered three vehicles containing a gross of axes for the Indian market, vermilion and other paints, glass beads, small looking-glasses, tawdry trinkets, cheap knives, buttons, nails, hammers, and other articles on which young Indians of both sexes set a high value and white men little or none.

Again and again in the early tales of the expansion of the nation westward and southward, we find travellers making note of these itinerant merchants. They would pop up in the most unexpected places. Even Horn's *Overland Guide to California*—the Baedeker of the forty-niners—contains the advertisement of a Mr. Sypher in Fort Des Moines, who is willing to supply peddlers with drygoods, groceries, hardware, cutlery, caps, boots and shoes, books and stationery, drugs, medicines, paints, oils and dye-stuffs at the lowest possible rates.

In many instances peddling was the means of support by virtue of which migrating settlers made their way to their new homes. An Ephraim Davis (to note one instance out of many) when he reached the age of 21 and was seized with a lust for frontier life, invested his adolescent savings in Yankee notions and, filling two tin trunks, slung them over his shoulder and peddled his way westward across the New England States and up through the Mohawk Valley until, in the autumn of 1791, he reached the spot he planned to settle in. There he made his home, founded the first iron forge and cotton mill in the locality, and served a useful purpose in his chosen spot. His simple annals were brought to a close in 1854.

But there was more to the Yankee peddler's rôle in the

widening of the frontier than the mere selling of goods. These young men with packs on their backs were the forerunners of whole groups that left their New England farms to settle in the new West. They surveyed the possibilities of various regions and, on returning home, reported their findings. They were the scouts for that great migration westward and southward of the hardy New England stock which first peopled the frontiers—part of that half million souls who between the Revolution and 1800 moved into western New York, Virginia, Tennessee, and Kentucky.

Scarcely a town in New England but was represented on the road by one or more itinerants. Meriden, Connecticut, sent thirty to forty of its young men constantly on the roads of the South and the West. From Wolcott, Connecticut, ten youths fared forth every year. Weare, New Hampshire, was represented by fifteen peddlers at one time. Such were the young men who brought back to their New England homes news of the land Manasseh Cutler led his people to in the Marietta region of the Northwest Territory, news of the rich Mississippi Valley, of the wide prairies of Illinois, of the vastness of Texas, and of the possibilities that lay at the ends of the Oregon and California Trails.

THE PEDDLER AS A NATIONAL FIGURE

The Yankee peddler was the whipping-boy of our early national life, the butt of national jokes and the target of all visitors to America. To-day foreigners in our midst make invidious comparisons with regard to our over-heated homes, our over-pampered wives and our unnecessary skyscrapers. Previous to the Civil War they found the peddler and the American spitting habit two great points of divergence between the crude life of this country and the older civilization of their own.

The peddler observations of these visitors would fill many pages. Let us be satisfied with one—a torrid one—from

Thomas Hamilton who came here in 1833 and wrote "Men and Manners in America"—"The whole race of Yankee peddlers in particular are proverbial for dishonesty. They go forth annually in the thousands to lie, cog, cheat, swindle, in short, to get possession of their neighbour's property in any manner it can be done with impunity. Their ingenuity in deception is confessedly very great. They warrant broken watches to be the best time-keepers in the world; sell pinchbeck trinkets for gold; and always have a large assortment of wooden nutmegs and stagnant barometers." Evidently Mr. Hamilton had reason for his acrimonious attack, but we question his statement about the nutmegs. No case in court has been found to prove this wooden nutmeg charge.

And yet, despite his unsavory reputation, we must realize that the peddler was such a national figure that the fiction of early America could not be written without him. It is a poor Colonial or post-Revolutionary novel that has not somewhere a peddler character. Cooper's "Spy"—Harvey Birch—was a peddler; Rip Van Winkle's wife died from a fit of anger at a peddler. In 1877 a German novel published in Cincinnati, and written by Otto Ruffins, was called "The Peddler," and used a Jewish notion hawker for its hero. In later days, Robert W. Chambers' "Cardigan" centres around a peddler's activities and even so recent a Revolutionary novel as "Drums" gives the peddler prominence. Indeed it is a significant fact that the first humourous figure in American literature was a peddler—Sam Slick—who travelled through New England and Canada selling clocks to people who didn't want them and at a price far beyond their value. Tales of Sam's wise sayings and sly dealings tickled the humour of our forefathers, because Sam was a type familiar to them everywhere before and after the Revolution.

Even poets conceded him a niche in their gallery of worthies. One Connecticut bard, Joseph H. Nichols, years ago drew this pleasant picture of the Yankee peddler:—

With what a gay and tidy air
 The tavern shows its painted sign,
Causing each traveller to stare
 And cypher out the gold-leaf line.
And yonder is the merchant's stand,
 Where, on the benches round the door,
Gather the story-telling band.
 And all burst out in hearty roar
As some wild wag, at his tongue's rote
 Deals the convulsive anecdote.

Why is the dust in such a rage?
 It is the yearly caravan
Of peddlers, on their pilgrimage
 To southern marts; full of japan,
And tin, and wooden furniture,
 That try to charm the passing eye;
And spices which, I'm very sure,
 Ne'er saw the shores of Araby;
Well skilled in that smooth eloquence
 Are they, which steals away your pence.

CHAPTER II

THE RISE OF THE YANKEE PEDDLER

INCE such a pronounced sectional type as the Yankee peddler does not spring full-fledged from a people, how, then, was he evolved? How did the Yankee become a trader? Why was he sharper than other traders? Whence came the articles he sold?

After blowing away the dust of pious and pretty legends, we find that, like anyone else, the Yankee peddler and his goods were the result of a struggle against geographic environment.

Geography plays strange tricks on settlers in a new land. Two bands of emigrants driven out by the same sort of governmental and ecclesiastical pressure, leave the same rack-rented areas of the Old Country. Those who go to the rolling country and fat agricultural lands of Pennsylvania and the Carolinas become farmers. Those who go to the rock-riven terrain of New England become petty manufacturers, merchants, and peddlers. In North Carolina the McCullocks are owners of plantations; in Connecticut the Pattisons establish the tinware industry and start the tin-peddling trade.

The Puritans may have given New England the formula of a town built around a church, but subsequent settling and developing of the country and of commerce changed this to a town built around a factory. The geography of New England, the lay of the land, decided this.

Spread out a map of the Atlantic seaboard, and you will see how geography plays its hand. In the South and up to New York, the Appalachian Mountains are quite a distance from the coast. At New York they pinch in nearer the shore. Thereafter, through New England, they form a series of uplands and valleys and ridges. This position of the mountains made a difference in the areas of easily tillable land along the coast and this, in turn, bore its effect on the nature of the settlements.

The location of this first mountain range also affects the rivers of the Atlantic seaboard. In the South, the rivers are broad and deep and leisurely in flow and, not being broken by falls near the coast, permit navigation far inland. They are highways. In New England the rivers are smaller, swifter, more constant, more capable of supplying power to turn mill-wheels, and they are broken by cascades and falls that do not permit great distances of water transportation or invite inland travel.

There is also the difference in the soil. New England has a thin, boulder-filled clay for the most part, with a richer soil along the rivers and good upland pastures in New Hampshire, Vermont, and in parts of Maine. In the South most of the soil of the coastal plain is alluvial, deposited by rivers and floods. The one is difficult to work, the other relatively easy.

Several other factors shaped the destiny of New England —the rigorous climate, the hostility of the Indians, the dense forests that clothed the mountain sides and the proximity of the French in upper Maine and Canada. Because of these several influences, the New England settlements were, in the beginning, compact villages located in restricted areas along the coast and the main rivers.

The settling of the South, on the other hand, was more scattered. The Indians were friendly, the climate gentle, settlements of other European countries at a great distance, the soil easy to work, the rivers easy to navigate. These factors, together with the early introduction of slaves, fostered a system of large estates owned and controlled by an aristocratic class of proprietors. The South had few towns. Although legislatures of the Southern provinces attempted to create trading towns by law, they were unsuccessful. Even as late as the Revolution, these cross-roads "paper towns" were inconsequential.

Thus with its large plantations and scattered farming population, the South became a land of agriculture. New England became a neighbourhood of small farms, of compact villages and, when the rivers were dammed, as at Manchester, Lowell, Lawrence, and Holyoke, a land of manufacture.

The pinching in of the mountains and the intervention of the Dutch at New Amsterdam at first isolated New England. During this isolation the several Yankee provinces evolved a a similarity in political and religious codes. These factors tended to give New England a homogeneous character. Its people developed a distinctive type—the New England type. The peddlers from this district became distinctive peddlers— Yankee peddlers.

In Colonial days the average Pennsylvanian may have differed from the son of Maryland, and the Carolinian from the Georgian, but in no case would the difference have been so pronounced as in the case of the Yankee. Nicholas Creswell, a young Englishman travelling here in Revolutionary times, reports that no country dialects were to be distinguished between Americans "except it be the New Englanders, who have a sort of whining cadence."

This homogeneous character of New England was maintained for many years, owing to the fact that after 1640 she received practically no emigrants until about 1820, when the Irish and French Canadians began coming in. During that long time the birth rate was high. From this source came those men and women of distinctly New England type who went as pioneers to all sections of the country. From this source sprang the youths and men who penetrated all parts of the South and West as itinerant hawkers of goods.

In New England the attitude of the people toward trading was much more sympathetic than in the South, where the trader was considered poor trash by the upper classes. For years the majority of the manufactured goods bought by these classes was imported from England. The agricultural barons became the leaders of the people. Such trade as the South had was in the hands of representatives of English mer-

Backwoods types such as were encountered by the itinerants who travelled through the South. These were sketched by Captain Basil Hall in his travels through America in 1827-28

The product of the wood-turner's shop was often hawked around by the owner of the shop or one of his assistants

Coopering was a craft that employed journeymen workers
Sometimes the work was done on farms

chants and the coastwise trade in the hands of northern merchants who took their pay in tobacco and other local produce. North of Maryland, the influential class was composed of ministers and merchants.

The compact settlement which characterized New England was also a more sympathetic environment for manufacture than the scattered population of the South.

In manufacturing, one trade competes with another in ingenuity and skill, and one trade is dependent on another for mutual help and stimulation. The early blacksmiths needed occasional help from the cobbler and the wheelwright; the spinners and weavers called on the wood-turners, beammakers, and timber-sawyers; and they all competed with each other. The widely separated plantations of the South offered no such opportunity for competition and aid, consequently manufacturing was not likely to thrive there. Moreover, slave labour was not especially suited to manufacturing.

MANUFACTURING BEGINS

The sources of New England's domestic manufactured goods were first, the home and then the commercial factories of these provinces. Household industries of all sorts began early in New England. This is true especially of Connecticut, for there the household industries soon developed into commercial industries, whereas, in Massachusetts, the chief business of the beginning years was building and navigating ships, the fishing industry, and the resultant trade in fish.

Agriculture, of course, remained the backbone of the wealth of this section, together with shipping, fisheries, pelts, and cattle. Meantime, however, household industries were slowly laying the foundation of New England's industrial life. The transition from one to the other was very gradual. Not until the Civil War had New England finished her evolution from an agricultural to an industrial country. Not until the Civil War had the quaint creak of the domestic loom grown to the mighty chorus of ten thousand spindles in factories.

3

One of the first endeavours of the provincial governments was to encourage commercial manufacturing. Both in the North and the South bounties were offered to stimulate the growth of wool and the sowing of flax and their manufacture into cloth, the making of silk, paper, firearms, iron, and others. Despite this encouragement, for the first hundred years after the colonization of this country these attempts to introduce commercial manufacturing were unsuccessful. The Colonists had to depend on imported goods or goods made in their own homes.

In the years prior to the Revolution and immediately afterward, practically every household did some form of simple manufacturing. The majority of them were self-contained so far as clothing and crude equipment were concerned. Their women could spin and weave, their men build and repair. This self-contained state was the first step in household industries. Next the home was used as a place for making goods intended to be sold. One or two processes might be carried on at home and the remainder at a local factory. This was the second stage. Then the work went out of the home and the factory handled all the processes. Thus were household industries gradually transformed into commercial industries.

The same manufacturing tendencies were evident in some of the other colonies. Pennsylvania, with its political and religious freedom, attracted a polyglot population, and Philadelphia soon became a manufacturing and commercial centre.

Since manufacturing is a product of demand, and since the initial demand was local, the New England market first absorbed the output of its primitive household factories. As communications improved and the production was more than the local market required, there sprang up a brisk trade with the other colonies and with Canada, Bermuda, the Barbadoes, Jamaica and the mother country.

When the sales of the products of New England and the middle provinces began to cut into the business of English manufacturers then, in 1731, the first of many acts was passed restricting the manufacture of goods which could be made in New England. When Yankee ships began taking their wares to the Carribean Colonies and to England itself, the situation assumed the ominous proportions of a trade war.

These taxations and prohibitions invariably stimulated local manufacturing. The coastal blockades of the first two wars—The Revolution and 1812—sent the women to their spinning wheels and looms and the men to their anvils and lathes. Patriots refused to buy foreign-made goods. Consequently, the home industries and the distribution of the products of these industries increased a hundred fold. By 1820, however, the household industries in New England were being overshadowed by the first factories. Another twenty years found them going out completely.

These wares, both the home-manufactured and those imported, were distributed in two ways—through the retail shops of town merchants, and through the itinerant vending of peddlers who carried them from house to house and even to the most distant settlements.

EXPANDING MARKETS

The peddler's markets expanded with the growth of the Colonies and the States, the pushing westward of the frontiers, and with the establishment of roads, canals and other means of travel. Transportation then, as now, was essential to the success of manufacturing.

Once again geography exerts its influence. The broad rivers of the South were highways of commerce, and good roads developed slowly in that region because they were not required. Virginia was the only exception. In New England, where the narrow and falls-broken rivers compelled local governments to build roads and many of them, road traffic began as soon as the various settlements became established.

The order in which transportation advanced in this country was as follows: First, Indian trails and rivers; then the trails were developed into "tote" roads and new roads were

cut. By 1790 private companies and the nation began building turnpikes. At the same time rivers and lakes were connected by canals built under governmental and state direction.
Finally came the steamboat and the railroad. Each of these
steps bore its effect on the peddler's trade.

Since he carried his own stock of goods with him, and since
he often was, in the beginning, the maker of those goods, the
first peddler filled the triple rôle of manufacturer, salesman,
and transportation agent. Later, being employed by a manufacturer, he served in only the last two capacities. In the early
nineteenth century, many of the peddlers financed their own
stock or bought it from the manufacturer on time payments.

When travel between settlement and settlement was by a
blazed Indian trail, the peddler was limited in the area of his
route and in the quantity and kinds of goods he carried, because he went by foot or on horseback. With the trail widened
to a road and new roads cut, he took to a wagon, although in
those days the roads were not the graded and surfaced highways we know, but merely cleared alleys through forests,
across country, and through streams, at the fords. So poor
were the roads that in 1780 a horseman with a light load could
make no more than ten miles a day, and carts were out of the
question in many sections. The river traffic used canoes, small
sailing vessels, and flatboats poled along. The canal brought
into being the barge. With the introduction of steamboats
and with the coming of the railroads, all other forms of traffic
were reduced to secondary importance as carriers of goods.

HOW THE EARLY PEDDLER SOLD

The difference in currency between the colonies before
the Revolution and the confusion in currency that followed
it, made barter the only feasible method for rural sales. Practically all the trade of the countryside and the small towns
was carried on this way. The business of retail stores, taverns,
the doctor's bills, the minister's salary, the hire of labour and
such, were paid in kind, in farm produce—corn, rye, wheat,

flax—or in articles of household manufacture—blankets, coverlets, baskets. It was called "country pay." The merchants of a general store in Danbury, Connecticut, for example, advertised:

> "All kinds of country produce will be received in payment and every favour gratefully acknowledged. Good rock salt exchanged for flax seed or rye, even."

A person driving out of town took a bag of grain or a bundle of carded wool in his wagon or on his horse to pay his tavern expenses. We can scarcely realize what a dearth of cash means, we who have it jingling in our pockets. Yet our sturdy ancestors managed to survive without it. In the country areas actual money was often a rarity.*

The principle of a deal in bartering was to outwit the customer, to use such methods of what we call "salesmanship" that the peddler invariably got the better end of the bargain.

In cities some effort was made before the Revolution to arrive at a dependable price list. This is indicated by the legislation of various provinces and by the combination of merchants who in 1762 composed the United Company of Spermaceti Candlers. These manufacturers of candles in New England and Pennsylvania formed a trust that fixed market prices, controlled the supply of raw materials and attempted to oust competitors from the field. Isolated country districts, on the other hand, knew no such fixed prices. The era of one-price wares, of goods marked with prices, had not dawned; in fact, that era began within the memory of our generation. The peddler could ask all the traffic would bear. He was like

---

*Frederic Law Olmsted, in his travels in the Southern Cotton States during 1853-4, heard of men in isolated country districts who had never seen a dollar in their entire lives! For years in some sections of the South, the Spanish dollar was about the only silver known. It was cut with a hammer and chisel into halves and quarters (hence our common names for such values) and the quarters into "bits" and these again into "picayunes."

the medicine vendor in O. Henry's story: he respected his profession, and was satisfied with 300 per cent profit!

From the town, where he had acquainted himself with current prices, the peddler went into a thinly settled region and bartered his goods for farm produce and local wares. Having no notion of current town prices, the straw-chewing yokels could be persuaded to accept goods and pay for them in produce that, in the town, had a marketable value far in excess of what they had received in exchange.

The peddler always had the genial habit of "accommodatin'" his customers. He took an old book, or a chair or a piece of pewter in exchange for their purchases. Of course he always knew the value of these articles—which leads us to believe that peddlers were the first dealers in early American "antiques!"

There wasn't anything unusually dishonest about this sort of sharp transaction; business standards up to fifty years ago were of that nature.

THE YANKEE PEDDLER'S CONSCIENCE

That the Yankee peddler should put his local brand of conscience in his pocket when he started business is not so much the fault of that conscience as it was the fault of contemporary business standards. Commercial honesty had not yet cut its teeth.

Far greater than his work with kites and electricity, his invention of stoves and musical glasses, was Benjamin Franklin's resurrected fact that honesty is the best policy. To the commercial world of his day it was what the discovery of a new planet would be to the world of astronomy. His axiom (however unethical) put honesty on a business basis. It could be made a commercial asset. It paid! Hitherto it had been too fragile a virtue to be bandied about the mart. The early dealings with the Indians were about as disgraceful as anything could be. Vast tracts of lands had been filched from them for a few strings of beads and a bottle of whiskey. By

1622 Virginia had a glass-works whose sole output appears to have been beads for trading with the Indians! Quantities of pelts were bought for a handful of trinkets. Were some of the great fur merchants of early America—those who founded our alleged aristocracy—alive and carrying on their business to-day in their accustomed way, the Atlanta and Fort Leavenworth prisons would be nowhere near big enough to hold them. Pick out a later date, and you find that stones and sand were commonly slipped into bales of cotton to increase their weight. At one time before the Civil War, there lay on the wharves at Liverpool thousands of bales of American sanded cotton that the spinners refused to buy at any price. Examples could be produced by the hundreds. These are typical, however. And, if such was the standard of dealing alike with the savage native and with civilized countries, is it surprising that the smaller merchants and country peddlers displayed no rigidly upright ideals of commercial probity? Besides there was eminent Biblical authority for all this (and the Yankee was strong for Scriptural support); the son of Sirach in his *Wisdom* proclaimed that "a merchant shall hardly keep himself from doing wrong; and a huckster shall not be declared free from sin."

Early in their careers both Massachusetts and Connecticut enacted laws regulating the amount of profit a trader might make, but these seem to have been forgotten as the years passed, for the New England merchant soon managed to acquire an unsavory reputation for taking more than his share. Stephen Collins, a pre-Revolutionary Philadelphia merchant, called the Boston merchants "deceitful, canting, Presbyterian deacons." William Beekman, of New York, charged Connecticut business men with selling goods underweight and said, "Seven-eighths of the people I have credited in New England have proven to be such damned, ungrateful, cheating fellows that I am now almost afraid to trust any man in Connecticut though he be well recommended from others."

While all Yankee peddlers and merchants may not have

measured up to these standards, many of them did attain rather steep records for business acumen.

WHAT MADE THE YANKEE PEDDLER SHARP

Just as the struggle against geographic environment made the Yankee a producer of marketable goods, so it made the Yankee itinerant salesman of these goods smarter than the others.

The climate of the South creates easy living and a slow pace of life; whereas the climate of New England makes for keenness and a quicker pace. The Southern colonist took life as it came to him, abundantly; the New Englander had to fight for every necessity of life. This struggle gave the people a resilient vitality; it made them industrious and quick-witted. Having once sharpened his wits against the wits of his fellow Yankees, trading and bartering with people in more easy-going regions was child's play to the New England peddler.

True, the South had its household industries—each plantation made its shoes and its common clothes and simple necessities—but it made practically no surplus, and its social attitude was not conducive to the rise of a trading class. Consequently, it was in the South that the Yankee peddler found most of his trade. He had penetrated to the Carolinas as early as 1676 and gained such a monopoly of the local sales that a restrictive law was aimed against him.

The passing of the years and the industrial development of the South did not change this situation materially. Until long after the Civil War the South remained the happy hunting ground for Northern commerce. The seeds of some of the ill-feeling between the North and the South unquestionably were first planted through the activities of these Yankee peddlers.

It is unfortunate that the New England peddler bore the entire blame for the slick reputation American peddlers had. This is due simply to the fact that the majority of peddlers hailed from New England. To the outside world—to the islands in the Carribean, to England and to Continental countries whither some of these traders penetrated and their reputation doubtless preceded them—no local distinction was made. The Yankee trader was officially the American trader. To this day American commerce enjoys—or suffers under—the reputation it gained when the first Connecticut peddlers set forth with their packs of tinware and Yankee notions.

CHAPTER III

YANKEE NOTIONS

N THE course of their activities some of the Yankee peddlers laid the foundations of the big business of our present times. Others served an economic need that passed, and they passed with it. Still others bore descendants who figure almost unchanged among the itinerant salesmen of to-day.

The tinware peddler, as we shall see, started the great tin-plate industry. The indigo peddler answered a need that no longer exists. The book peddler finds his persisting progeny in our door-to-door book agents, and the medicine peddler was sire to those glib salesmen who go through parts of the country selling a "hoss" liniment that contains 60 per cent alcohol, and, although peppery, serves as a rural intoxicant when none other is available.

Since he was the dealer in the smallest articles, let us start with the trunk-peddler of Yankee notions of about the year 1800. He halts at your house, sets down his trunk, spreads out his stock and reveals an amazing assortment. Where do all these items come from? What part is he playing in the rise of their manufacture?

COMBS AND BUTTONS

In his stock are always found combs. The making of these began at West Newbury, Mass., was fathered by the peddling system, and for generations has been centered in the town of Leominster.

The first American combs were crude, wooden affairs, whittled out with a knife. In 1759, at West Newbury, Mass., Enoch Noyes began making horn combs with primitive machinery. These he peddled around the neighbourhood. Quite a local character was Enoch, a wit of sorts and a persistent old Tory. Like most of the people of his class and time, he went hatless and shoeless in summer. So fast did his business prosper that neighbours—farmers mostly—took it up, and the Provincial Congress of Massachusetts in 1774 recommended encouragement to this infant industry of the hornsmith. The women of Leominster also had a hand in the work; they polished the combs at home with wood ashes and water. At first these combs were wrapped in rough paper; by 1835 they were put up in boxes, a great aid to the itinerant salesman. Enoch Noyes and his descendants were in the comb business for 162 years. To-day Leominster is the centre of the world's horn comb industry. It is from that town and from smaller factories in Philadelphia and Meriden, Connecticut, that the trunk peddler's comb supply came. Brass and wooden combs, made for the Southern negro trade and distributed by peddlers, also had their source in Meriden.

Bone buttons, a later side-line of the horn industry, followed the brass, silver and pewter buttons of Colonial and Federal days, and all of them were peddled. E. C. Maltby of Northford, Connecticut, made buttons of bone, ivory, horn, and wood and kept four peddlers' carts on the road. By 1860 Connecticut was making 55 per cent of the buttons produced in the country.

JEWELLERY

Since jewellery is a mark of luxury, one does not expect to find much of it in the first years of this country. Men and women were too busy carving out a living for themselves and their children to afford or enjoy such luxuries. In the inventory of one New England housewife, Mistress Anne Hibben, we discover a gold wedding ring valued at sixteen shillings and a ring with a diamond at eight shillings. (It couldn't have been much of a diamond!). This was in 1656 and is a rare instance for primitive New England. All classes of the Dutch in New York wore jewellery and so did the French Huguenots and English of that city and neighbourhood. In

Pennsylvania, the attitude of the early Friends was not conducive to a sharp rise in jewellery sales.

So soon as the Provinces became established, however, there was a marked increase in the use of personal adornment. In vain were men and women in New England prosecuted for wearing gold and silver lace, and in other colonies we find the same rebelling to the poverty, economy and stern discipline of primitive days. Visiting Boston in 1740, Whitefield, the itinerant preacher, laments the jewels, black patches, and gay apparel of the women. Rings, gold necklaces and lockets, and gold sleeve buttons were common among the wealthy of New England at this time. Sarah Knight on her journey from Boston to New York in 1704 discovered that even the country girls adorned their hands with rings. Thomas Hamilton, covering the same area in 1832, is impressed by the earrings worn by waitresses in country taverns. In the South, among the luxury-loving plantation owners and their wives, jewellery was found, but the owning and wearing of jewellery cannot be said to be a marked propensity among other classes in the South until after 1800.

Goldsmiths and silversmiths there were aplenty, and brooches and buckles were common, and were bought from town dealers. The cheaper and more popular lines of jewellery—breast pins, rings and ear-rings—such as would appeal to the farmwife and the country girl, found their distribution in the peddler. Some of this cheap jewellery or "pinchbeck" came from Birmingham in England, and some, from Attleborough, Massachusetts, and Providence, Rhode Island. It was made of soft material, stamped and pressed and soldered together and thinly washed with gold. But the Attleborough gold wash was not so successful as the British, for the Yankee manufacturers used to complain that with three dollars' worth of gold they couldn't get the effects the British did with six cents' worth. The English gauds were contemptuously called "Brummagem" from their Birmingham source, and the American, "Attleborough." Attleborough started making cheap jewellery as early as 1780. Electroplated brass jewellery appeared there in 1843; rolled gold plate was introduced in 1849. This Massachusetts town becomes the home of cheap jewellery for the itinerant trade.

In his travels through the back country of the South before the Civil War, Olmsted encountered a trinket seller who was typical. He hailed from Düsseldorf in Germany and had followed various odd jobs in many towns. He made and lost money,—probably drank and gambled it away—but finally managed to scrape together enough to buy "a leetle coach-dray" and a stock of cheap jewellery and calico, handkerchiefs and patent medicines that he peddled among the poor in the back country of Mississippi. These people never had any money so he traded in kind. And this was how he did it: "All poor foks, dam poor; got no money; oh, no; but I say, 'dat too bad, I don't like to balk you, my friend; may be so, you got some egg, some fedder, some cheeken, some rag, some sass, or some skin vot you kill.' I takes dem dings vet dey have, and ven I gets my load I cums to Natchez back and sells dem, alvays dwo or dree times as much as dey coss me; and den I buys some more goods. Not bad beesnes—no. Oh, dese poor people dey deenk me is von fool ven I buy some dime deir rag vat dey bin vear; dey calls me 'de ole Dutch cuss.' But dey don't know nottin' vot it is vorth. I deenk dey neever see no money; may be so dey geev all de cheeken vot dey been got for a leetle breastpin vot cost me not so much as von beet. Sometime dey be dam crazy fool; dey know not how do make de count at all. Yess, I makes some money, a heap."

PINS

For a long time pins were imported from England. George Washington ordered them, especially the smallest size called "minikins" or "minifers." At first they came in a loose lot wrapped in paper; by 1744 we find them in boxes; forty years later "sheet" pins were sold, arranged in rows on a sheet of paper as we know them. And there was almost as great a variety as we have—black pins for mourning, "corkins, middlings, short whites, lillikins, and lace pins." They weren't cheap. The Revolutionary price for a dozen was seven shillings, sixpence. Since pins are made of drawn brass wire we would expect to find their initial manufacture in this country shortly after the first machines to draw wire were introduced. An abortive attempt at this manufacture was made in Massachusetts and Rhode Island previous to 1750, but most of the output of the machines was wire for wool cards. The industry really did not get under way until about 1831 when pins began to be made in Connecticut by a machine invented in that year, designed to make complete pins at a single operation. Previously the heads had been made separately and clamped into place. They had a tantalizing way of jumping off, leaving the point to go where it liked. Thereafter the importation slowed down. The pins carried by peddlers after this date were mainly from the Connecticut source.

SHOELACES

The short and simple annals of shoelaces help clear up some questions regarding the footwear of our Colonial forefathers. The New Haven colonists used shoestrings instead of buckles and we even find shoestrings mentioned in an old will in Massachusetts. They were cut from raw hide and must have been crude affairs. "Whang" was the colloquial name for them. In the nineteenth century they were made from leather scrap. "Shoestring Pratt" of Randolph, Massachusetts, devised a way of cutting these waste bits of leather concentrically, pulling them straight, rolling them in their own fat until they were round and then cutting them to standard lengths. He went about with a wagon to the various shoemakers' houses and factories and gathered up the waste from which he made his product and his fortune. This is typical of Yankee shrewdness—out of waste he created a necessity.

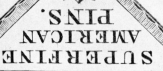

SUPERFINE
AMERICAN
PINS.

THOS. HAYNES & CO.

AMERICAN

PIN

BONNET WIRE ASSORTED.

KNITTING NEEDLES ASSORTED

MANUFACTORY

NEW-YORK.

HARD & SOFT WIRE DRAWING

BEST AMERICAN

PINS.

EARLY PAPER PIN-COVER

The loom room of the established weaver became the centre of the
town's gossip in early days

Comb-making began in Leominster, Mass. Combs were regular items
in the peddler's pack

JEW'S HARPS

Among the more frivolous of the peddler's notions was the Jew's harp. This has its own little history. The legendary Blue Laws of Connecticut* forbade its citizens playing any instrument of music except the drum, trumpet, and Jew's harp. Perhaps it had an Old Testament flavour that appealed to these rigorous worthies who founded and ruled their colony on Old Testament theology.

For a matter of fact it was called a Jew's harp because in England such things were peddled by Jews. Where they came from is difficult to say—perhaps Germany at first, then, perhaps the German colonies of Pennsylvania—Ephrata and Germantown especially—where musical instruments played a large part in the daily life of the people.

Indication that the Pennsylvania Dutch used many musical instruments can be found in the argot of their early settlers. The Jew's harp was *Rumpel;* the harpsichord, *Gloria;* the melodeon, *Bosorgel;* the bag pipe,—brought into the back country of Pennsylvania by the Scotch-Irish—*Dudelsok;* and they also had a strange instrument made from a mule's teeth and jawbone, called *Kinboka.*

In later times melodeons were peddled. The dealer would drive out to a farmhouse, set up the instrument in the parlour and give a demonstration of hymn-playing and singing in which the family was urged to take part.

---

* No one seems to have heard of these Blue Laws until they appeared in "A General History of Connecticut" published in 1829 and written by the Rev. Richard Peters. That eminent divine, with a blithesome disregard for the truth, created out of the whole cloth the following quaint regulations for the citizenry of Connecticut: "No one to cross a river but with an authorized ferryman. No one shall run on the Sabbath day, or walk in his garden or elsewhere, except reverently to and from meeting. No one shall travel, cook victuals, make beds, sweep house, cut hair, or shave on the Sabbath or fasting day. No one shall read Common Prayer, keep Christmas or Saints-days, make minced pies, dance, play cards, or play on any instrument of music, except the drum, trumpet, and jews'-harp. Married persons must live together, or be imprisoned. Every male shall have his hair cut round according to a cap."

KNIVES AND WOODENWARE

The jackknife or Barlow knife was an early concomitant of homemade wooden ware. This implement was essential to the life of men and boys in the early days, especially in New England where whittling was raised to a fine art.

In the back country families may have had a little pewter to start with, but cups, bowls, and trenchers were cut out of wood and served everyday table purposes. White ash knots were used for making bowls and constantly the woodworkers were grubbing around the forests for knots in old sugar maples, soft-maples, ash, beech, and birch trees. A single large knot would make a whole nest of bowls. Such wood was referred to as "dish timber." There were itinerant whittlers who came through the country, and wooden ware peddlers as well. At Henniker, New Hampshire, Timothy Gillette and his son established a woodenware works in 1817. The son turned the lathe by hand while the father controlled the blades. Bowls, plates, skimmers, cups, and saucers were turned out of ash. When they accumulated a stock, the father filled his two large leather pouches with the goods, placed them on horseback, and peddled them around the countryside. The valley of the Sauquoit in New York boasted a poet who was also a woodenware maker and peddler, and who went from house to house distributing his rolling pins and butter stamps and regaling his customer with examples of his homemade verse. Boston of 1799 sang a popular song called, "Come Buy My Woodenware."

Well up into the nineteenth century, Hingham, Massachusetts, pointed with pride to its various coopering industries. Loads of their output were peddled, in winter especially, when the local makers' stock accumulated too fast. They were bartered by their makers along the road. The Hingham bucket gained fame throughout New England, as did the tubs, hoop and nest boxes, dumb-bettys, washtubs, keelers, piggins, and other wooden products.

In addition to these, we find wheelwrights making spinning wheels and peddling them on horseback. They were carried in parts, and when a sale was made, the wheelwright set up the machine.

Up to 1832 most of the cutlery sold in this country was imported from England and was crude in design and finish. In that year, at Saccarappa, Maine, D. N. Ropes began making ivory-handled cutlery. Later the business was moved to Meriden, Connecticut, where the wastage from the handles was used for making combs. Wood was also employed for handles, and subsequently vulcanized rubber. 1839 is the momentous date for the first vulcanizing of rubber by Charles Goodyear. And that began a vast industry, of which many products were distributed by peddlers.

COTTON AND SILK

American-made piece goods of cotton and silk came into the peddler's pack in quantity around 1800, as did ribbons, handkerchiefs, garters and suspenders. Most of these goods hailed from New England and Philadelphia, which were early textile centres. Northern housewives would often exchange homemade tow cloth—made of the tow of hemp and flax—for woollen, checked linen, and dress goods. The tow cloth eventually was sold to plantation owners who provided it to their slaves for clothing. There were even specialists in these textile lines. The poplin peddler, who carried the new styles in ribbed silk, fresh imported from Ireland, caused a flurry among country housewives when he arrived in town.

Middletown, Connecticut, was responsible for the "gum elastic" suspenders, or "galluses" and garters that the peddler hawked, and to this day Middletown leads in the manufacture of elastic webbing.

Among the items carried by the first Yankee peddlers previous to 1750 were home-knitted goods—socks, mitts and such—which were peddled, together with cheeses, among the French Canadians to the North and the Dutch to the West.

Although practically every housewife knitted hosiery, the industry really started in Pennsylvania, at Germantown, shortly after Penn's arrival, when the Mennonites and other Germans made stockings on crude frames at home. They were taken to Philadelphia to sell. Women were paid half a crown a pair for knitting these stockings. After 1800 the Philadelphia stocking industry went into the hands of English knitters (many of them coming from Ipswich, Massachusetts, after the stocking business failed there) who did their work in their own houses. These stockings eventually found their way into the peddler's pack. Philadelphia still maintains its leadership in the manufacture of knitted goods.

THE PEDDLING OF BOOKS

In one form or another the book agent has been with us from the beginning; perhaps he will linger on to the end. At first he appeared as a peddler of broadsides, ballads, and popular books. Then, when he began to distribute religious books he assumed the position of a necessary influence for good. At least, that is what Cotton Mather thought of him, for when the Assembly of Massachusetts passed laws restricting peddlers that divine was worried lest this would also restrict those who were to "scatter books of Truth and Goodness in all Corners of the Land." Doubtless the town bookseller used the peddler to distribute his wares, employing both the notions peddler and men specializing on books. Some of them carried such popular pieces as chapbooks, which were occasionally imported from England. Then came Wigglesworth's "Day of Doom," Cotton Mather's pious writings and his "Life of Sir William Phipps," together with catechisms and primers.

"The New England Primer," one of the oldest of American publications, contained things supposedly of interest to very small children—the alphabet, religious disquisitions for the infant mind and the Assembly's "Catechism." These were regularly peddled around New England and were stock books in shops and general stores.

PETITION OF THE MAIDS OF NEW-YORK.

WE, the maids of New-York city,
(Maids, good lack! the more's the pity,)
Do humbly offer this petition
To repreſent our ſad condition,
Which once made known, our hope and truſt is,
That men of *parts* will do us juſtice.
Now, you muſt know,---ah! can't you gueſs
The ſubjeſt of a maid's diſtreſs?
(Plague on the widows that compel us
Thus to petition for young fellows,)
But we were ſaying, you muſt know,
(Tho' bluſhing we declare our woe,)
A virgin was deſign'd by nature,
A weakly and imperfeſt creature,
So apt to fall, ſo apt to ſtray,
Her wants require a *guide*, a *ſtay*.
And then ſo timorous of ſprites,
She dares not lie *alone* at nights;
Say what ſhe will, do what ſhe can,
Her heart ſtill gravitates to man;
From whence 'tis evident as light,
That marriage is a maiden's right;
And therefore it's prodigious hard
To be from ſuch a right debarr'd;
Yet we, poor ſouls, can't have the freedom
To get good men, howe'er we need 'em.
The widows, firs, the rankeſt goats
That e'er polluted petticoats,
Thoſe plagues, more odious than ſmall-pox,
Thoſe jades, more cunning than a fox,
Still *cut us out*, are ſtill before us,
And leave no lovers to adore us.------*Oh!*

THE CHOICE.

LO! here's the *bride* and there's the *tree*,
Take which of theſe beſt liketh thee.------
" The bargain's bad on either part---
" But---hangman, come, drive on the cart."

FROM AN ALMANAC OF 1801—"HUTCHIN'S IMPROVED"
Sold by the canvassers of that day

The firſt important book items of the early peddler, however, muſt have been catechisms, New Teſtaments and psalm books. Catechisms especially, for these even preceded primers. In Conneċticut, Ludlow's Code of 1649 required children to be taught some "shorte orthodox catechisme." Almoſt every parson seems to have concoċted his own, although all are more or less faithful versions of the Shorter Weſtminſter code. They were produced in Ipswich, Cambridge, Dorcheſter, Roxbury, Chelmsford, New Haven, Hartford, Norwich, Salem, and Andover. We know of over 300 of these variations. It was part of the miniſter's duty to go from house to house and catechize not only the women and children but the servants as well. Men and women were fined for not being able to recite the catechism! Consequently there muſt have been quite a demand for these books, because one never knew when the parson would drop in and ſtart asking what the whole duty of man was!

Between 1749 and 1766, Franklin & Hall of Boſton printed 37,000 copies of "The New England Primer." It has been eſtimated that between 1680 and 1830 over 6,000,000 of these primers and catechisms were issued in this country.

Religious books dominated the publishing business in the early days. Two-thirds of the books and pamphlets published between 1700 and 1750 were on religious subjeċts. After 1750, spelling books began to appear along with Noah Webſter's "Seleċtions" and Jedidiah Morse's "Geography," and later, peddlers hawked Ezekiel Cheever's Latin "Accidence" or grammar. Other curious book items carried by the peddler were "The Book of Knowledge," a manual of aſtrology, palmiſtry, and physiognomy by "Erra Pater, a Jew Doċtor in Aſtronomy and Physic, born in Bethany near Mount Olivet in Judea" and "made English" by W. Lily, aſtrologer; such romantic titles as "Female Policy Deteċted," "The French Convert," "Robinson Crusoe," "Pilgrim's Progress" and "Little King Pippin"; and there were also cheap little pamphlets, joke books, pretty "garlands," almanacs and treatises on farming. Often apprentices of printing shops, in their spare time, and, for their own private profit, were allowed to print pamphlets and sheets of ballads which were sold to peddlers. And people bought books in these early days—in some years Franklin's "Poor Richard" would sell as many as 10,000 copies. Often the peddler bartered books, taking in exchange the old for the new.

The subscription book business, with which most of us, more or less regretfully are acquainted, started in Hartford about 1810 and depended for distribution, as to-day, on canvassers. These combined peddlers sometimes managed to sell 150,000 to 200,000 volumes of a single work. "The Cottage Bible," a two-volume commentary, and "Webster's Unabridged Dictionary" were early favourites in this trade.

Nathaniel Hawthorne in his "American Notes" describes an itinerant subscription agent he meets in Shelburne Falls, "getting subscriptions for a religious and abolitionist paper in New York—somewhat elderly and gray-haired, quick in his movements, hasty in his walk, with an eager, earnest stare through his spectacles, hurrying about with a pocketbook of subscriptions in his hand—seldom speaking and then in brief expressions—sitting down before the stage comes, to write a list of subscribers obtained to his employers in New York. Withal a city and business air about him, as of one accustomed to hurry through narrow alleys and dart across thronged streets." A clever thumb-nail sketch, that.

The early book peddlers form a distinct class. John Dunton of Massachusetts was an early bookseller and so was the estimable James Gray, who, when he died in 1705, left an estate of £712 in bags of coins. One amusing book peddler hailed from Philadelphia. Bell was his name and Scotch his nationality. He travelled through Virginia in 1725 in a cart that held his family and his books, and he invariably paid his way at inns by giving the local Boniface a copy of Sheridan's "The School for Scandal." Another book hawker, Mr. Benham of Meriden, Connecticut, drove a one-horse wagon with a large square cabinet fitted to the rear in which he carried his books. When he arrived at a farmhouse, he opened the back of his cart and there was his travelling library! Just the sort of person Christopher Morley would delight in. Another queer character from the same town was Joseph A. Coe, known the country over as "Bible Leaf Joe." For years he bought Bibles, tore off the bindings and distributed the disjointed leaves to passersby. He travelled along the roads, in canal boats and even went through the early trains, travelling as far south as New Orleans, passing out his sheets of the Word. We suspect that Joe was a little "touched."

The best known and most romantic book peddler of all was Parson Weems, the same one who is responsible for fixing upon the youthful innocence of George Washington that abominable tale of the cherry tree. His biographer says: "For thirty years there was no more familiar figure on the roads of the Southern States than this book peddler and author who, provided gypsy-like with horse and wagon, travelled his long route year after year, sleeping in wayside inn, farmhouse, or forest, fiddling, writing, selling books, living in the open, and learning some new road lore, field lore, or wisdom of the road with each new day that passed."

Mason Locke Weems was his full name, and he appears to have been born October 1, 1759, at Marshes Seat, the family homestead near Herring Creek in Anne Arundel County, Maryland. In his fourteenth year he was sent abroad to study medicine and for three years this purpose held him in London and at the University of Edinburgh. In 1772 he returned to England and took Orders, then back again to his native land where for eight years he was one of the most active clergymen of the Maryland diocese. Desirous of spreading the Gospel truth,—too active, in fact, for his parishioners found means of persuading him to give up local work,—he started on the road, selecting for his churches, inn parlours, courthouse steps, ballrooms, village greens and the cottages of labourers. About 1800 was the date he began wayfaring as book agent for Matthew Carey of Philadelphia. Five years earlier, he had married Miss Fanny Elwell and settled in the town of Dumfries, Prince William County, Virginia, where he established a basis of supplies in a bookstore. To this town and this wife he returned occasionally from his journeys.

On these long tours he carried his fiddle with him, and at nights played for dances, for the "hoe downs" of the negroes, and even for a puppet show, it is said. What a merry picture he must have made, this white-haired parson who would play for you to dance, would sell you a book, pray with you, or preach you a sermon! So famously did his trade prosper that in one year he sold three thousand copies of an expensive Bible! His stock included books for children, Bibles, philosophical and historical works, prayer books and hymn books and, of course, his own biographies, moral pamphlets and famous sermons which he himself published. Marshall's "Life of Washington," an expensive five-volume set, he sold by subscription, just as our modern book agents do. Or if he had a job lot of moral works, he unloaded his cart on the courthouse steps on the days the court was sitting, and exposed them to public gaze. Sometimes he armed himself with a sheaf of pamphlets and invaded tavern barrooms, preached a little good-natured sermon, delivered himself of a diatribe on the evils of liquor and drunkenness, and then sold his beery audience a handful of his "Drunkard's Looking Glass" at twenty-five cents a copy.

For thirty years this fine old parson continued his literary vagabondage through the South—playing his fiddle, selling books and preaching the Word. Finally one day while he was on business in Beaufort, South Carolina, he reached his last inn. He died there, far from the wife and home he loved. The year was 1825.

Combs and buttons, jewellery, pins, shoelaces, Jew's harps, knives and woodenware, piece goods and books—all these are only a few of the Yankee notions that the packpeddler carried. As the years passed and manufacture grew more diversified, his stock became more varied. Carpet slippers, razors, snuff-boxes, tobacco, spectacles with tin or copper frames, and hair and clothes brushes appear in his pack. By 1830 the stock grew so large that many of these itinerants were forced to take to wagons, and we find miniature department stores going about the country in a cart. For many years some of the foot-goers who could not afford a cart kept to the road; they are occasionally still to be found.

The first two generations of these pack peddlers were Yankees; by 1836 the German Jew had seriously invaded the trade. Being ambitious, he remained on foot only so long as was necessary for him to accumulate the money to buy a horse and wagon.

CHAPTER IV

PEDDLERS IN LITTLE THINGS

INDIGO AND ESSENCES

OR half a century, the indigo peddler made his regular visits to the Connecticut Valley, going from town to town on horseback, and he was a welcome salesman.

In the days before and after the Revolution, the average farmwife carded, spun and wove her own wool. Before weaving, the wool thread was dyed, and indigo furnished the favourite blue that tinted the bedcovers and those sporty blue and white striped and checkered shirts for which the men of the Connecticut Valley were famous. The indigo tub was a regular feature of the big kitchens in early houses.

This indigo at first came from the South. In South Carolina Mrs. Charles Cotesworthy Pinckney introduced the cultivation of indigo in 1745, and for half a century, until cotton took its place in the fields, indigo was a profitable crop for the people of that province. An acre of good land would produce eighty pounds of indigo, and one negro could take care of two acres without straining his accumulated inertia. After the Revolution, indigo was raised so cheaply in the East Indies that its cultivation here stopped.

Other dyes were made from roots, leaves and flowers gathered in the woods and meadows. Sometimes the indigo peddler saved the housewife the trouble of making them up, and carried brown, black, and saffron, and other colours in his stock.

The essence peddler was quite a different sort. Usually a free-lance, he managed to scrape together ten or twenty dollars which was enough capital to set himself up in business, that is, fill his tin trunk with peppermint, bergamot, and wintergreen extracts and bitters. In the backwoods these

56

bitters were in great demand. They were mixed with the local brand of homemade liquor which, in those pre-Revolutionary days of innocence and freedom, and for a time afterward, it was every man's privilege to distil. Other extracts were used as remedies and antidotes.

In his "American Notes," Hawthorne describes one of these essence peddlers—"Toward night (we) took up (on the stage coach) an essence vendor for a short distance. He was returning home after having been out on a tour two or three weeks and nearly exhausted his stock. He was not exclusively an essence peddler, having a large tin box, which had been filled with drygoods, combs, jewellery, etc., now mostly sold out. His essences were of aniseed, cloves, red cedar, wormwood, together with opodeldoc, and an oil for the hair. These matters were concocted at Ashfield, Massachusetts, and the peddlers are sent about with vast quantities. Cologne water is among the essences manufactured, though the bottles have foreign labels on them. . . The peddlers find satisfaction for all contumelies in making good bargains out of their customers. This man was a peddler in quite a small way, and carrying no more than an open basket full of essences, but some go out with wagon loads."

THE DRUG PEDDLER

Closely allied in the beginning to the essence peddler was the itinerant dealer in nostrums. He started as a vendor of medicinal herbs, later he handled various brands of patent medicine. Philadelphia has always been an active drug centre and many of the peddlers represented Philadelphia houses. Even the wandering herb doctor can still be remembered by older Philadelphians, for one used to cry his wares—sassafras, bergamot, wormwood, rhubarb, and sweet basil—on Chestnut Street near Independence Hall as late as twenty-five years ago. His trade was mostly with negroes.

At one time these simple herb remedies were in the closets of every country house. Next, patent nostrums began to find favour—Ward's Anodyne Pearls, which were worn as a necklace by babies during teething; Bezoar Stone, for curing bites of snakes; Bateman's Pectoral Drops, for colds; Seneca Snake Root; Turlington's Original Balsam; and Duffy's Elixir.

A diverting trade, this peddling of nostrums, and it must have required a sense of humour. The peddler generally bought his pills in quantity lots, put them up under his own label and hawked them about under his own name. The next peddler sold the same pills under a different name—and recommended them for quite a different illness! Hawthorne meets one of these medicine vendors, "a Dr. Jacques, who carried about with him recommendatory letters in favour of himself and drugs, signed by a long list of people. I believe he comes from Philadelphia."

Just as the tin peddler later became a tinker and the clock peddler a repairer of clocks, so these early hawkers of remedies added a side line of simple doctoring in order to gain a standing in those backwoods communities where every housewife had her own set notions of materia medica. Much of it was bluff, a lot of it, crude superstition; but a young Yankee with a trunkful of patent medicines and a smart head on his shoulders could be depended on to gain a medical reputation in no time. Down South druggists and vendors of medicine were called "Doctor," just as all men with beards or goatees were dubbed "Colonel."

From this Yankee medicine peddler grew a countryside attraction that flourished in this land and still thrives in some sections—the Medicine Man and the Medicine Show. The Medicine Man, carrying the nostrums of some drug house, sets himself up wherever the people gather, in the public square or at country fairs. There under the flare of a gasoline torch he barks his wares, using a small boy as a terrible example. He is really a circus figure—wears flashy clothes, sometimes a silk hat, an array of large and dazzling imitation diamonds, and he usually has a fearsome black waxed mustache. His flow of language is comparable only to the Fourth of July oratory of present-day senators, although in horrors it sometimes attains the blood-curdling colour of the sermons once preached by Jonathan Edwards.

POTTERY

Perhaps the first reference to American-made pottery is found in a letter from old Josiah Wedgwood, written in 1755, and expressing apprehension over the proposed establishment of a pottery in South Carolina. Hitherto, all the pottery used in this country had been imported from England, and Wedgwood feared lest these inroads would embarrass his business. Vast quantities of enamelled earthenware were imported from Holland and England prior to the Revolution. However, before the end of the century, many potteries along the Atlantic seaboard were turning out a crude stoneware. Yet not until after the Revolution did china become a common household furnishing. By 1810 various New England towns had kilns where a "Queensware"—a heavy, white ware—was produced. The first porcelain seems to have been made in Jersey City and Philadelphia in 1825. Gradually the business gravitated to Trenton, New Jersey, which is still a centre of the industry.

It might be surprising to find such fragile articles as pottery being peddled over the rough roads of our countryside, yet in some districts they were. Even before the tin peddler's carts were seen in Connecticut, a potter sold his ware from house to house in that state. A pottery established at Ellicott, New York, in 1814, kept several men on the road. The first pottery in Vermont was started at Bennington in 1793 by Captain John Norton and his sons, and continued working in Bennington till about 1825. Some of this ware was peddled around the country in carts, although most of it was sent in quantities to stores, whence it was retailed. It was a common, rough, red earthenware—milk pans, bowls, cider jugs, crocks, etc. The Bennington pottery, now so highly prized by collectors, belongs to a later date. It was packed in strong tierces, and transported in gaily-painted wagons, to distributing points such as Albany, Troy, Boston, and Keene, New Hampshire; it was not peddled, however. Pottery made by the Clarks at Lyndeboro, New Hampshire, was peddled, and so was the lava ware or so-called Parian, popular in New England.

Recollections of several octogenarians in South Jersey paint pretty pictures of porcelain and plaster figure peddlers who went through that country in the mid-fifties of the nineteenth century. They carried a tray on the head, loaded with china dogs and cats, the kind displayed in our antique stores to-day. Others report that to their isolated farms came peddlers with trays of plaster birds, vases and images. The birds were highly coloured parrots and canaries. These are still to be found in the Pennsylvania Dutch districts and are much sought after by collectors. The Pennsylvania Dutch doubtless made them, for there were several potteries in their locality in the early days of the last century.

The Germans of Pennsylvania were also famous for their slipware which was made by farmer-potters from 1720 to 1850, and produced both for local use and commercial sale. It was known as *hefa* and the potter's wheel on which it was turned, as *hefnarawd*.

Also there were occasional Italian peddlers of plaster casts of famous masterpieces and statuettes who used to go through New York and Philadelphia streets and the countryside hawking their wares. They were mainly Lucchese, for the business of making plaster casts has been an institution of Lucca for centuries.

SHAWLS AND LACES

Lace was a necessary item in the dress of both the Colonial wife and her husband. It was worn on his shirt bosoms and cuffs and on her *fichus*. In the earlier times, the word "laces" meant what we now call "lacings," that is, gilt and silken braids for liveries and uniforms. These lacings are found regularly among the items of ships' cargoes before the Revolution.

Linen and silk thread laces were first made in this country at Ipswich, Massachusetts, and later, Connecticut housewives produced a surplus that was sold. The lace pillow was among the prized possessions of the more genteel women of the Colonial era.

Our grandparents spoke of bone, pillow and thread lace; the first two meaning bobbin lace, regardless of its sort. Blonde lace was used for ruffles up to the time of the Civil War. Black Chantilly lace shawls and carriage parasols were fashionable at the same time. But Blonde and Chantilly were not cheap enough for ordinary hawking, whereas the narrow edgings of Buckinghamshire were—lace frequently spoken of as "Baby Bucks," which came from the Midlands of England where also it was peddled. It was introduced into England by the French Huguenots, for it really is a coarse Lille. These plebeian sorts were the kinds the peddler handled. The Ipswich lace was taken by stage coach to Boston and sold, but it is questionable if enough of it was produced to supply peddlers except, perhaps, in the immediate vicinity of Ipswich.

Tatting, crocheting and embroidery often employed the time of housewives and servants and this handiwork was apt to be used for bartering with peddlers. Hawthorne pictures one such deal—a peddler with "girls' neckerchiefs—or gauze—men's silk pocket handkerchiefs and a variety of horn combs, trying to trade with the servant girls of the house. Laura attempts to exchange a worked vandyke, which she values at two dollars and a half."

The East India trade that had its American centre in New England brought in the first shawls; the *Salem Gazette* of 1784 advertised the arrival of a shipment of assorted shawls. At this time shawls were just coming into fashion in Europe. A later style was the colourful Paisley shawl with its East Indian arabesques.

A well-authenticated story tells how Jim "Jubilee" Fisk made his first money peddling these Paisley shawls. He was associated with Volney Haskell, a travelling jeweller, who lived for years in Otis, Massachusetts, and later in Great Barrington. One of the partners would go ahead to a small town, seek out a woman well known and beautiful, and give her a Paisley shawl suggesting that she wear it to church the following Sunday. Imagine the stir when she "sashayed" up the aisle! Imagine the envy of her admiring friends after church! The following week Haskell or Fisk appeared in town with a carriage load of Paisley shawls, and found a ready market among the women whose appetite had been so cleverly whetted. From this Fisk passed into finance, and his later history is bound up with the development of the Erie Railroad, until it was interrupted by a bullet from Stokes's revolver.

CHAIRS AND BASKETS

In some backwoods sections of the country—in rural New England and in the mountains of the South, manufacturing peddlers of baskets and chairs are still to be found. Many of them are the second generation in the trade and some the third. Many repeat the same designs that their forebears made and distributed. In Morrison, Tennessee, to cite one example, is a chair- and basket-maker and peddler whose father before him made chairs and baskets and peddled them in a two-horse wagon, going as far south as Atlanta, Georgia. To-day the son uses a motor truck which makes it possible for him to carry his wares to the Florida line. In the neighbourhood of Amherst, Massachusetts, definite types of baskets—and good baskets they are, too—are made and peddled by a second generation. The Gypsies also carried a line of baskets.

The first makers of baskets doubtless learned the art from the Indians. These natives seem to have had different designs and materials according to their locality, and in many of these original localities the designs still persist in the work of basket-weavers. In her "Stage Coach and Tavern Days" Alice Morse Earle tells of an Indian basket peddler near Shrewsbury, Massachusetts, who came to peddling after an exciting life—"His real name was the gentle title Basil, but he had been a pirate on the high seas, and Brazil was more appropriate. He and his wife thriftily ran their little farm and industriously wove charming baskets and peddled them around the neighbouring towns." The Indians of New York, Pennsylvania, and Louisiana made and peddled, in their localities, baking trays, wooden dishes, ladles, spoons, shovels, brooms, embroidered birch-bark baskets, and fancy figures of coloured porcupine quills.

Occasionally, one finds a record of an itinerant basket-weaver, usually a tinker who has basket-weaving as a side-line. Many farm women were adept at making baskets, and their production was part of the housewife's duties. On some farms there were willows from which was cut the material for these baskets—for the coarser potato and corn baskets; the finer peeled reeds being used for household use. These reeds we find in the first broom-peddler's stock.

All manner of country chairs eventually found their way into the peddler's cart. It wouldn't be surprising if even the Windsor chair, which first saw the light of day in Philadelphia and was soon spread over the Atlantic seaboard, had some of its initial distribution in this way.

BROOMS

The making of brooms here is directly traceable to the Indians. Sticks of birch or ash were used for handles and two tough splints for the brush, or sometimes the brush part was made by splitting a block of birch into slender strips. These were called "splinter brooms" and were sold from 8d to 9d apiece by the Indians and their squaws who peddled them around the neighbourhood. Later the Colonists made Guinea-wheat brooms. It became one of the household chores, for in her diary of 1775, Abigail Foote, a young girl of Colchester, Connecticut, speaks of having to make one. Oven brooms were made of husks; others of birch and hemlock twigs and rushes. Down South, brooms were often imported from England.

Although there was some sporadic planting of broom corn under the direction of Franklin in Pennsylvania and under Jefferson in Virginia, it was not undertaken systematically until about 1798, when Levi Dickenson planted a few hills in his garden at Hadley, Massachusetts, from which he harvested enough material to make twenty brooms. The next year he planted half an acre and was able to make 200 brooms. These he peddled, together with reeds for basket making, around the neighbourhood. The third year he seeded down an entire acre, made more brooms and extended his peddling route. Seeing his success, others in the neighbourhood took to planting broom corn. Part of the barn or a shed near the house was turned into a workshop and broom-making became a fall and winter industry. The farmers cut their own handles and the twine was spun from their own flax. By 1799 Dickenson was carrying his brooms to Pittsfield; in 1805 his agents went as far as New London, Albany and Boston. The Shakers of Enfield also took up the trade in 1830 and made the Shaker broom; it had narrow shoulders and was tied with twine.

The broom business prospered so that by 1810 Hampshire County, Massachusetts, was producing 70,000 brooms annually. But it met competition when the farmers of the prairie regions of Ohio and Illinois grew stronger, longer, and better broom corn. To-day tobacco and onions are raised in those meadows of the Connecticut Valley where once Yankee broom corn plumes waved, and the farmers are—Poles!

While the broom peddler started as a local man and a specialist, his line was eventually taken over by the tin peddler, and brooms became a regular part of the tinware peddler's stock. He carried them stacked in bundles on the back of his wagon, like great aigrettes.

It is interesting to note, apropos of this industry, that the Fuller Brush Company, of Hartford, Connecticut, still prides itself on its successful though archaic peddling system. It employs some 5000 peddlers, usually young men, who sell from door to door, and, in the isolated sections of the country still accept farm produce in exchange for their wares.

AN ASSORTMENT OF PEDDLERS

The fish dinners of New England, one of the few items on the Yankee cuisine worth preserving, followed the course of vagrant commerce. History records that, from 1800 on, oysters and fish were peddled through New England. In that year oysters were first planted in Connecticut waters, and between that date and 1825 they were regularly carried into the interior by vendors. South Norwalk, New Haven, and Stamford were the centres of the trade. The oysters were packed in kegs, piled into saddle-bags, and carried by horseback to towns in the interior of the state. Soon enterprising dealers loaded up spring wagons with oysters and fish, and went even to Hartford, Springfield, and northern New York, Vermont, and Canada. While the stock was usually sold for cash where it was available, many of the oyster caravans returning from the northern parts of New England brought back exchange merchandise—butter, cheese, pork, brooms, Vermont gray cloth and other inland commodities. Imagine swapping a pair of home-knit wrist-warmers for a dozen oysters on the half-shell!

Although many farmers did their own butchering, the itinerant butcher was also known in the early days. In 1700 his charge for butchering a beast was five shillings and his meals. He served both as a salesman of goods and a worker in that he might sell meats and could also butcher for the farmers. The meat he carried in paniers on horseback. He did his butchering, so it is said, only at favourable phases of the moon, lest the meat should shrink in the corning barrel. Autumn was the favourite season, and the attic and the smoke house would be filled with the winter's supply of hams, sausages, corned beef, and pork. When he did butchering he would barter for the fats and tallow, which he turned into the candlemaker's hands. Often he himself was a candlemaker,

5

and a candle-peddler who had a side-line of butchering, and he would swap finished, dipped or moulded candles for the tallow, in that way procuring his raw materials.

Quite a diversity of trades were carried on by itinerants. From Connecticut would come a blacksmith who made and peddled steel-yards and axes, taking them through South Carolina and Georgia. With him went his brother whose line might be mules, of which he would collect a drove in Vermont and New Hampshire, and gradually work them down to the Carolinas where they were sold.

Quite a neat little history could be written about the early American horse trade. It has a bad reputation from the beginning, and since most of it was done on the fly, it comes under our head of itinerants. Before 1700 horse "coursers" or horse thieves were a pest in Connecticut. The colony was obliged to hold a court especially for them at New London, and the penalties were from £10 to £30 and an equal number of lashes. Great quantities of horses were bought in Canada and driven down south where they were sold to the farmers or else shipped from Boston and New York to the West Indies. It was also not unusual for a man who owned an especially fine stallion to travel with it around the immediate country; his charge for service in 1780 was fifteen shillings.

The most picturesque horse coursers of the past century were the notorious gang in New York state which stole draft horses in New York, drove them down South and sold them, and stole driving horses in the South, drove them north and made a handsome profit. The gang was finally caught and broken up. The leader, arrested on a different and much more serious charge, was run out of the state, and went West and became a peddler. His descendants are now prominent in church and prohibition affairs.

HATS AND SILVER

To two more infant industries did the peddler lend his support—the distribution of hats and plated ware.

While Danbury, Connecticut, has always been synony-
mous with the hat-making trade, there seems to be little evidence that these hats were peddled; most of them were taken
to New York or Boston and sold in quantity lots. On the
other hand, from New Britain, Connecticut, and from other
New England towns, we do find hats hawked about the
countryside by their makers. One New Britain peddler-
manufacturer was Amos Stanley. In winter when he had
accumulated a considerable number of hats, he loaded them
on his two-horse team and went to western New York, where
he bartered them for beaver and other furs, which were
brought home and made into hats for another season.

There was some peddling of cheap hats by makers who
rode on horseback through Salem, Boston, and thereabouts.
Subsequently these hat peddlers acquired a pair of wheels
and shafts with a rude seat and carried the hats in big boxes
slung under the axle. Later they took to carts. By 1804 only
a few of these manufacturer-peddlers were to be seen in that
neighbourhood, and it is the supposition that the hats, like
many other articles, went into the general peddler's stock.
These were of several grades—common wool hats, sometimes
called "Negro hats" which sold for a couple of shillings each;
and the raccoon and beaver hats, made principally for farmers and common people. Seven dollars was not too much to
pay for a good beaver hat. It was intended to last a lifetime.

We have no record that the straw bonnets, made first in
Framingham, Massachusetts, in 1800, were peddled, but it
is likely that they were, because they appealed to the women-
folk of the country districts and the peddler was quick to
meet the needs of his women customers.

Plated ware, of course, is another story. Up to 1750 ster-
ling silver was the proud possession of the well-to-do; then
Yankee manufacturers began making alloys—German silver
and Britannia. Meriden and Wallingford, Connecticut, became the home of this industry in plated ware. Except spoons
which were sold by the dozen, plated ware was sold by weight

and was known as "weight ware." By 1800 these items went into the peddler's pack—spoons, plates, and platters. He also carried tin and pewter spoons.

PEDDLERS OF BROADSIDES AND BALLADS

The early broadsides were proclamations, posted in public places and passed around for the enlightenment of the community. In New Orleans, broadsides were also used to carry on personal quarrels; lampoons and pasquinades were posted in public places, which must have added a fillip to the delight of living in that city.

Practically every early printer turned out broadsides and ballads, Boston printers being especially active in this production. Benjamin Franklin, when young, used to pick up pennies selling ballads that he wrote and his brother printed. But the best story of all is that told of Thomas Fleet (1685-1758), a printer, editor, and auctioneer of Boston. One day in 1740 there came into Boston Harbor, under convoy of a British cruiser, a Spanish ship that had been captured. Aboard her were several bales of Papal bulls intended for the Florida and Louisiana trade. Fleet bought these all up and printed ballads on the back of them and advertised them in his paper, *The Boston Evening Post*, as being available "either by the single Bull, Quire or Ream at a much cheaper rate than they can be purchased of the French or Spanish priests and yet will be warranted to be of the same Advantage to the Possessors."

After the proclamation stage of the broadside, it developed a yellow-journal touch. It became the medium for the confession of criminals, especially those sentenced to die and who took this chance to tell their story to the world. The ballads of this era also celebrated tragic events, and were printed with woodcuts of coffins and other grim decorations. Even in pre-Revolutionary days our forefathers relished their tit-bits of crime. The broadside peddler was welcome.

Later on, after 1812, popular ballads were commonly hawked—the words written to tunes everyone knew. They

DEATH AND THE LADY

A broadside of the type that amused our ancestors. Sometimes popular ballads were printed and often the confession of a criminal about to be executed. They were sold by peddlers

Courtesy of H. D. Eberlein

Groups of cobblers worked together in shops after the initial era of itineracy

Danbury, Ct., was the first great centre of hat manufacturing. Hats and caps found a place in the peddler's pack

were popular up to the Civil War. When John Davis travelled through this country in the early years of the last century
he made a note of these ballad peddlers. A peddler came to
the door, and exhibited his ballads. "Here," said he, "is the
whole trial, examination and condemnation of Jason Fairbanks who was executed at Philadelphia for cutting off Peggy
Placket's head under a hedge on the road to Frankford..."
"And here," cried the peddler, "is the account of a whale
that was left ashore by the tide in the bay of Chesapeak, with
a ship of 5000 tons in his belly, called the Merry Dane, of
Dover..." So the broadside was the first tabloid newspaper.

THE ITINERANT NURSERYMAN

In his travels through the Southern States previous to the
Civil War, Frederick Law Olmsted met up with an itinerant
nurseryman, a substantial citizen who apparently believed
in advertising. His catalogue reads not unlike some of the
catalogues of nurserymen to-day. The writers of this type of
imaginative literature haven't changed much! His business
was conducted by itinerant dealers who carried mixed nursery
and seed stock and who went from farm to farm.

The one Olmsted encountered in Mississippi purported to
represent a M. Rousset, a "member of several societies at
Paris (France), Boulevard of Hospital, and at Chambrey,
faubourg de Mache." The circular of this peddler states that,
"Mr. Rousset beg to inform they are arrived in this town,
with a large assortment of the most rare vegetable plants,
either flowered on fruit bearer, onion bulbous, seeds, etc., etc."
Among other things he lists are "Rhododendrums, Bubbs
Paeony, and Rosiers, Golden Renette, yellow, backwards
plant, The Chinese Strawberry, weihing 16 to a pound, produce fruit all year round, of the fine apple's taste, The Per-
petual Raspberry Tree, imported from Indies producing a
fruit large as an egg, taste delicious, 3 kinds, red, violet, and
white." But the pinnacle of horticultural temptations is
found in "The Judgment Trompette," which is introduced
to the marvelling yokels of Mississippi as follows:

"The admirable and strange plant called Trompette du Jugement (The Judgment Trompette), of that name having not yet found its classification.

"This marvellous plant was send to us from China by the clever and courageous botanical collector, M. Fortune, from l'Himalaya, near summet of the Chamalari Macon.

"This splendid plant deserves the first rank among all kinds of plant wich the botanical science has produce till now in spite of all the new discoveries.

"This bulbous plant gives several stems on the same subject. It grows to the height of 6 feet. It is furnished with flowers from bottom to top. The bud looks by his form like a big cannon ball of a heavenly blue. The centre is of an aurora yellewish colour. The vegetation of that plant is to fouitfull that when it is near to blossom it gives a great heat when tassing it in hand, and when the bud opens it produces a naite Similar to a pislole shot. Immediately the vegetation takes fire and burns like alcohol about an hour and half. The flowers succeeding one to the other gives the satisfaction of having flowers during 7 or 8 months.

"The most intense cold can not hurt this plant and can be cultivated in pots, in appartments or green houses.

"We call the public attention to this plant as a great curiosity."

Incidentally, the itinerant agent of nursery stock is still with us, and his wares are often as sublime fakes as some of M. Rousset's.

CHAPTER V

PEDDLERS AND BIG BUSINESS

TINWARE PEDDLERS AND THE TINWARE INDUSTRY

N 1738, two Irishmen from County Tyrone settled in the town of Berlin, Connecticut. William and Edgar Pattison were their names. A sister Anna accompanied them. They were tinsmiths by trade but they found little chance to practice it because tin was scarce. Two years after their arrival in Berlin they began importing sheet tin from England, working it up into cooking utensils. At that time most of such utensils were brought over from England and fetched high prices. The Pattisons did their work at home, beating out the vessels on anvils with wooden mallets. When they had accumulated a stock, they themselves sold it from door to door in Berlin. The local demand filled, they began walking to near-by settlements carrying their wares in sacks on their backs. They met with many sales because this new bright and shining ware was a welcome relief from the dull, drab, dented pewter generally in use. Their endeavours were celebrated by a local poetess, Emma Hart Willard, who describes the guests at a wedding as clamouring:—

"Oh, what's that lordly dish so rare,
"That glitters forth in splendour's glare?
"Tell us, Miss Norton, is it silver?
"It is from China or Brazil or . . . ?"
    Then all together on they ran.
    Quote the good dame, "'Tis a tin pan,
"The first made in the colony,
"The maker, Pattison's jest by,
"From Ireland in the last ship o'er.
"You all can buy. He'll soon make more!"

Not only did he make more, but so prosperous was his trade that other Berliners took up the manufacture of

tinware, and the town soon became the centre of the tin
industry, which continued there until 1850. From the small
beginning of a household employment, the work went into
factories located along streams that supplied water power.
Improved methods of manufacture increased the output
until it was not unusual for Berlin to consume 10,000
boxes of sheet tin a year most of it made up into culinary
utensils. Other tinware shops sprang up in Farmington and
near-by towns.

The methods of distributing and selling this output also
improved and increased. As we saw in a previous chapter,
the condition of the roads before the Revolution made wagon
travel difficult except along the main highways. Consequently, for some time the Pattisons and their imitators
carried their wares on foot or a-horseback. The dishes were
packed in large tin trunks, each weighing about 50 pounds
and two of these were slung on the peddler's back. Later
these trunks were slung on the horses.

By 1790 when the newly-fledged nation began building
turnpikes, the tin peddlers took to wagons. A special form of
cart was built for the purpose—a cart with a boxed body, one
that would contain as many tin vessels as a horse could con-
veniently draw. Later the size of the wagons was increased
and the team and the load were doubled.

Although the Pattisons and their immediate competitors
were at first their own salesmen, the industry grew so fast and
proved so lucrative that apprentices and peddlers had to be
hired. The early journeys of these peddlers' wagons were
limited; then, as the countryside was opened up by more
roads and by canals, the cart went farther and farther from
its initial base of supplies. It was not unusual for them to
cover 1200 to 1500 miles on a single trip, going down South,
up to Canada, and westward through the interior. Timothy
Dwight tells of having met tin peddlers on Cape Cod, on Lake
Erie, in Detroit, in Canada, and Kentucky, and says that
they made their way even to St. Louis and New Orleans.

Practically every inhabited part of the United States was visited by them.

The peddling trip generally began in late summer or winter, according to Dwight. As the peddler went farther from his factory, his stock grew less. To keep him supplied the following method was devised by the home manufacturers. The tin workers at Berlin would pile up a large stock through the spring and summer months—five men working at home could keep twenty-five selling on the road. Then the tinsmiths would be sent to various towns in the South, where they would make up another supply and where a stock of general goods was kept on hand. These workers carried their tools and tinplate with them and travelled, where possible, by water. Richmond, Newbern, Charleston, Savannah, Albany, and Montreal were the usual points of temporary manufacture. Here the workers stayed through the winter. The peddlers always managed to route their journeys so that when they had finished their stock they were in the neighbourhood of one of these towns. Here they handed their profits over to an agent and, re-supplied, started off on the road again for their spring and summer shifts. Then the workers returned to Connecticut. On the northern routes the peddlers started in early spring and the workers went to their temporary factories during the summer. As summer began, the wagons of the tin peddlers headed toward home. They usually foregathered in New York, where they sold their teams and wagons and went by boat back to Connecticut.

Very soon, of course, the tin peddler took on more than tin. By 1823, his stock was composed of "tinware, pins, needles, scissors, combs, buttons, children's books, cotton stuffs. . . A number set out with large wagons loaded with drygoods, hats and shoes together with tinware and the small articles already mentioned. These loads will frequently cost the proprietor from one to two thousand dollars, and are intended exclusively for the Southern and Western." It was the tin peddler, then, who was the original Yankee peddler.

In succeeding years the tin peddler exchanged his wares for linen rags, generally known as "paper rags," which were turned into the paper factories. In its early days, the great Crane Company of Pittsfield, Massachusetts, advertised the sentiment that patriotic housewives should save paper rags for the peddlers and thus help build up their infant industry. The tin peddlers also collected wood ashes for the potasheries and would barter notions and knick-knacks for this by-product of households. Thus the peddler played a role in the building up of other great industries besides his own.

PEDDLER HONESTY

Since most of the customers of the tinware peddler lived in isolated country areas, the peddler, as we have seen, was obliged to take farm produce and articles of home manufacture in exchange for his cooking utensils. His wagon was always filled. When a town was reached all this barter had to be converted into cash.

On the face of it, this bartering and this double responsibility of the early tin peddler would seem like taking a big risk. The first tinware peddlers weren't working for themselves; they were representatives of manufacturers in faraway Connecticut. Here were hundreds of young men trusted with a stock, trusted with a team, trusted with bartering, and depended upon to make honest reports and honest returns. In the light of their legendary reputation for dishonesty and slick dealing, this would seem almost expecting the impossible of the peddlers, certainly a too artless confidence on the part of their employers, for the Connecticut Yankee has never enjoyed the reputation of having confidence in any one except himself. Doubtless there were fraudulent and absconding peddlers in these first days, but the greater part of their evil reputation lies not in their dealings with their employers but in their overreaching of uninformed customers. Later on both the tin peddler and the other sorts were "staked" to a stock by the manufacturer or they bought it outright themselves.

Before we leave the tin peddler, let us quote an old Connecticut poem about him. Hugh Peters was the author. The title is:

A YANKEE LYRIC

There is, in famous Yankee-land
A class of men ycleped tin-peddlers,
A shrewd, sarcastic band
Of busy meddlers;
They scour the country through and through,
Vending their wares, tin pots, tin pans,
Tin ovens, dippers, wash-bowls, cans,
Tin whistles, kettles, or to boil or stew,
Tin dullenders, tin nutmeg graters,
Tin warming-platters for your fish and 'taters!
In short,
If you will look within
His cart,
And gaze upon the tin
Which glitters there,
So bright and fair,
There is no danger in defying
You to go off without buying.

One of these cunning, keen-eyed gentry
Stopped at a tavern in the country
Just before night,
And called for bitters for himself, of course,
And fodder for his horse:
This done, our worthy wight
Informed the landlord that his purse was low,
Quite empty, I assure you, sir, and so
I wish you'd take your pay
In something in my way.

Now Boniface supposed himself a wag—
And when he saw that he was sucked,
Was not dispirited, but plucked

Up courage and his trousers too!
Quoth he t'himself, I am not apt to brag,
'Tis true,
But I can stick a feather in my cap
By making fun of this same Yankee chap.
"Well, my good friend,
That we may end
This troublesome affair,
I'll take my pay in ware,
Provided that you've got what suits
My inclination."
"No doubt of that," the peddler cried,
Sans hesitation:
"Well, bring us in a pair of good tin boots!"
"Tin boots," our Jonathan espied
His landlord's spindle shanks,
And giving his good Genius thanks
For the suggestion,
Ran out, returned, and then—"By goles!
Yes, here's a pair of candle-moulds!
They'll fit you without question!"

PEDDLERS AND THE BRASS INDUSTRY

The tin industry well under way, there arose another—in brass. And it began very simply, in the making of brass buttons for clothes.

Practically every suit worn by men in the days prior to 1825 was garnished with innumerable brass, silver or pewter buttons, which at first were imported from England. Pewter was the material first used by American manufacturers and after the Revolution buttons of pewter were made at several towns in Connecticut, at Attleborough, Massachusetts, and at Philadelphia. The next step was to buy up old brass kettles and pots—peddlers used to collect them—hammer them out flat and convert them into buttons with punches and dies. But the first domestic manufacturers struck a snag in their distribution. Ordinarily the hardware dealers of those times handled clothes-buttons, but it appears that British buttons, or agents for British buttons (these agents of British manufacturers were generally shrewd Scotchmen) had so thoroughly convinced the dealers of the superiority of the British-made article that they refused to carry the American product. The English buttons had a colour the Americans were unable to imitate. So the Colonial manufacturers were obliged to turn their product over to the tin peddlers who, without the least inconvenience, added them to their tinware stock. And just as the tin peddler collected rags for the paper manufacturer, so he would pick up old copper and brass which was turned in to the brass-button maker at the end of the journey. When sheet brass became available, large objects were turned out—kettles and lamps—and the assortment varied to include cowbells, harness buckles and quantities of small Yankee notions.

The Naugatuck Valley of Connecticut, with Waterbury as its palpitating centre, saw the beginning of the brass industry. There was a brass factory in that town as early as 1750, making buttons, and knee and shoe buckles. At first the sheet brass was imported from England, then it was rolled here for the first time in 1823 with machinery brought from the Old Country by stealth. From these small beginnings, fathered by the peddler who carried brass wares to Canada and as far west as the Mississippi, started the American Brass Company.

CLOCK PEDDLERS AND THE CLOCK BUSINESS

It is said that the house of every substantial farmer in the days following the Revolution had three ornaments—a polyglot Bible, a tin reflector and a wooden clock. The tin we have discussed. The polyglot Bible "all in English" (one Yankee peddler is alleged to have sold £16,000 worth of them) is a myth. But the wooden clock was very real. And the wooden clock industry was another that depended on the peddler for its initial distribution.*

Up to 1800 the majority of clocks were imported from England in parts and assembled here by watch and clock-makers. The usual kind was what we know as a tall or grand-father clock, made to stand in gracious dignity in hallways and on landings of stairs.

A Connecticut Yankee conceived the idea of reducing the size of the clock so that it could be set on a shelf. Hitherto, itinerant clock salesmen had sold only the works, and the purchaser had to provide the case for the long clock, either making it himself or having the local cabinet-maker build it for him. Or else the open works were merely hung on the wall and in that *décolleté* condition came to be known as "wag-on-the-wall." The new design in clocks gave the purchaser a completed article. It was smaller. It could be transported easier and the price was reduced accordingly.

Eli Terry was the name of this Connecticut Yankee. He hailed from East Windsor. In 1793 he went to Plymouth, Connecticut, not far from Waterbury, where he took up clock-making as a business. The parts were cut out of hard wood and finished with a file. The cords were spun by women from their own flax. Twice a year, when he had accumulated a number of finished clocks, he started out on the road with them, going as far West as the Hudson and bartering them for salt pork and other produce. Sometimes he would go to southern Pennsylvania and Kentucky with his clocks. He

---

*G. W. Featherstonbaugh, an English scientist, who travelled through the middle west in the early '40's had the strange experience of being surrounded in one frontier settlement in Arkansas by excited women who insisted that he must have something to sell or must be a tailor. "These worthy people," he says, "think if you are not looking for land to settle, that you must be peddlers: there are no markets or shopkeepers in the country for them to go to, and therefore the markets come to them—peddlers to sell goods and tailors to cut coats and make their new clothes. As to the Yankee clocks peddler * * * in Kentucky, Indiana, Illinois, Missouri and here in every dell of Arkansas and in every cabin where there was not a chair to sit on there was sure to be a Connecticut clock."

carried four at a time—one forward on the saddle, one behind and one on each side in a portmanteau. The price asked was from $20 to $40 a clock, which is equivalent to four times that sum to-day.

The clocks of these early days were marked with Yankee canniness, "Warranted if well used." Most of the clocks were sold on the trial basis, and the price for them collected when the peddler came that way again. Often customers would give their notes for clocks and the notes would prove worthless, showing that peddlers weren't the only dishonest people in those days.

Terry's sales increased to such an extent that in 1807 a number of business men in Waterbury formed a company to finance him. They bought a mill on a stream where there was waterpower, installed machinery, and started in to lay out 500 clocks at a time. Quantity production of this kind was unknown in those days. Terry was a standing joke in the community until he proved that there were enough people in the world to buy five hundred clocks. There must have been, for we read that at one time eight or ten two-horse covered wagons would stand in a row opposite Terry's house, filled with clocks to be sent South. These goods were carted to the nearest port whence they were shipped to the cities, many of them to be afterward distributed by peddlers.

In the development of his business Terry was helped by a young mechanic, Seth Thomas, from West Haven. A few years later Thomas and an associate—Silas Hoadley—bought the original Terry factory and set up in business for themselves.

By 1837 brass had become cheap enough, even with hand labour, to compete with wood in clock-making. Three years later, at Bristol, Connecticut, Chauncey Jerome, who had been associated with Eli Terry, began stamping clock parts out of sheet brass by machinery. This put the wooden clock industry completely out of business. The finished brass parts for a one-day clock sold for five or six dollars. Thousands of

these were turned out—the output of Bristol alone was
100,000 clocks a year by 1840—and they became a regular
part of the peddler's stock.

Among the famous clock-makers who also peddled clocks
was Simon Willard, who gave us the Banjo clock. After the
death of his wife, Willard found surcease of his grief in roam-
ing about the country peddling. Another, hailing from Bristol,
Connecticut, was Gideon Roberts, who peddled clocks
before 1790; by 1812 he had a regular market, especially
in the South.

Some of the clock peddlers through the South traded
their clocks for mules, which they drove north for sale.

The clock peddler also acquired the knack of repairing
clocks and added that to his accomplishments. "The itinerant menders of clocks were more strongly marked than the
makers," Wallace Nutting observes in "The Clock Book."
"More than half a century since, the tinker and clock-repairer
and general exponent of mechanical genius went from house
to house in the country and gave a new lease of life to the
old tall clocks which had become rheumatic through
age or abuse."

This, then, is the story of the beginning of the clock business in America, and the part the peddler played in it. To-
day more than 80 per cent of the world's output of clocks
comes from the same state in which the peddler bought his—
Connecticut.

SAM SLICK

Though a character of fiction, *Sam Slick the Clockmaker*
portrays vividly the peddler of these wares; his salesmanship
was amazing. Here is an example:

"But how is it," said I, "that you manage to sell such an
immense number of clocks which certainly cannot be called
necessary articles, among people with whom there seems to
be so great a scarcity of money?"

Mr. Slick paused as if considering the propriety of answer-
ing the question and, looking me in the face, said, in a confi-

dential tone, "Why I don't care if I do tell you; for the market is glutted, and I shall quit this circuit. It is done by a knowledge of soft sawder and human natur.' But here is Deacon Flint's," said he, "I have but one clock left, and I guess I will sell it to him."

At the gate of a most comfortable looking farmhouse stood Deacon Flint, a respectable old man who had understood the value of time better than most of his neighbours. . ."

After the usual salutation, an invitation to alight was accepted by Mr. Slick, who said he wished to take leave of Mrs. Flint before he left Colchester.

We had hardly entered the house before the clockmaker, pointing to the view from the window, and addressing himself to me said, "If I was to tell them in Connecticut that there was such a farm as this away Down East here in Nova Scotia, they wouldn't believe me. Why, there ain't such a location in all New England. The Deacon has a hundred acres of dyke——"

"Seventy," said the Deacon, "only seventy."

"Well, seventy; but then there is your fine deep bottom. Why, I could run a ramrod into it——"

"Interval we call it," said the Deacon, who, though evidently pleased at this eulogium, seemed to wish the experiment of the ramrod to be tried in the right place.

"Well, interval if you please—though Professor Eleazer Cumstick, in his work on Ohio, calls them bottoms—is jist as good as dyke. Then there is that water privilege, worth three or four thousand dollars, twice as good as that Governor Case paid fifteen thousand dollars for. I wonder, Deacon, you don't put up a cardin' mill on it; the same works would carry a tunin' lathe, a shingle machine, a circular saw, grind bark, and——"

"Too old," said the Deacon, "too old for all these speculations——"

"Old!" repeated the Clockmaker. "Not you. Why, you are worth half a dozen of the young men we see now-a-days.

6

You are young enough to have——" Here he said something in a lower tone of voice which I did not distinctly hear; but, whatever it was, the Deacon was pleased: he smiled and said he did not think of such things now.

"But your beasts, dear me, your beasts must be put in and have a feed. . ."

As the old gentleman closed the door after him, Mr. Slick drew near to me and said in an undertone, "That is what I call soft sawder. . ."

"Now I find——"

Here his lecture on soft sawder was cut short by the entrance of Mrs. Flint.

"Jist come to say good-by, Mrs. Flint."

"What, have you sold all your clocks?"

"Yes, and very low too; for money is scarce, and I wished to close the concarn. I am wrong in sayin' all; for I have jist one left. Neighbour Steel's wife asked to have the refusal of it, but I guess I won't sell it. I had but two of 'em, this one and the feller of it that I sold Governor Lincoln. Gineral Green, the Secretary of State for Maine, said he'd give me fifty dollars for this here one—it has composition wheels and patent axles; it is a beautiful article, a rael first chop, no mistake, genuine superfine—but I guess I'll take it back. And, besides, Squire Hawk might think kinder hard that I did not give him the offer."

"Dear me," said Mrs. Flint, "I should like to see it. Where is it?"

"It is in a chest of mine over the way, at Tom Tape's store. I guess he can ship it on to Eastport."

"That's a good man," said Mrs. Flint, "jist let's look at it."

Mr. Slick, willing to oblige, yielded to these entreaties and soon produced the clock, a gaudy, highly varnished, trumpery affair. He placed it on the chimney piece, where its beauties were pointed out and duly appreciated by Mrs. Flint, whose admiration was about ending in a proposal when Mr.

Flint returned from giving his directions about the care of the horses.

The Deacon praised the clock. He too thought it a handsome one; but the Deacon was a prudent man—he had a watch—he was sorry—but he had no occasion for a clock.

"I guess you're in the wrong furrow this time, Deacon. It ain't for sale," said Mr. Slick. "And if it was, I reckon Neighbour Steel's wife would have it; for she gives me no peace about it."

Mrs. Flint said Mr. Steel had enough to do, poor man, to pay his interest without buying clocks for his wife.

"It's no concern of mine," said Mr. Slick, "as long as he pays me, what he has to do; but I guess I don't want to sell it. And, besides, it comes too high; that clock can't be made at Rhode Island under forty dollars."

"Why, it ain't possible," said the Clockmaker, in apparent surprise, looking at his watch, "why, as I'm alive, it is four o'clock, and if I ha'n't been two hours here. How on airth shall I reach River Philip to-night. I'll tell you what, Mrs. Flint, I'll leave the clock in your care until I return on my way to the States. I'll set it a-goin' and put it to the right time."

As soon as this operation was performed, he delivered the key to the Deacon with a sort of serio-comic injunction to wind up the clock every Saturday night. . . .

"That," said the Clockmaker, as soon as we were mounted, "that I call human natur.' Now, that clock is sold for forty dollars. It cost me jist six dollars and fifty cents. Mrs. Flint will never let Mrs. Steel have the refusal; nor will the Deacon larn until I call for the clock . . . how hard it is to give it up. We can do without any article of luxury we have never had, but . . . it is not in human natur' to surrender it voluntarily. Of fifteen thousand sold by myself and my partners in this Province, twelve thousand were left in this manner; and only ten clocks were ever returned. . . . We trust to soft sawder to get them into the house, and to human natur' that they never come out of it."

The yarns about Yankee clock peddlers are legion. Perhaps the most amusing is the one about the peddler who always sold a clock on the understanding that he would return in a few weeks, and, if the clock did not run satisfactorily, would replace it with another. It was also his rule to sell all the clocks in his stock but one. When he reached the end of his route he turned back with his one remaining clock. At the first house, the clock he had sold did not run, so he replaced it with the one that remained. At the second house, he replaced the unsatisfactory clock with the one he had taken from the first house. And so on, he went, selling and replacing clocks that never would work, and waxing fat on the proceeds!

THE WHOLESALE PEDDLER

The peddler was a dealer apart from the town merchant—often his strongest competitor—but in his later development the peddler took on a wholesale function and served the town merchant to their mutual advantage. Commercial drummers from New York, Boston, Philadelphia, and other wholesale houses were not so common then as now. In the mid-nineteenth century, the town merchant usually made an annual or semi-annual stock-buying trip to the big cities, but between these trips his stock often ran low. Also, if his town was located far from a railroad, quick supplies were not available and he was forced to forego profitable trade. This demand gave rise to the wholesale peddler who, in his day, was a well-known figure on the roads.

The "merchant prince" of wholesale peddlers in New England was Henry W. Carter of Vermont, for he had practically a monopoly in this line. His headquarters were first at Chelsea, Vermont, then at Lebanon, New Hampshire. Here his warehouses were kept stocked and from them drove the flashy teams that, in their day, were a sensation. Evidently a believer in advertising, Mr. Carter had five teams of four horses each, and one of six—beautiful, well-matched

Aspiring artists often served their apprenticeship in a shop such as this
Then they took to the road

Candles, both the moulded and the dipped, were peddled and itinerant candle-makers
were known to our early roads

horses with silver-mounted harness. The wagons, huge affairs, were brilliantly painted, some with scenes on the sides, and always kept highly varnished. They made an impressive sight as they dashed up the main street of a country town and drew rein before the general store or the local hotel. In winter the wagons were put on runners.

These wagons were rolling, wholesale jobbing establishments, for they carried a complete stock equal in variety to the large wholesale stores of the cities. Each load was worth several thousand dollars. There would be a complete line of Yankee notions, silk and linen, suspenders, knives, scissors, soap and perfume, pins and needles, buttons, edgings and trimmings. Various side lines were also carried—tableware of silver and plate, china, cups and saucers, jewellery and choice brands of tobacco and cigars. It is recorded that in seven weeks one of Carter's teams disposed of $11,000 worth of cheap watches! The country merchant might buy $25 worth of stock from these wagons, or he might plunge as much as $200, or more. The stock of these teams was kept up-to-date and occasionally they made bargain-sale trips to clear out old style and shopworn goods. Carter bought in large quantities from the manufacturers and could stock his wagons at rock-bottom figures. No wonder he amassed a fortune!

These Carter teams covered routes in New Hampshire and Vermont up to the Canadian line and through Massachusetts and Connecticut. Each team was so routed that it could cover forty or fifty towns on the outward and return trip four times a year. In the spring and fall the wagons returned to headquarters for inventory and re-stocking. There were also small warehouses on each route where the drivers could replenish their stocks.

THE WAGON DOCTOR

Mr. Carter's passion for gaudy teams reminds us that the Wagon Doctor had the same. In many places there were light wagon and sleigh peddlers—makers of wagons who hawked them around the immediate country districts, but the Wagon Doctor was a much more picturesque figure and much more of a scamp. His methods are aptly exhibited in the life and labours of an ancestor of one of our families now renowned for philanthropy.

This slick cadger went through the central New York countryside buying up discarded light wagons, broken old carcasses that their owners were ready to throw on the dumps. A few cents was a reasonable price to pay for them. These he would pile aboard his cart and haul home, where they were put into shape—a wheel or a swingle-tree from one being attached to the wagon that lacked them. Then a local painter willing to work for fifty cents a day, covered their palpable imperfections with glistening paint. When a number of them had been put into shape so that they would stand up under a few days' driving, the Doctor would lead his caravan into a country town on market day, and plaster the walls with posters announcing his monster sale of new light wagons. In his own cart he always carried a jug or two of homemade "hooch" which he dispensed liberally to the crowd before starting the sale, a custom in those days at vendues.

Then the sale would commence, with much banter and rustic persiflage and hyperbole. In the crowd were the Doctor's "comers-on" who bid in the first two wagons. These sales made, the whiskey was passed again. The farmers started to bid. A nice light wagon to take the wife to church in! A pretty painted wagon you wouldn't be ashamed of! Sixty dollars was the average price brought by these miserable hulks.

Toward dusk the gullible farmers hitched their priceless acquisitions to the back of their carts and drove home. If the wagon lasted till they reached there, they were lucky. Some even stood up long enough to take the wife to church the next Sunday. Then the rutted country roads proved what junk they had been swindled into buying.

The Wagon Doctor never tried to repeat a sale in the same town; he always chose a distant county for his new endeavours.

CHAPTER VI

THE DECLINE OF YANKEE PEDDLING

N THE tap-rooms of cross-road Pennsylvania taverns, once on a time, the drivers of Conestoga wagons used to foregather and pound their beer mugs to a curse that ran this way:—

Bad luck to the man who invented the plan,
For he ruined us wagoners and every other man.

The "plan" referred to was the canal system then being built which put them out of business.

If the Yankee peddlers had some such swan song, it is not recorded. Perhaps at the inns of Connecticut they groused and cursed as the wagoners did. But theirs would have been a different ballad, because not one plan or one man or one circumstance ruined their business; they were the gradual victims of the progress and development of the country.

The same improvement in means of communication that increased their markets and spread their trade also contributed to their downfall. The steamboat and the railroad reduced them to a subsidiary place as carriers of merchandise. The farther the railroads went, the deeper into the rural and frontier districts was driven the peddler.

By 1860 railroads, highways, and river traffic—railroads especially—made it possible for factories to supply the needs of a far larger proportion of the people for manufactured goods. Steamboats and trains brought stock to the inland merchants who lived at a great distance from manufacturing centres, and carried raw materials to inland factories and finished goods to inland warehouses. At the same time better roads made it easier for the rural populations to get into towns for their purchases, although it is well to bear in mind that the great paved arteries that now cross and recross the continent are concomitants of the automobile. Of course the

The "Best Friend," the First Locomotive built in the United States for actual service on a Railroad.

The "Best Friend" was built at the West Point Foundry Shops in New York City, for the South Carolina Railroad, arrived in Charleston by ship Niagara October 23d, and after several experimental trials, in November and December, 1830, made the first excursion trip, as shown, on Saturday, 14th January, 1831, being the anniversary of the commencement of the construction of the road. (Copied from Charleston Courier, page 152.)

From "The History of the First Locomotive in America", by William Henry Brown, a celebrated silhouette-cutter

Exciting Trial of Speed between Mr. Peter Cooper's Locomotive, "Tom Thumb," and one of Stockton & Stokes's Horse-Cars.

The trial took place on the Baltimore and Ohio Railroad, on the 28th August, 1830. The sketch represents the moment the Engine overtook and passed the Horse-Car, the passengers filled with excitement.

HORSE-POWER LOCOMOTIVE.

SAILING-CAR.

Pedlars Licences

1770

Date	Name		Mode	Amount	Total
Dec 14	Andreas Steel Recd 3 Ins.t		Travels on foot	1..1..0	1..1..0
1771 Jan.y 15	Alexander Ewren Recd th Inst		Travels on foot	1..1..0	1..1..0
Feb.y 1	Bartholomew Stole 28 Jan.y		with Horse	1..11..0	
4	Martin Franks		on foot	1..1..0	
11	Peter Gallagher		with horse	1..11..0	4..3..0
March 7	Michael Meyer (Recd the order)		Ditto	1..11..0	
21	William Kerr (Recd this day)		Ditto	1..11..0	3..2..0
April 19	Jacob Riser Do this day		on foot	1..01..0	
30	John Barron Do this day		with horse	1..11..0	2..12..0

The following Licences were issued in Mr.
Hamilton's names — Viz

May 1771
15	Joseph Scott Recd th Inst		Travels with Horse	1..11..0	1..11..0

June 1771
14	John Grate		Travels with Horse	1..11..0	
18	Frederic Ane		Do	1..11..0	
24	James Alexander		Do	1..11..0	4..13..0

July 1771
20	Robert Lilley		Travels with Horse		1..11..0

August
7	Barney Riney		Do	1..11..0	
14	James Brown		Do	1..11..0	
17	David Burnside		Do	1..11..0	4..13..0

September
5	John Henry		Travels on foot	1..01..0	
14	Peter Biss		Travels with Horse	1..11..0	2..12..0

October
10	Daniel Gillin		Travels on foot	1..1..0	
19	Matthew Thompson		Travels with Horse	1..11..0	2..12..0

November
1	John McCartney			1..11..0	
9	James Homer			1..1..0	
13	Isaac Wolf			1..11..0	
16	John Shedder			1..11..0	
29	William McCandlass			1..11..0	7..5..0

From the original in the possession of The Historical Society of Pennsylvania

Yankee peddler was almost a memory years before the first motor-car made its appearance.

To a degree the free-lance peddler was also a victim of conspiracy.

In the beginning he was one of the few means for the distribution of manufactured goods. Quantities of these goods were sent to shops in towns, but, had there been no peddlers there would have been no countryside distribution, and with no distribution, manufacturing, even of the humblest household sort, could never have thrived. Despite this service, the peddler's foe was the established, settled, town merchant.

We can trace the dislike of the town for the country through practically all phases of itinerant life. We shall meet it when we come to the wayfaring preachers. We find it among the wandering trades. In the history of merchandising manufactured goods in this country it gathered force at an early date.

THE PEDDLER UNDER THE LAW

In both New England and in Pennsylvania there was evolved, in the years previous to the Revolution, a distinct and strong merchant class, and these merchant groups operated to force the peddler out of existence by legislating against him.

In 1717 Connecticut peddlers paid to the town which they first entered, 20 shillings for every hundred pounds worth of goods they carried. Ten years later a group of Connecticut town merchants petitioned the Governor and House of Magistrates to suppress the "Multitudes of foreign or Peregrine Peddlers who flock into this Colony and travel up and Down in it with Packs of Goods to Sell." They claimed that the town merchants paid taxes and these peddlers paid none; also they professed great fear lest peddlers would introduce into the Colony "many raging and contagious Diseases." Since Connecticut was the home of the Yankee peddler, this petition reads very much like the proverbial and acrimonious conversation between the pot and the kettle.

The pressure against the peddler was constant. In 1765 the Connecticut Assembly was induced to raise the cost of the peddler's license from £5 to £20, a prohibitive figure. This date, it will be remembered, was only twenty-five years after the Pattison brothers sent out their first tinware vendors from Berlin. And as soon as this tax was imposed, the Assembly of Connecticut was bombarded by all manner of citizens who begged for peddling licenses without having to pay the exorbitant tax—ex-soldiers, men in poor health, the maimed and the halt, who could not do steady work. In 1770, all peddlers, hawkers and petty chapmen were forbidden doing business in Connecticut, save those who dealt in pelts and the produce and manufacture of that and neighbouring colonies. This was aimed not only at foreign peddlers but at the sale of imported goods.

In Rhode Island in 1698 we find a law stating that the peddlers injured regular trade. A heavy tax was imposed in 1700; in 1713 peddlers were forbidden to sell drygoods anywhere in the state; in 1728 a general law, more comprehensive than the last, forbade peddlers selling every sort of merchandise on penalty of forfeiture. And in 1750 we find the complaint which tells the whole story—that peddlers were objectionable to town merchants because the town merchants were taxed, paid rent and were under other expenses that the peddler did not have to bear. The town merchant insisted that the peddler be meted the same justice as he. Being a wily person, the Rhode Island vendor dodged the law by hiring a shop in which he carried on his trade for a short time, but for which he was not taxed because he was not an inhabitant!

In Pennsylvania, forty-five years before the Revolution, peddlers were licensed, but the fees were to be remitted if they sold only those goods manufactured in the province. This Pennsylvania statute—dated August 15, 1730—was directed against "idle and vagrant persons who come into the province under pretence of being hawkers or peddlers and carrying goods from house to house . . . and have greatly imposed upon many people as well in the quality as in the price of their goods and under colour of selling their wares have entered houses and committed felonies." Such peddlers as were granted licenses were to first obtain a warrant of good character from the justice of their county court, put up a bond not to exceed £40 and for the license pay twenty-five shillings if they went by horse and fifteen if they went afoot. Those found doing business without a license were to be heavily fined and treated as common vagrants. There is no record of this bill having passed; for in 1762, according to the Provincial account books, a peddler with wagon paid £1 11s and those afoot £1 1s.

These laws against peddlers can be found in many province and state records. And there is much to be said for the case of the established town merchant who supported them. In Louisiana in 1820, for example, the storekeeper was assessed $110 a year, whereas the peddler paid only $12. The peddlers of New Hampshire paid the same sum for their licenses in 1815, but were forbidden to sell feathers, distilled spirits, playing cards, lottery tickets and jewellery.

However, one good came out of these assessments on peddlers—the House of Burgesses of Virginia voted to the College of William and Mary all proceeds from peddlers' taxes, whereas in other provinces the money was divided between the justice of the peace and the public treasury, and the fines went to the treasury and those who informed on peddlers selling without licenses.

THE COMING OF THE JEWS

Another factor that hastened the decline of the Yankee peddler was the coming of the German Jew to America.

Jews were in this country almost from the beginning. We find them in Rhode Island very early; they arrived in Carolina shortly after Oglethorpe had laid out Savannah; New York had Portuguese Jews from Holland and Brazil, and the first congregation formed by 1682; Philadelphia and the back country around Lancaster saw them settled there by 1734.

In New York both the Dutch and the English forbade the Jew entering retail trade, so they took to keeping taverns, distilling, goldsmithing, auctioning and butchering, but mostly they went into importing and exporting. Luis Gomez became one of the leading merchants in pre-Revolutionary New York; his country residence at Marlborough-on-Hudson is still commemorated by the name of the creek that flows near by, known to the older inhabitants as Jew's Creek.

The Census of 1790—the first—shows the Jews to be less than one-tenth of one per cent of the total population. Not until 1835 did the great Jewish migration to this country begin. It followed the oppressive marriage laws promulgated in Bavaria. The peddlers among them had been legislated against in their native land. They came here in droves and many of the men immediately took to peddling. First they were trunk-peddlers. After a few weeks they were able to pay off their original liability and, when the necessary funds had been saved, they bought a horse and wagon and increased both their stock and the distances they were able to cover. Many well-known department stores in various sections of the country were established by these Jews, or their descendants who came here in '35 and started their commercial careers as pack-peddlers.

The latest migration of Jews came from Russia and Poland from 1882 on, following the pogroms and reactionary movements of the Russian police under M. von Plehve after the assassination of Alexander II. They, however, did not take to peddling so much as did the Germans, but were absorbed in the growing industrial system of the country. Such of them as did peddle were rather apt to become push-cart merchants in their own ghettos.

The Pennsylvania Provincial Accounts for 1760–1766, which contain the names of those taking out wedding, tavern, and peddler's licenses, record only two Jews in those six years. When the German Jew did come in quantities, he soon crowded out the Yankee peddler. The peddlers who are remembered by old inhabitants to-day are mostly men of this nationality, together with a few local native characters who carried on an itinerant trade traditional to their families or supported by certain local areas.

The years following the Revolution saw the merchant class grow stronger and more widely spread. Since these merchants were combined to an extent and since the peddlers were more or less free-lances, the itinerant was a competitor easy to legislate against. Doubtless some of the peddler's undesirable reputation was due to propaganda fostered by merchants.

In later years any dealing with peddlers was apt to give the city merchant who indulged in it a bad name, yet there were countless wholesale houses in Boston, New York, and Philadelphia that did a backdoor business with peddlers. Some did nothing else.

THE PEDDLER'S SERVICES

The peddler's reputation for sly tricks has completely overshadowed any appreciation we might be ready to express of the many worthy and useful purposes he served in his generation. In leaving him it is only fair to mention his other side.

Previous to his coming, practically all of the time of the men, women and children in the scattered country areas was devoted to making and growing of things necessary to their existence. With his arrival some of this burden of domestic manufacture was lightened. The householder bought from the peddler's stock that which hitherto he used to consume hours and days in making.

A vast amount of sentiment has been wasted over this Homespun Era. It has been spoken of as a Golden Age. The women of it have been lauded for the constancy of their work and the men for the way they bent their back to the arduous farm chores. Indeed they deserve all the praise we can give them, but the era was far from ideal. It was an age of merciless toil. So engrossed were they in the labour of the day-to-day existence that they had no chance to improve their condition, either the women to refine their home surroundings or the men to initiate and develop better farming and cattle breeding methods. In coast towns, whither imported goods came, the situation may have been brighter; the back country areas present anything but a reassuring picture.

While in the beginning the articles that went into the peddler's pack and cart were all that the market might afford, in later days he was the outlet for merchant's remnants and factory seconds. To-day some of the five-and-ten-cent stores sell what the peddler used to dispose of.

The merchant was the dealer of the town; the peddler was the dealer of the thinly settled countryside. The merchant who ran a general store, was, however, the outgrowth of the peddler's system of general merchandising. From the peddler's pack of early days to the great metropolitan department stores of to-day is a vast distance, but the line of descent is unbroken.

The peddler brought the store in miniature to the consumer's door. To-day, with every farmer owning an automobile, the consumer goes to the store or buys from a mail-order house. The economic need of the peddler therefore has passed.*

But if he is gone, he served a purpose in the frontier life of young America that cannot be forgotten as long as history endures. For he was a social figure in the existence of the common people, and in that lies his immortality.

As we have seen, spring and autumn country fairs and the

---

* In central New York, however, itinerant grocery stores on trucks are beginning to revive the old peddling system. Theirs is a strictly cash business. They handle "package" groceries, and it is said that town grocers, who once enjoyed the trade of the farmer who came into town, are feeling this loss of business. Does this mean that the improvement of roads, which helped put the peddler out of business, is now bringing him back again?

weekly or semi-weekly markets in town and the Training Days were his happy hunting ground. He flew to them as steel to a magnet. Here he would open his pack or display goods on his cart and hawk to the passer-by. And he always seems to have had a way with the ladies. John Dunton, the roving bookseller, states that a virtuous woman could be distinguished as one who did not go to fairs "in order to meet with chapmen" or peddlers. What possibilities that picture opens up!—the dour New England household, the psalm-singing husband and the atmosphere of suppression under piety and poverty in which the women lived. What a relief on market days was the garrulous chapman! He may even have gone so far as to have exchanged a wink! Let's hope he did; for the Pilgrim wives deserved every little iota of enjoyment a merciful Providence might spare them, even if it came from a peddler!

A later bookman, Nathaniel Hawthorne, describes in his "American Notes" the peddlers who made the commencement at Williams College in 1838 more than a scholastic fête:—"The most characteristic part of the scene was where the peddlers, ginger-bread sellers, etc., were collected. There was a peddler there from New York State who sold his wares by auction, and I could have stood and listened to him all day long. Sometimes he would put up a heterogeny of articles in a lot—as a paper of pins, a lead pencil, and a shaving box—and knock them all down, perhaps for ninepence. Bunches of lead pencils, steel pens, pound cakes of shaving soap, gilt finger-rings, bracelets, clasps and other jewellery, cards of pearl buttons, or steel, bundles of wooden combs, boxes of matches, suspenders and, in short, everything—dipping his hand down into his wares, with the promise of a wonderful lot, and producing, perhaps, a bottle of opodeldoc, and joining it with a lead pencil."

The result of their travels made the peddlers literally walking directories. They knew the old Indian trails and the white man's road as well; they could help stranger and native find the way, and locate kin and shelter. As patriots, time and again they served to rally the isolated country folks to the nation's support. Politicians used them as election touts. It was not uncommon for an office-seeker to refer contemptuously to his opponent as "a peddler's candidate." He carried good news and bad, gossip, scandal, droll stories and love missives from house to house. Imagine how welcome he was to the women folk and men of the isolated frontiers! And then, when he returned home, what great things he had to relate—tales of different people, of new environments! And what a new man he was—a man of broader visions and more liberal ideas!

CHAPTER VII

WORKMEN OF THE ROAD

S WE have seen, the tinware peddler added tinkering to his vocation, the clock peddler became a repairer of clocks and the vendor of nostrums an amateur physician. These, however, represented only an insignificant section of the itinerant workers known in various early times to our country roads.

Just why the vagabond worker became a vagabond, and how he eventually settled down, is an interesting story. In telling it we touch on a number of romantic pictures—the economic evolution of the worker, the household industries of early America, the nature of the early emigration to these shores.

During Colonial days the energy and time of nine-tenths of the people were devoted to cultivating the soil. Labour in those years was not highly specialized as we know it, although practised and experienced craftsmen were constantly coming here from abroad. Where common labour was required, the colonist depended on indentured servants, apprentices, convicts, and slaves.

SLAVES, CONVICTS, AND REDEMPTIONERS

In addition to the importation of hordes of negro slaves, certain parts of the Atlantic seaboard served as the Siberia of England. Between 1717 and 1775 over 40,000 convicts were shipped to the middle and southern provinces. Maryland was made a penal colony and after 1750 four or five hundred of these dregs and slops of society were each year poured on her people. Up to the Revolution no less than 20,000 of them—despite protest—had been landed in that province alone. These felons were brought over by regular contractors who were paid at the rate of £5 per man, f.o.b. London landed in Maryland.

The indentured servant falls into a different class. Vast numbers of the men and women who came to America previous to the Revolution and for some years afterward, were unable to pay their passage and so bonded themselves to work out this cost as indentured servants. Some, indeed, did not come of their own volition. There used to be quite a thriving little trade among the underworld of London and other parts of England in kidnapping men and delivering them to ship captains for passage money indenture in the Colonies. The men who drove this trade were called "Spirits." The majority of the redemptioners, however, were just lacking in funds, or were unfortunate in their political affiliations and so were banished to America.

The captain of the ship that brought them, representing the owners of the vessel, sold them when port was reached. A Philadelphia paper of 1817 displayed the following advertisement:

THE PASSENGERS

On board the brig Bubona, from Amsterdam, and who are willing to engage themselves for a limited time, to defray the expenses of their passage, consist of persons of the following occupations, besides women and children, viz.: 13 farmers, 2 bakers, 2 butchers, 8 weavers, 3 taylors, 1 gardner, 3 masons, 1 mill-sawyer, 1 white-smith, 2 shoemakers, 3 cabinet-makers, 1 coal-burner, 1 barber, 1 carpenter, 1 stocking-weaver, 1 cooper, 1 wheelwright, 1 1 brewer, 1 locksmith. Apply on board of the Bubona, opposite Callowhill-street, in the river Delaware, or to W. Odlin and Co., No. 38 South Wharves.

The time of these indentured servants, or redemptioners, was priced at from £2 and £4 a year according to their age, strength, and health. The term of service lasted from five to seven years, during which a man or woman might learn a trade, or practise one he already knew. Or he even might buy his freedom. The master clothed and fed him. At the end of his term he was given two full suits of clothes, a set of tools necessary for his trade and some money, called "freedom dues." He then went on his own. Either he settled in that locality or moved to another. In the Middle Colonies, where manual labor was considered a decent calling, these servants became substantial citizens; in the South, they were generally unable to rise in the social scale until after the Revolution. The early "poor white" class may be attributable to this fact, and to the convict element.

Virginia, as well as Massachusetts and the rest of New England managed to resist the dumping of paupers and convicts on their shores, and this bore its effect in the type of men these two great commonwealths produced during the Revolutionary and Federal periods. One traveller to New England in 1822 comments on the use of the term "hired man," indicating an economic status in the North that the indentured servant would not have attained elsewhere. The shipping of these redemptioners stopped about 1820.   37764

This form of voluntary slavery left behind it all manner of legends. Some are sad, and some are funny. The most amusing is the tale of the Irish redemptioner who, like so many of his fellows, had been peddled around Philadelphia. Finally he was bought in by a farmer who started to take him home. They had to stop over night at an inn. The next morning the Irishman arose very early, sold his master to the keeper of the inn, and, as he pocketed the money, gave the rustic a good character, "Only," he said, "he's addicted to lying!"

APPRENTICES

Another source of workers was furnished by the apprentice system whereby young men and boys were bound over to a master to be taught a trade. They were clothed and lodged and fed, and, after a term of years, turned loose to work out their own careers. In a number of cases, in towns especially, these newly fledged journeymen set up in business for themselves or were employed by their old masters. Generally the journeymen had to go from place to place seeking employment, according to the demand for his type of labour, and along the way did any kind of work that might come to his hand and afford him meals and lodging. This was called "Whipping the Cat" and "Whipping the Stump"—why, it is difficult to say. When a young journeyman found a profitable section, he might settle down and become identified with that community. Others, lured on by the persisting temptation of the road and the ever-widening frontiers, remained nomads to their dying day.

That the nomadic skilled worker should find employment in the thinly populated country districts was due to the fact that practically every household represented one or more domestic industries. In the towns along the coast merchants could supply clothing and household wares, but in the back country districts, where distances isolated families, they had to depend on their own skill and resourcefulness for the production of these items. Certain branches of the work were either too heavy or too difficult for the unpractised settler, and in these lines the itinerant worker found some of his employment.

In New England and the Middle Colonies many industries that later grew into large and stabilized concerns had their beginnings in the home, and from the household class were recruited their first workers. It was not a far cry from the loom at home to the loom in the factory. Again, in the stabilizing of an industry, many nomadic workers disappeared from the road. Examples of these two influences are found in the rise of the boot and shoe industry and in the woollen industry.

SHOEMAKERS AND COBBLERS

In the primitive days, when the head of the house was a jack-of-all-trades, the father or the elder brother made and repaired the family shoes. The family was self-contained as to footgear. When apprentices and lately indentured servants began to "whip the cat," the shoemakers among them went from house to house making and repairing shoes. In this stage of the industry—when it was just beginning to issue forth from the cocoon of the home—the householder supplied the leather (which he obtained from the local tannery) and the findings and often a workbench; the cobbler carried only his tools—lapstone, hammer, and awls—and a few lasts wrapped up in a leathern apron and slung over his shoulder, or pushed along in a hand cart. Itinerant shoemakers in the South also provided wooden heels for women's shoes, since they were generally covered with silk provided by the mistress of the house. Sometimes, when his route was small, he went about with his workbench on his back or in his cart. Often these journeymen shoemakers farmed in spring and summer, and cobbled for the neighbourhood in winter. People would date up the cobbler ahead of time, and often determine the price of work. He was generally paid in board and lodgings. By 1700, journeymen cobblers of Pennsylvania and New Jersey earned two shillings per pair of shoes plus food and lodging. In country pay this was equivalent to three pecks of corn. The ranks of the shoemakers were recruited from farmers' sons in Massachusetts and from negroes, Germans, and English in Pennsylvania and the South.

In "The Book of Daniel Drew" Bouck White remarks as to the visits of this itinerant shoemaker: "We used to learn the news in a general way when the cobbler came to the house once a year to make up the year's supply of shoes and boots for the household. This visit of the cobbler was quite an event each year. Father would prepare for it by swapping a pair of cattle or a load of potatoes down at Foster's tan-yard for a few sides of leather. Then the cobbler would come for a week or so and make the leather up into footwear. When the the cobbler came, it was the boy's work to whittle out the pegs for him."

This picture must have been drawn after 1811, for wooden pegs were not used until that year; previous to that time shoes were hand-sewed throughout.

The second stage of the industry was reached when the journeyman shoemaker, finding a likely town, settled down there. Then his customers would bring leather to the shop to have their shoes made. This was called "bespoke work." Between times the shoemaker, from his own stock of leather or from leather left over from bespoke jobs, might make up a few shoes that he peddled, or bartered with the farmers for leather and foodstuffs. These were called "sales" or "shop" shoes. At first these shoes were carried to market by the maker in panniers or in a cart.

From this stage on, the industry begins to stabilize. Merchants supply leather, and cobblers in their own shops make shoes in quantity and on different lasts and sizes. A system of sizes is drafted in 1700. Gradually groups of cobblers begin to work together in one shop under supervision. All grades of shoes are made, including the cheapest, called "market" shoes, because they are sold at low prices in the public markets, just as we find them to-day on push-carts in New York.

These quantity-made shoes were shipped by boat in barrels, tea chests, sugar boxes, and hogsheads, without regard to quality or size and went to Philadelphia and Baltimore where they were bartered for produce. On their arrival at these ports, people trooped down to the wharf. The captain hoisted up a barrel or a box of shoes, and converted his deck into a retail shoeshop.

Not until 1836 did the manufacturers of Lynn, the great New England shoe centre, begin to use regular shoe boxes, and, indeed, not until 1830 was there machinery for preparing leather or making shoes; up to that date the work was all done by hand.

Towns around Boston and Philadelphia were the two centres of the shoe industry, and salesmen went thence through the South taking orders—custom shoes for the gentry and quantity stock for their slaves. One New England firm—Batcheller of Brookfield, Massachusetts—in 1831

began making a special line of russet brogans for Southern slaves. These became the chief product of the firm and
enjoyed immense popularity among the negroes. Can this
account, we wonder, for the negro's prevailing passion for
yellow shoes?

Wherever you find him, the shoemaker respects his calling,
and from almost the beginning these sons of St. Crispin were
banded into a guild. The first was The Company of Shoemakers in Boston in 1648; then came the Society of Master
Cordwainers of Philadelphia in 1789, the Federation of
Journeymen Cordwainers in 1794, the United Beneficial
Society of Journeymen in 1835 and in 1868 the Knights of
St. Crispin. The first strike called in this country was ventured by the Philadelphia shoemakers in the early part of the
nineteenth century.

It was natural that men of this noble and respected calling
should resent the inroads of poor workmanship. The established cordwainers of the towns despised the vagabond
cobbler of the countryside whose work, not being supervised,
was apt to be poor and whose charges were below the current
market prices. So we find the better-trained Boston cobblers,
who worked in their shops, petitioning the courts for redress
against these nomads, and, "the damage which the country
sustains by occasions of bad wear."

However, the vagabond shoemaker made a place for himself in the hearts of the country people. He was generally
good company—could whistle and sing and crack jokes and
spin yarns. Up in New Hampshire in the neighbourhood of
Weare, one nomad shoemaker was long remembered. John
Anderson was his name, a Scotch-Irish emigrant, popular at
young people's parties for his Scotch songs and stories. He
always wore leather breeches.

WOOL AND FABRICS

For the first hundred years after the colonization of this
country the attempts to introduce commercial manufacturing

could scarcely be called successful. The household industries
held down the demand for factory-made goods and, whenever
manufacturers managed to accumulate a surplus and sell it,
laws were quickly enacted against them through the influence of British manufacturers who brooked no competition.
By 1731, for example, more than 10,000 beaver hats were
being made annually in New York and New England. So
strongly did they compete with the British product that
the English hatters supported a law prohibiting the expor-
tation of hats from the Colonies and limiting their manufacture. Constantly American Colonial manufacturers were
inhibited and suppressed. Nevertheless, the home industries thrived, and the greatest of them was the making
of cloth.

In practically every household women and children carded
and spun wool. At first only the rich could afford looms on
which to weave this into cloth. When looms were made here,
cloth weaving became common. Since weaving was heavy
work, it was often done by itinerant weavers who went from
house to house. Sometimes the poorer neighbours were hired
to do the work. These vagabond weavers provided themselves with linen warp and raw cotton. Any surplus of cloth
over that which the family required, was taken to the nearest
town and sold or bartered. By 1740 merchants began send-
ing agents through the country districts, supplying the
weavers with the thread and raw cotton, and receiving cloth
in exchange. The cloth was finished at a fulling mill, where
the grease on the wool was blotted out by covering the
cloth with fuller's earth. This grease was worked into
the wool before carding. Linens were bleached at home
on the grass. By 1800 country families were averaging
from 100 to 600 yards of linen, cotton and coarse woollen
cloths a year.

This spinning and weaving of cloth was part of the custom-
ary household duties of every wife, along with making
bread and the hundred other chores, for the recreation of the

DESIGNS FOR BED-COVERLETS FROM THE PATTERN BOOK OF
AN ITINERANT WEAVER
Courtesy of William Jay Robinson

early American woman was found in industry. She certainly could never be accused of eating the bread of idleness. Often the loom stood in the corner of the farmhouse kitchen, and whenever she had a free moment the wife would mount the bench and do a few inches. "In those days there was the whiz of the shuttle, the jarring of the lathe, and the clattering of the treadles, while buzz-buzz went the rapid wheel and creak-creak the windle from which ran the yarn the rosey daughter was quilling."

Governor Moore of New Jersey, in a report of 1767, says of the household weaving: "The custom of making these coarse cloths (woollen and linsey-woollen) in private families prevails throughout the whole Province, and in almost every house a sufficient quantity is manufactured for the use of the family. . . . Every home swarms with children, who are set to work as soon as they are able to spin and card; and as every family is furnished with a loom, the Itinerant Weavers, who travel about the country, put the finishing hand to the work." These weavers averaged twelve pence a yard.

Like other itinerant workmen of the day, the wandering weaver was welcomed by the isolated family, for he carried the tattle of the countryside, and the early weaver soon acquired a towering reputation as a gossip. Even when he settled down, his loom-room became the centre of the town's news and scandal, just as did the general country store of later days.

The weaving of bed coverlets by itinerant workers was an art that persisted for many years. Books of designs these men carried are still preserved.

Not only were the services of the itinerant weaver in demand, but there were loom repairers as well, who travelled about the country, and, in the flax districts, flax hecklers. Most of the latter were Scotch-Irish. These estimable people introduced linen manufacture to New England. No less than 10,000 Scotch-Irish weavers, thrown out of work by the decadence of the linen manufacture in Ireland, came to this country between 1771 and 1774.

What became of these itinerant weavers would afford pleasant speculation. One, at least, we know of—Alexander Wilson—eventually one of the greatest ornithologists this country has ever produced, who thus began his career on the road. For many years a weaver and poet in his native Paisley he migrated to Philadelphia, became in turn a weaver, school teacher and peddler. On the road he pursued his observations of birds. In 1812 John Bartram, the Philadelphia botanist, discovered him and began giving systematic direction to his studies. Thereafter Wilson devoted the remainder of his life to ornithology and, before he died, had completed nearly nine volumes on the subject.

TAILORS

In the beginning, and for quite a number of years, the making up of cloth into clothes was another common household industry, especially in New England and the Middle Colonies and among the poorer classes down South. The better-off were accustomed to send to London for their clothes. They had their measurements filed with their tailors and ordered one or several suits at a time. This was not always a satisfactory procedure, as some of the old correspondence shows.

Later on the itinerant tailor became a figure on country roads. At first, like the shoemaker, he merely did the work, and the householder supplied the cloth which had been made at home or bought of a local merchant. Wool was worked up into linsey-woolsey and the tailors made up the suits for the men and boys, suits that were counted on to last a year. The journeyman tailor in 1700 was paid twelve shillings a week and "diet." Later he carried cloth with him. It is a legend at Brooks Brothers in New York that the genesis of that firm was in the sale of cloth to these itinerant tailors.

Although it was a profitable trade, tailoring seems to have

been despised in Colonial days, especially in New England. Few would engage in it. In no uncertain terms did the Rev. Nathaniel Ward, of Ipswich, Massachusetts, berate tailors. "If taylors were men indeed," he writes, "well furnished but with mere moral principles, they would distain to be led about like apes. . . . It is a most unworthy thing for men that have bones in them to spend their lives in making fidle-cases for futilous women's phansies."

Women heretofore had always made the clothes. When men took up the needle and sat around crosslegged inside the house gossiping—doing a women's job—it was not to be expected that tailoring should be highly respected. Sometimes these tailors were referred to as "goose-herders" because they carried their tailor's goose with them. Later on the tailor gained a respectable position, and in Virginia we find them being sufficiently trusted by planters to hold a power of attorney.

Here are the bills of an itinerant tailor who visited Waterbury, Connecticut, and made up the clothing specified for one native Beau Brummel:

1818
October 28   To making pantelloons............$ .32
              To footing stockings............... .25
1819
January 14   To making vest................... .42
              To silk and twill for vest.......... .12
April 30   To cloth pantelloons and making the
              same......................... 2.50
June 8   To four yards of cotton shirting..... 1.32
              To making two cotton shirts........ .60
              To one yard and a half of stripped
              linen and making the same....... .75
November 10   To two yards of woollen cloth, one
              dollar and thirty-three cents per
              yard......................... 2.66
              To trimmings and making pantel-
              loons......................... .33

1820

January 12	To one pair of woollen stockings.....$	.50
May 5	To two yards and quarter of woollen cloth........................	3.95
	To making coat..................	1.50
	To 14 gilt buttons...............	.50
	To silk twist and thread for coat....	.20
	To cloth for pantelloons and making.	1.50
June 8	To two yards and half of linen cloth, thread, and making same........	1.00
	To four yards of cotton cloth, thread and making....................	1.75
	To trimming and making vest......	.33
		$20.50

In later years the dressmaker appeared—the "mantua maker" as she was called, who went to ladies' residences and made gowns, hats, cloaks, and riding habits. Her circuit, of course, was restricted.

TIDES OF WORKMEN

Constantly flowing up and down the Atlantic seaboard in pre-Revolutionary times and for years afterward, were tides of workmen of various sorts, driven from one district by lack of work or hard times, lured to another by the chances for employment, just as to-day these same tides drift about the country. On the other hand, there were numerous workmen who kept moving because they were not high class men. Good workers could readily find stationary employment in towns. The nomads represented a lower order of skill or a lower order of character. Many of them enjoyed the hospitality of the tavern too much for their own good.

We find records of even so humble a calling as the itinerant wood-chopper, tramping from town to town and farm to farm, in search of work. "His baggage a bundle, a handkerchief, and a pair of coarse boots. His implement, an axe, most keenly ground." To this solitary wood-chopper must be added those woodsmen who in later years drifted from place to place in groups through the back country of Pennsylvania, Kentucky, and Tennessee and laid their axes to the virgin forests of pine, hemlock, beech, and maple that clothed the mountainsides. A rough hardy crew, they travelled in canoes or overland to the forest, and when it was cut, made rafts of the felled timber and floated them down the streams to sell. They lived, meantime, on the produce of the forest and rivers. They, too, carried with them their own body of legends and their own songs. Wherever they stayed you find, among the older people, memories of these legends and songs—"Kitty Wells," "The Irishman's Shanty," "Tim Finnegan's Wake," and such like.

There were also candle-makers who travelled about with their moulds and helped the housewife to make candles. The moulds were usually in nests, making up two dozen at a time. Wicks were suspended from wires laid over the mouths of the moulds and the melted tallow poured in around them. The housewife furnished the tallow, in the early days rendering it from deer suet, moose fat, bear grease, and the fats left from cooking and butchering. In some places bayberry was used. Later spermaceti, taken from the heads of whales, supplanted tallow, being harder and giving a much better and less smoky light.

In addition to these we find reminders of chair seaters and makers of hickory chairs, millwheel cutters and tombstone cutters who came around to add new names to tombstones! Cooperers sometimes drifted from job to job and in western New York there were itinerant thatchers. In the towns were queer trades, such as the whitesmith who went about making and mending smoke jacks, locks and hinges, and hanging room bells. He had a fellow queer trader in the skillful Londoner who came to Salem in 1809 and served that section of Massachusetts as a professional rat killer! Down on the plantations of the South even the itinerant barber managed to make a living.

CABINET-MAKERS AND CARPENTERS

The cabinet-maker and the carpenter were both apt to drift, and they have left traces of their wanderings in many country districts. The finer pieces of furniture were made by established cabinet-makers in cities—the Saverys and Phyfes of the time—but for ordinary and crude country purposes, the itinerant cabinet-maker's services would be used. He carried his tools with him, stopped off in the house and stayed until he had made all the furniture the family required.

In Philadelphia, at least, the carpenters were so many, so prosperous, so influential and so well established, that by 1724 they formed a guild patterned after the Worshipful Company of Carpenters of London. Their guild house— Carpenter's Hall—is still preserved. In addition to these settled workmen were many that were drifters, and, through the country districts, they also left their impress. The architecture we have inherited from them, while not always of the highest order, is something of which we need not be ashamed.

The question is often asked: How did the wandering carpenter know such excellent designs? Where did he gain a sense of scale? Whence his taste in mouldings and other architectural details? The means of knowing these he carried with him along with his tools.

The eighteenth century saw a remarkable flood of building-books put on the market in England, books that were bought in great quantities here. Their names indicate that they were not intended merely for appreciation by gentlemen architects—architecture was considered a gentleman's hobby in the early days—but were definitely designed to meet the need of working carpenters and builders. "A Sure Guide For Builders," "The Art of Brickwork," "The Art of House Carpentry," "Builder's Complete Assistant," "The Builders' Jewel or the Youth's Instructor and Workman's Remembrance," "The Builder's Golden Rule," "The Carpenter's Treasure"—such were the pleasant names of some of these

THE

.BRITISH CARPENTER:

OR, A

TREATISE

ON

CARPENTRY.

Containing the moſt Conciſe and Authentick

RULES of that ART,

IN

A more Uſeful and Extenſive METHOD, than has been
made publick.

The SIXTH EDITION, corrected,

And illuſtrated with Sixty-Two COPPER-PLATES.

By *FRANCIS PRICE,*

Late Surveyor to the Cathedral Church of *Saliſbury,* and Author of a Series
of Obſervations on that admirable Structure.

LONDON:

Printed for A. PALLADIO, J. JONES and C. WREN, M,DCCLXVIII

TITLE PAGE FROM ONE OF THE SOURCES OF AMERICAN COUNTRY ARCHITECTURE

THE TRAMP PRINTER AND HIS WORK
He was a congenital itinerant

Fitch's Steamboat.

John Fitch, who invented an early steamboat, was a picturesque and constant wanderer

volumes. Some of them were later published in this country. There were also works on the construction of chimneys and how to remedy those that smoked.

With such complete guides in his tool chest, the wandering carpenter could not possibly build houses that were ugly.

PEWTERERS

Only a negligible amount of pewter was made here previous to 1750. The better class had it; the poorer and rural folks used wooden ware for everyday purposes. Most of the pewter to be found here earlier than that date was imported from England. From 1750 to 1825 vast quantities of pewter were made here and it was used by all classes. Finally cheap china and Britannia ware supplanted it.

That pewter got out of shape, was broken and had to be repaired, would follow naturally on its daily use. The number of spoon moulds that have come down to us indicate that they were pretty widely owned in the Colonies, and it was easy for the man of the house to melt down an old plate, or two, or melt the broken spoons and recast or "run" them in the moulds. For more difficult work they called on the itinerant tinkers, who carried in their saddle bags soldering irons and moulds for eight-inch plates and for spoons. These men were thoroughly capable of plugging up holes and straightening out crumpled dishes, and of repairing teapots and turning old pewter basins into new. Most of them were equipped to tackle brass, tin, and pewter indiscriminately.

THE TRAMP PRINTER

Some trades carry with them the nomad tradition, of which the most pronounced is the craft of printing. Why the printer first became a tramp, why the tradition should continue in America even into our day, is a question that is puzzling but not beyond conjecture.

Printing started at Mainz in Germany about the middle of the fifteenth century. In 1462 the city was partially destroyed and most of the printers dispersed to neighbouring German cities—Cologne, Wurtemburg, Strasbourg, and Bamberg. They took with them the hand moulds in which type was cast. Some travelled from place to place, producing books as they went along. Sweynheym and Pannartz went over the Alps into Italy with a small printing outfit strapped on the back of a donkey and settled at Subiaco. From this beginning we leap the years to the tramp printer of America who drifted from one printing shop to another. Benjamin Franklin went from Boston to Philadelphia, from Philadelphia to France and England, and wherever he went he was always a printer.

The cause for these wanderings may be attributed to the same circumstance that made the journeyman shoemakers and tailors and potterers "whip the cat"—the newly fledged apprentice travelled about to find work and he wanted to perfect himself by seeing the world. The apprentice printer was indentured to a master printer, lived in his house and did odd jobs until his time was up, when he actually started to journey, gaining various information, good and bad, while he was doing it. The printer, however, had a heritage of scholarship that other trades lacked; in his life (although he may not have been conscious of it) was the tradition of those early learned printers who were also editors and scholars, and he constantly sought new environments and new experiences in the attempt to follow the traditional footsteps of the forebears of his trade. Moreover the printer carried on the work of the itinerant scrivener or letter and document writer who, in his day in Europe, was a commonplace and necessary figure where schooling was rare.

One of the most famous of our botanists started as journeyman printer—Thomas Nuttall, who came to Philadelphia in 1808. He showed an aptitude for botany and travelled all over the continent studying the trees of North America, even penetrating to the Pacific Coast—a great feat in those days. Later he became curator of the Botanic Gardens at Harvard and was author of many books on his subject, including a monumental work—"North American Sylva," in three volumes.

However, not all the wandering printers turned out so well. Many of them were good workmen and had literary talent of sorts, but were not capable of sustained effort. The bottle was often their worst enemy. They drank up their earnings or lost their jobs to better men, then had to go on the road again to another centre where they found employment, and this meant considerable wandering in the early days.* The centres of book and newspaper publication were few and far between before the Revolution—New England and Pennsylvania mostly, but fifty years later the country had grown a fine crop of journals. An observer, travelling here in 1831, says that nine-tenths of the people read nothing but newspapers. These increased and far-flung opportunities for work beckoned the printer on. His later history as a tramp has been commented upon by countless writers, for during the last half of the last century, the tramp printer was an unmistakable character of the road. To-day he rides brake-beams or drives a broken-down flivver.

THE STORY OF JOHN FITCH

There are many examples of these industrial nomads of the days before and after the Revolution, but few cover so varied a range of activities and few, indeed, attain such a height as does the life of John Fitch, an early inventor of a steamboat.

A Connecticut Yankee, he was born at Windsor in 1743, and, like other youths of his day, was apprenticed at eighteen. The clock-maker and brass-worker to whom he was assigned apparently taught him little or nothing of the trade, but the boy did manage to pick up the knack of cleaning clocks. At twenty-five he also managed to acquire a wife who brought

---

*It is touching to discover that Artemus Ward, himself once a printer, left practically all his money to establish an asylum for indigent printers.

8

him a son and daughter. Since Fitch was apparently a congenital unbeliever and his wife a deeply religious girl, their marital life was not altogether happy. After two and a half years, the young husband, wearied of his pious incubus, deserted her bed and board, and took to the road. A young lord of his own destiny, he wandered through New York State to Albany, thence to Pittsfield, Massachusetts, then south through Connecticut and New York to New Jersey, where he travelled around Princeton and Trenton. He cleaned clocks *en route* and did odd jobs for his food and scant lodging.

At Trenton he settled down to making brass buttons, repairing clocks, and—the effrontery of it!—to the gentle art of silversmithing. The customers did not come, so he determined to go to the customers. With eight or ten shillings in his pocket, his clothes much the worse for wear, and with a stock of fifty or sixty pairs of brass sleeve buttons, he started on the road. These he peddled through the county, adding to his profits by cleaning clocks. In a tour of two weeks he managed to sell all his buttons and clean twelve clocks. Returning to Trenton, he bought up a lot of old brass kettles and pots, and worked them up into more sleeve buttons. Once more he did well with this stock on the road; in fact, he prospered to such an extent that he acquired enough capital to set himself up in business in Trenton as a manufacturer of brass and silver buttons, in a promising way. He took on twenty hands, meanwhile continuing his peddling trips. The business grew. He added silverwork to his line. On some of his trips he would carry as much as £200 worth of it with him. By the time the Revolutionary War broke, he had made £800 profit, a tidy little sum in those days.

He joined the Revolutionary Army, was promptly made lieutenant, and later exempted from military service because he claimed to be a gunsmith, and gunsmiths were more valuable at their workbenches than behind stone walls with the embattled farmers. Fitch supplied arms to the New

Jersey troops until the British destroyed his tools and the equipment of his factory. The gun-supplying business stopped, he went with the American army to Valley Forge and there, so it is said, drove the trade of supplying beer to the American forces. The story goes that he made a clear profit of £5 per barrel—which certainly put him in the war profiteer class.

From all accounts he was not an ardent patriot, for from this beery episode he went back to his brass and silversmithing while the war was still on. But, somehow, they had lost their tang for him. His foot was restless to be on the road again. In 1780, he wandered down through Kentucky as a surveyor, and worked along the Ohio. Here, one day, the Indians descended on him, and he was taken a prisoner to Canada. While held there by the British he made buttons and wooden clocks and cultivated a garden that was a marvel to his captors. Finally he was exchanged, and returned again to the Ohio to make surveys. During the next few years he made several journeys into this Northwest Territory and even engraved a map of it, of which he sold 800 copies while travelling through the countryside.

In 1785 he came east again and settled down on the Delaware where he conceived the idea of building a boat that could be propelled by a steam engine driving paddle wheels. He apparently was not acquainted with the progress that had been made in this field. His first model was tried out. He asked for Government help, which was refused, but finally did acquire a grant from New Jersey whereby he was permitted to navigate the waters of the state for fourteen years. Pennsylvania later gave him the same permission. His attempts to capitalize a company met with little success, but he did raise enough money to build a steamboat in 1787. Virginia also gave him a grant at this point, and he looked for a happy future. But his claims infringed on those of earlier experimenters and he was unable to protect his design. He built a second ship that for fourteen years ran between

Burlington, New Jersey, and Philadelphia. Refused a patent
and lacking capital, he went to France. Here again he met
with disappointment. He returned to America, settling in
Kentucky to continue his experiments, but everything
seemed to go against him. Finally in a fit of despondency he
took his life. The year was 1790, and his age, fifty-five.

CHAPTER VIII

HEALING AND JUSTICE TAKE TO THE HIGHWAY

HE first doctor trudging out of a primitive settlement to an isolated hut in a forest clearing, and the modern specialist zooming along a cement road in a high-powered car, are both on the same errand. From the very beginning doctors have gone on just such errands. They probably always will. By virtue of their calling the sons of Esculapius are, in a measure, itinerant.

We find physicians among the early settlers on the boats going to Massachusetts and to Jamestown and even the Swedes in Delaware had their barber-surgeon. The Dutch provided not only for preachers and teachers but for "comforters of the sick"—*Zieckentrooster*—who were often schoolmasters. Penn brought two doctors with him, but Pennsylvania appears to have been a poor place for them in the beginning, for in his diary Gabriel Thomas writes, "Of lawyers and doctors I shall say nothing, because the country is peaceable and healthy." We find them in almost every settlement, however, and, when not present, the community depended on barbers, midwives and the doctors who chanced to be on boats for medical attention.

In those beginning days, as we have already noted, practically every householder had some primitive notions of materia medica and depended on herbs for nostrums—sourdock ointment for the itch, poultices of everlasting, mullein for the bowels, and blackberry root for dysentery. Much of this sort of medication they learned in their native lands and some they may have learned from the Indians. Later they consulted medical books and almanacs. Dr Jaynes's "Guide To Health" enjoyed a wide distribution—a pamphlet filled with advertisements of the good Doctor's specifics and extra-

ordinary testimonials of cures effected by them. Or they had
such a handy little work as "The Experienced Botanist or
Indian Physician" by J. W. Cooper of Pennsylvania, who
advertised himself as both of these.

Many men of affairs took up doctoring as a gentleman's
side-line. Governor John Winthrop of Connecticut practised
medicine as an avocation, rode about treating patients in
Massachusetts and Rhode Island as well as in his own province, and he even dared prescribe for them by letter. He
used a famous cure-all called "rubila." Some of the physicians were storekeepers, some teachers, some parsons. Dr.
Abram Staats of New Amsterdam was also a fur trader. Dr.
Jasper Gunn of Connecticut practised surveying and mended
kettles to make ends meet between sick calls. Bishop Seabury
the first Anglican Bishop of America, studied medicine as part
of the missionary's equipment for Holy Orders. Griffith
Owen, a physician who came to America with Penn, visited
the neighbouring provinces preaching and healing as well.

Crude treatments were used in those early days. Medicine had not yet completely crept from under the incubus of
the "Doctrine of Signatures," whereby one could tell the
disease a plant would cure by a mark on the plant. Nicholas
Culpepper was the last supporter of this doctrine, and his
books were found in the libraries of our first physicians. In
those times surgery was little short of torture and diag-
nosis was in its most elemental forms. The first medical
advance made in the country was in 1721 when Dr. Zabdiel
Boylston of Boston, supported by Cotton Mather and
soundly denounced by the clergy and other physicians,
dared to vaccinate for smallpox. For this his fame spread,
and he was made the first American member of the Royal
Society of London.

During the first hundred years there were no medical
schools, no great medical libraries and no hospitals at which
young, aspiring doctors could study. A youth who wanted to
follow the calling was accredited to a Scotch or English uni-

versity, or else he went to reside with a doctor, read such books as he had, and visited about with him on his sick calls. Eventually he picked up enough knowledge to venture practising alone. When medical schools were established— the first equipped hospital being opened in Philadelphia in 1752* and the first medical school in 1765—they became the centre of much education and research, although in country districts for many years the local physician still served as tutor to the medically-inclined youth.

The physician also served for many years as pharmacist, since druggists were scarcely known outside the big towns. He made up his own drugs and carried them about with him in his saddle bags. He would prescribe "my pills" or "my syrup." Samuel Thompson, a New Hampshire itinerant herb doctor, grew so famous for his decoctions that his method of medication became known as Thompsonism. He wrote "A New Guide To Health" that was once popular. In Massachusetts he was prosecuted as a quack.

Among the illustrations will be found a travelling physician's box, with its bottle and instruments, that he carried from bedside to bedside through the country. There are also the instruments used in child delivery, indicating that this physician came later than the middle of the eighteenth century. Previous to that time it was not considered proper for a man to have anything to do with maternity cases; the delivery of children was in the hands of midwives.

THE MIDWIFE

The midwife occupied a position of great importance in the Colonial community; in fact, she was a community institution. New Amsterdam gave its first midwife, Lysbert Dircken, a house built at public expense, and one of her successors, Hellezond Jaris, was paid a yearly salary of 100 guilders.

Some of the midwives made for themselves records of

---

*The Dutch had what they called a hospital at New Amsterdam in 1658, of which Hilletize Wilbruch was matron.

which they might justly be proud. On her tombstone in the Phillip Street burying ground at Charleston, you find it recorded of Mrs. Elizabeth Phillips (and we have no way of disputing the good lady's mortuary boast) that she assisted at the delivery of some 3000 children. Mrs. Lydia Robinson of New London, Connecticut, claimed to have helped deliver 1200 in thirty-five years of practice—and never lost a case!

Early New England also had its women doctors. Margaret Jones, the first woman to be executed for witchcraft in Massachusetts, was "a physician and doctress."

The transition from midwife to male physician was gradual. Dr. James Floyd of Boston returned from London in 1752 equipped to handle obstetrics, and had the temerity to offer himself as a "man midwife." Further South, Drs. Atwood and Tennent, in New York, Dr. Shippen in Philadelphia, and Dr. Moultrie of Charleston, all began the same practice. Many, however, deemed the employment of a male accoucheur scandalous, and for years the old Granny midwife— whose fees ranged from $3 to $8—was still the favourite. The change came about, it is said, because on the Continent fashionable women began to employ men doctors for such cases, and American women of those times (as now) followed whatever Continental styles dictated.

NOSTRUMS AND FAKERS

Legitimate practice soon gathered in its train the quack, and serious medication, the fake nostrum. By 1711 a Mrs. Sibylla Masters of Philadelphia was making "Tuscarora Rice" out of Indian corn and selling it as a sure cure for consumption. The stuff was ground out in a mill near Philadelphia and doubtless found its way into the peddler's pack. Seneca rattlesnake root appeared in 1739 and Dr. John Tennent was awarded £100 by the Virginia Colony for curing pleurisy with it. This was a popular nostrum with itinerant medicine vendors for many years. In 1745 there came to Philadelphia (which was early a thriving medical centre) a

Frenchman by the name of Francis Torres, with a Chinese
Stone and sundry mystic powders that, he claimed, would
cure, with equal ease, snakebite, cancer, toothache, gout and
labour pains! Then in quick succession followed a flood of
fakes and quacks—Perkins' metallic tractors,* galvanic wires
and Brandreth's pills, and a vast company of itinerant mes-
meric healers who gave out medicine, cast horoscopes, and
felt head bumps. When La Rochefoucauld was here in 1799,
he encountered a German medical faker who had been an
actor, and who drew teeth, bled patients, vended nostrums
and sold ballads. Quite a versatile fellow!

In cities the associations of doctors could fight these impostors, but in the country and on the frontiers they had an
uncontested field. Once again we see the settled town representative (and rightly) combating the itinerant. Connecticut
legislated against these impostors in her queer old law forbidding mountebanks. Other states subsequently followed
suit, so that the itinerant medical faker has always been
under the eye of the sheriff.

THE COUNTRY DOCTOR

The practising physician of early America was not highly
rewarded for his services. In Boston, prior to 1782 one shilling sixpence to two shillings was the charge for the ordinary
visit; night calls were double these sums. The country doctor
usually took his fees in kind.

Those who can recall the old country general practitioner
on his "ride" have a fairly faithful portrait of the devotion
and untiring labours of the peripatetic physician of earlier
days. His clothes are different—for he wore knee breeches
and a cocked hat—maybe a beaver hat—and in rainy weather
an oiled linen hat cover and a large shoulder cape or roque-
laure. His method of getting about is different—horseback

---

*These were metal rods passed over the patient's body. In New York Perkins
tried to cure himself of yellow fever with his own "tractors." He died three days
after the symptoms appeared. That, somehow, discouraged their sales.

and afoot through the wilderness instead of a joggling shay along a rutted country road. His medicines are different and more diverse. But the spirit of the man is the same. By night and by day, in sunshine and in storm he rode on his errands of mercy. No angel at Bethesda stirred more healing waters than did these physicians of the early American frontier and countryside. Nor did any profession produce more picturesque characters.

In Connecticut, Jared Eliot visited practically every county in his state. This goodly physician made it a practice to read a book while his horse jogged along. And sometimes he became so absorbed that the old horse would stop and nibble grass until his bookworm master awoke with a start and set him on his way again. But this was before the day of emergency calls.

Imagine the courage it required for these simple physicians to undertake an operation! Imagine, too, the courage of the patient! For many of these backwoods doctors had only the crudest training and the crudest equipment; their ignorance of both anatomy and medicine was abysmal.

Nor were they always the idealistic figures we like to think them. The drinking doctor was well known. He would refuse to prescribe for a patient "until a square bottle of rum was placed under his entire and exclusive control." In those days grateful patients evidently presented their gifts before the cure was effected! Fort Orange (Albany) had an eccentric physician who worked on the legendary Chinese basis of patients paying to be kept in health. He offered to make yearly contracts with his patients, at the rate of ten beaver skins per annum and would work out this pay when his services were needed.

AN ITINERANT VACCINATOR

Smallpox was a scourge that regularly swept down on the settlements of the Atlantic seaboard. To his dying day, Washington carried its marks on his face, and because it was

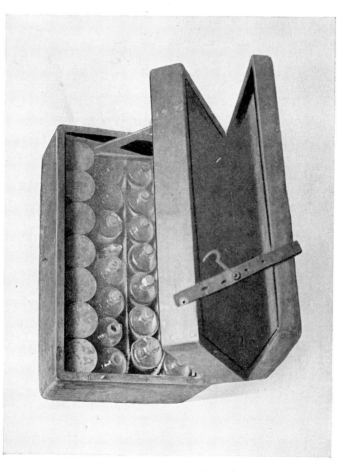

AN INGENIOUS MEDICINE-CHEST CARRIED BY A PHYSICIAN OF ABOUT 1820
The top held instruments; the bottom, 21 bottles of featherweight glass and 7 tins for medicines. The strap held the
box to the saddle. Courtesy of Samuel Hopkins Adams

For many years in this country the dentist was an itinerant

JOHN GREENWOOD, A DENTIST OF 1806

so feared, early American physicians made every effort to stem
or prevent its inception. We have noted the experiments at
vaccination made by Dr. Boylston. In 1798 Dr. Waterhouse
of Cambridge came out thoroughly for vaccination. He soon
had followers, not the least of whom was a Sylvanus Fancher
of Waterbury, Connecticut. Called Dr. Fancher by courtesy, this odd stick wandered about from town to town
and his fame spread all over New England. His appearance must have made him a fearsome person. He wore
"velvet small clothes, a parti-coloured waistcoat from which
dangled a half a dozen watch-chains and trinkets for the
amusement of the little folks, and a faded blue coat—all
these surmounted by a slouched hat overhanging green gog-
gles." Despite his appearance, he seems to have known his
business, for he invented and used a vaccinating instrument,
a silver bar tha. carried a concealed lancet with which the
incision was made.

WANDERING DENTISTS

Although to-day American dentists and dentistry are
famous the world over, they have no such ancient lineage as
the physicians. For many years there was practically no
specialization in that line. Just as the early surgeon in Europe
was a barber, so the doctor in early America was also a dentist, and that dual capacity was served for many years by the
country physician on his "rides." Up to 1830, only few of
the larger cities could boast a resident dentist. Charleston,
South Carolina, for example, had three in 1809, and it was a
dentist—John Gilliams, together with a young apothecary,
John Speaksman—who founded the Academy of Natural
Sciences in Philadelphia. Up to 1830 such dental practice as
existed apart from doctoring was generally itinerant. In
Vermont, for example, was practising a dentist by the name of
Brockway who, in 1822, was said to be the only one between
Canada and Albany and between the Rocky Mountains and
the White Mountains. These wanderers were untrained.

They made their own crude instruments. Many itinerant dentists were tinkers of sorts who practised dentistry as a side-line. In Pennsylvania a German clock-maker and repairer also drew teeth. Sometimes it was the barber, or the ivory-turner or the wig-maker who was the dentist of the neighbourhood.

Hippopotamus ivory was used for false teeth. Men who had many teeth extracted wore "plumpers"—little ivory balls to fill out their cheeks. We have portraits of Washington both with and without his plumpers. John Greenwood of Connecticut, a famous Revolutionary dentist, made false teeth for Washington and many famous men. Paul Revere advertised in the *Boston Gazette* that in two years he had "fixed some Hundreds of Teeth," that he cleansed teeth and —polite touch!—"will wait on any gentleman or lady at their lodging." Before 1819 gold was being prepared for dental use in Hartford and it is still made there.

So youthful is this specialty that it has yet to celebrate it hundredth anniversary. The first dental college was started in Baltimore as late as 1839, the first dental society organized in New York in 1840, and the first state law regulating dental surgery was passed in Alabama in 1841. The father of this college and this first dental society was H. H. Hayden of Baltimore, who had been trained in dentistry by John Greenwood.

Both the doctor who served as dentist and the itinerant dentist were encountered by Nathaniel Hawthorne on his wanderings in 1838. The doctor-dentist was in operation— "A young fellow, twenty or thereabouts, pained with a toothache. A doctor, passing on horseback, with his black leather saddlebags behind him, a thin, frosty-haired man. Being asked to operate, he looks at the tooth, lances the gum, and the fellow being content to be dealt with on the spot, he seats himself in a chair on the stoup with great heroism. The doctor produces a rusty pair of iron forceps, a man holds the patient's head. . . A turn of the doctor's hand, and the tooth is out. The patient gets up, half-amazed, pays the doctor ninepence, pockets the tooth, and the spectators are in glee and admiration."

The travelling surgeon-dentist is quite a different fellow. He "has taken a room in the North Adams House and sticks up his advertising bills on the pillars of the piazza and all about the town. He is a tall, slim young man, dressed in a country-made coat of light blue (taken, as he tells me, in exchange for dental operations), black pantaloons, and clumsy, cowhide boots. . . . He is not only a dentist, which trade he follows temporarily, but a licensed preacher of the Baptist persuasion, and is now on his way to the West to seek a place of settlement in his spiritual vocation." So this therapeutic nomad was also a peddler of the Word!

CIRCUIT JUDGES

Because of its far-flung settlements, this country soon faced the same problem of dispensing justice that England had long since known. In the days of Edward I, a man had to travel all the way to London to enjoy the King's justice, so there were created Assize Courts that sat in various parts of the shires and to these sittings came the judges who rode from one court to another on regular circuits.

When the first Congress met in 1789 one of its first labours was to establish a judiciary system, which provided for a Supreme Court with a Chief Justice and five Associate Judges, for thirteen Districts Courts, and for three Circuits. The country was divided into the Eastern, Middle, and Southern Circuits, and there was to be a court for each, consisting of two Justices of the Supreme Court and the Judge of the district where the Court was held.

The first Circuit Court sat in the Eastern Circuit at New York on April 4, 1790, with Chief Justice Jay, Judge Cushing, and District Judge Duane on the bench. Thus began the itineracy of the law under the new-born nation.

Previous to this time provincial courts had sat at stated

periods, but the itinerant life of the justices was not so pronounced since each province was self-contained in legal respects and the justices of one province had no jurisdiction in the courts of the other. Litigants and criminals came or were brought to the courts, minor cases were handled by local justices of the peace.

It is well also to remember that almost up to the Revolution, law was not the popular profession it is to-day. Connecticut's statute of 1698 classed lawyers with drunkards and keepers of bawdy houses, and in 1726 that Province limited their number to eleven. Rhode Island's law of 1730 forbade them being elected to the House of Deputies. In Vermont, during the land troubles there, they were denounced as "banditti." By 1768 Massachusetts could boast only twenty-five lawyers, and through the middle provinces they were equally scarce. Apart from the prejudice against them perhaps the reason for this absence was that their services were not needed. Prior to the Revolution there was not an abundance of the Hebraic race which, being constitutionally litigious, floods our courts to-day.

Whereas our modern Circuit Court judges travel by Pullman or motor, the early justices were obliged to ride their circuits by slower and less comfortable means. Judge Cushing, who travelled over the entire country and held courts in Virginia, Georgia, and the Carolinas, was accustomed to drive a four-wheeled phaeton drawn by a pair of horses. His was quite an ingenious equipage, for the Justice enjoyed his comforts and relished the pleasures of the table, and had the carriage built after his own design with storage spaces for books and choice foods. A jet black and faithful negro servant rode behind and gave the requisite touch of dignity to His Honour's peregrinations.

Mrs. Cushing always went along on the circuit, and it is said that as the Justice drove she read aloud to him. What a pretty picture this makes! Think how much chance he had for the preparation of cases, as he rumbled along the lonely

JAMES IREDELL, EARLY CIRCUIT-RIDING JUDGE
By permission of Albert Rosenthal

LINCOLN RIDING THE CIRCUIT

By courtesy of Wide World Photos and Collier's Weekly

roads! He doubtless had the briefs of forthcoming cases with him, and *en route*, Mrs. Justice could read the law applying to them. Let us hope, though, that for her sake, the reading was not always musty law. Perhaps, as they joggled along, she read him snatches from Mr. Sterne's "Life and Opinions of Tristram Shandy," or Mr. Swift's "Journal to Stella," or (for he doubtless read Latin with ease) verses from the immortal pen of Horace and the amorous and bacchic elegies of Sextus Propertius.

Not always was this legal going so romantic or so picturesque. The circuits were held in rotation, so that each justice managed to cover the entire Union, which consumed a great deal of time and occasioned no little hardship over the mud sloughs and rough ruts of the early roads. Judge Iredell complained that his life was nothing better than a postboy's. Many of the Justices rode their circuit on horseback. Justice Pinckney of Charleston started out early each morning and would consult with clients and lawyers *en route*. As they rode side by side he would listen to their case. If he had to give an opinion, he always made it in writing and cautiously endorsed it as "given on circuit," since he had no law books with him to consult. "Horseback opinion," it came to be called. Some of the pioneer lawyers, however, used to carry law books along with them—books in one saddle bag and refreshments in the other.

The Southern Circuit seemed to be the hardest to ride, as the areas covered were greater than those in the Eastern or Middle divisions. Judge Iredell, who commenced his first circuit in 1790, complained that "no Judge can conscientiously undertake to ride the Southern Circuit constantly and perform other parts of his duty. . . . I rode upon the last circuit 1900 miles." However, when this same Justice rode the Eastern Circuit, his New England hosts offered him so many courtesies that he was unforgetably charmed.

As the country grew, and other circuits were added to the

judiciary system, the circuit-riding judge became a not uncommon figure on the roads. In the Middle West he usually travelled by horseback. The years when Abraham Lincoln rode the circuit in Illinois form a definite and picturesque phase of his life.

CHAPTER IX

THE ARTIST AS AN ITINERANT

AS SOON as a people attain that point of self-consciousness where they desire to preserve their features for the delectation of descendants, then they may be said to have passed the primitive stage. So soon as the provinces along the Atlantic coast settled down into orderly communities, we find this desire manifested. By 1750 life had attained an ease which permitted the enjoyment of cultural luxuries. There were artists before that time (Cotton Mather speaks of an "English limner" being in Massachusetts in 1667), but we need do little more than mention them.

After 1750 those who were rich enough to go to England and interested enough to patronize them, might have their portraits painted by distinguished British artists. Such was Councillor Carter of Virginia, who sat to Sir Joshua Reynolds. The rest of the people, in the century between 1750 and 1850, depended on local talent, much of it itinerant.

However, the popular acceptance of the artist was, by no means, universal at first. Even a member of the General Court of Massachusetts classes painters—particularly inside house, miniature, and portrait painters—in the same category as "hairdressers, tavern keepers, musicians, stage players, buffoons, and exhibitors of birds and puppets!" He called them "unprofitable labourers."

The particular division of these "unprofitable labourers" which claims our attention, consisted of three grades—one or two outstanding men of real creative genius, several more of good honest talent, and a host of obscure and undistinguished journeymen. The lower in the scale the artist, the more is he apt to be itinerant. Most of them were self-taught. Not all of these men painted "ancestors." Some did miniatures (the subjects of which were mostly ancestors), some modelled in wax (and these were mainly portraits), some cut silhouettes, some painted signs and others did frescoes. Still others were satisfied if they found a job decorating household furniture and the homely objects of everyday use.

WANDERING PORTRAIT PAINTERS

Prior to the year 1800 the centres of culture in this country were Charleston, Baltimore, Philadelphia, New York and Boston; it was to these centres that even the great outstanding geniuses had to gravitate in order to find clients sufficiently cultured to patronize them—for culture is a product of cities. For other types of painting—landscapes and such—there was evidently little market in the early days.

Scarcely one of our best portrait painters but was obliged to wander seeking patronage. When they reached a city they opened what they called a "painting room." In those times the ubiquitous Bohemian and his studio were unheard of in America.

Before he went to Italy, Benjamin West painted first in Philadelphia and then moved on to New York. In his native city he received ten guineas a portrait, but managed to double the price when he reached New York. Copley visited Boston, New York, and Annapolis seeking jobs. Between June and December, 1771, he completed thirty-three portraits in New York City alone, being paid fourteen guineas for each half-length. Gilbert Stuart travelled to New England, New York, and Philadelphia to find sitters. Thus even the giants of those days were obliged to be itinerants. But, of course, so soon as they established a reputation, they could settle down in one city.

From the point of dates, we should begin this tale of wandering portrait painters with Gustavus Hesselius, a Swede, who in 1755 visited Virginia, Pennsylvania, and Maryland. The greater number of the portraits found in old Maryland mansions are supposed to have been done by him. He eventually toured most of the provinces, for when he was not painting, he was making and erecting church organs. He is said to have placed them in such widely scattered districts as Albany, New York, Lancaster, Easton, and York, Pennsylvania, and Salem, North Carolina. An advertisement in the *Pennsylvania Gazette* of December 11, 1740, informed the populace that painting was "done in the best manner by Gustavus Hesselius from Stockholm and John Winter from London. Viz.: Coats of Arms, drawn on Coaches, Chaises, etc., or any kind of Ornaments, Landskips, Signs, Shew-Boards, Ship and House painting, Gilding of all sorts, Writing in Gold or Colour, old Pictures cleaned and mended."

In those beginning days artists had to eke out their slender living by any jobs that came to hand. They filled a multitude of roles—house and sign painting was the usual way out. Charles Wilson Peale of Philadelphia was a coach-maker, silversmith, and saddle-maker, a modeller in wax and plaster, and he also preserved animals, conducted a famous private museum, served as legislator and was a dentist! Another Philadelphia artist, William Williams, advertised that he "was prepared to paint in general"—which meant everything from the side of a house to a tin coffee pot. Still a third Philadelphia artist added to his regular vocation of painting miniatures, the avocation of making lockets, rings and hair pins. But the really industrious fellow was Peter Pelham, who, to make ends meet, painted portraits, engraved, ran a dancing school, taught reading, writing and needlework, and now and then painted on glass.

The most popular of all the avocations among the second-rate and journeymen painters was the creation of tavern and shop signs. Many of their signs were much better than their portraits. In the years prior to the Revolution they really raised this to a fine art. The most amusing and amazing of our huge electric advertisements in no way compare with the beauty and skill of their productions.

Now and then these lowly itinerant artists used to make what were called "painted parsons," sign posts—which, like some ministers, always point the way but seem never to follow it themselves! Many of them started their careers in carriage shops as apprentices, and one of their tasks was to grind the colours. In later days when the trains appeared, some who had failed to make a go of the art game, painted and decorated the coaches.

Not only did the itinerant portrait painters welcome any kind of a commission, but, in order to find work, they used all manner of subterfuges. Some were brutally frank, some subtle. Imagine what Mr. George Mason must have been able to squeeze out in the way of a living from a portrait when he could advertise that, "with a view to more constant employment, he now draws faces in crayon for two guineas each, glass and frame included." Chester Harding, who eventually became one of the leading portrait painters of his day, was obliged both to wander and to use cut-rate methods. He travelled through Kentucky and eventually as far west as St. Louis, and his price was $25 a head. He managed to do 100 heads at this figure in a single vagabondage. But the hint direct is contained in very early years in the advertisement of Thomas Stuart White, in the *New England Weekly Journal* of July 8, 1724. He gives notice of his immediate return to London "unless he meets with sufficient encouragement to oblige him to stay." Something pitiful about that. He was one of those "foreign" artists with which we are now so much deluged; he had heard that America was a land of much and easy money—and he was doomed, as are some of the visiting foreign artists of our times, to disappointment.

Quantity production seems to have been the way out for some of these early artists. John Wesley Jarvis, for example, ran a portrait factory. He received six sitters a day at his painting room and limited each sitting to one hour. In that time he was able to do the face. Then the portrait was handed over to an assistant who painted in the background and the drapery. Jarvis is said to have averaged six portraits a week.

In this same class would fall Isaac Sheffield of New London, Connecticut, who specialized on portraits of sea captains. They were all painted with red faces, all stand before a red curtain and each holds in his hand a single telescope. Sheffield was gathered to his fathers in 1845, but his works survive him.

There is a legend (which may or may not be true) to the effect that the least skilled of the painters used to ply a quantity-production trade in this wise: These men were sign and house artists. In winter when jobs were few, they would paint several lines of busts, male and female; the male with a conventional coat and the female with a conventional breastpin. Then when Spring opened up the roads, these canvases were rolled up, put in the cart, and off on his way, the artist would go. Stopping at a house, he would suggest that it would be a nice thing if the old folks had their portraits done in real oil and paint. And he would display one or two lines of busts. If these didn't please, then he brought out his other lines. Finally a sale was made, and the sitter sat. The face was painted in, the hands touched up and the conventional breastpin changed to simulate one that the sitter actually owned. This, it is said, accounts for the fact that in certain country regions, the old family portraits have a sameness—certain lines of busts were popular in certain districts.

An example of these lowly and obscure itinerant artists can be cited in the cultural ascendency of one Frank Alexander, a farmer's son in Windham County, Connecticut. Without the slightest knowledge of painting technique he began to paint fish, at which the family marvelled, and from fish passed on to animals, and from animals, took the dizzy flight into human portraiture. He travelled about the countryside of Connecticut painting portraits for $3 a head and board. Saving his money, the lad went to New York for instruction in art, and after his return, he staggered the neighbourhood by charging $8 a head!

As pretty a story as you'd ever want is found in the wan-

derings of James Sharples the peripatetic artist. An Englishman, he was educated in France, and then came here in 1798.
His mediums were crayon and pastel. Seeing that the market
for his wares was scattered, he devised a special cart that
would comfortably hold his wife, two boys and a girl and their
clothes and food and his painting gear. It was drawn by one
large sturdy horse. In this *menage ambulant* he travelled all
over the country, going from town to town, and city to city.
In each city he would obtain letters of introduction to people
in the next city—military, civil or literary worthies. Sharples
would present the letter, beg the honour of doing a portrait
for his "collection," and, if this was granted, he would set to
work. As he was a good artist, he could manage to make a
faithful likeness in about two hours. Having seen himself so
faithfully portrayed, the sitter, of course, was easily induced
to buy the picture. The charges were $15 for a profile and $20
full face. Sharples' wanderings came to an end in 1811 when
he departed this life. His portraits could scarcely be called
masterpieces. Several of them are to be found in the
American Wing of the Metropolitan Museum of Art.

Perhaps the most favoured and elegant wandering por-
traitist of post-Revolutionary times was a Frenchman—
Charles Balthazar Julien Fevret de Saint Memin, who, one
day in 1793, found himself stranded in New York. He had
been entertained by the aristocracy of the city and, in leisure
moments, had amused himself making sketches of New York
harbour. Encouraged by this start, he determined to make
his living by portraiture. He understood the classic elegance
of the French eighteenth century and he began to apply it
to his work. He was joined by an equally unfortunate countryman, de Valdenuit—both of them exiles from their native
land. Saint Memin possessed both a talent for his work and
a cunning conception of salesmanship. He would do a nearly
life-size crayon portrait on tinted paper, then reduce this to
miniature size on a plate, from which any number of copies
could be run off for one's friends. The large portrait was

JOHN WESLEY JARVIS, PAINTER OF PORTRAITS
From a sketch by his pupil, Henry Inman

JOHN BANVARD, ITINERANT ARTIST AND POET

CHARLES B.J.F. de SAINT-MEMIN
1770 – 1852
Artist.

St. Memin, a French refugee, had the knack of always delineating his sitters as aristocrats,
which added to his popularity

WILLIAM HENRY BROWN
Itinerant Silhouette-Cutter and famous for his group portraits

CORRECT
Profile Likenesses,

Taken at Mr.   *from*

8 o'clock in the morning until 9 in the evening.

     M. CHAPMAN respectfully informs the Ladies and Gentlemen of   that he takes correct Profiles, reduced to any size, two of one person for 25 cents, neatly cut on a beautiful paper. He also paints and shades them, if requested, for 75 cents; specimens of which may be seen at his room. Of those persons who are not satisfied with their Profiles, previous to leaving his room, no pay shall be required. He makes use of a machine universally allowed by the best judges to be more correct than any ever before invented.

     ☞ Those who wish to embrace this opportunity of having their Profiles taken, will please to make early application, as he will positively leave town on

     N. B. *Frames* of different kinds, for the Profiles, may be had at the above place, from 50 cents to 2 dollars each.

AN ADVERTISEMENT OF AN ITINERANT SILHOUETTE-CUTTER

framed appropriately. For the framed crayon, copper plate and twelve miniature impressions he charged $33. In that day a lordly price. However, he met with instant success. His aristocratic connections brought him a big New York trade, and he was kept busy in that city for two years. Having exhausted the New York market, he went to Philadelphia, to Burlington, New Jersey (which used to be the smart summer place for old Philadelphia families), to Baltimore, Annapolis, Alexandria, Georgetown, Richmond, Washington, Norfolk, and Charleston, returning to Paris in 1812. How many portraits he did on these artistic wanderings we do not know, but 800 of them are recorded. They form a gallery of the worthies of that time. Saint Memin's great gift was not only that he made a faithful likeness, but he had the flattering knack of representing his sitters as aristocrats. His people all look like ladies and gentlemen. They have an elegant air.

Among the pre-Civil War itinerant artists would certainly come John Banvard. A New Yorker by birth, he drifted down to Louisville as a lad, clerked in a drugstore for a time, then, without any apparent schooling in art, began painting pictures and exhibiting them at New Orleans, Natchez, Cincinnati and other river towns, travelling from place to place in a boat. In 1840 he was seized with the ambition to paint the largest picture in the world and he set about to realize it. He acquired an open skiff and began making sketches of the entire Mississippi River, shooting game for food, and painting and showing pictures *en route*. Finally when he had finished his sketches he retired to Louisville where he transferred them to canvas, making a panorama. The picture required three miles of canvas. Surely this was the largest picture in the world! This he exhibited both here and abroad. A versatile fellow, Banvard; in addition to painting pictures he is said to have written over 1700 poems! The first chromo made in this country was reproduced from one of his paintings.

WAX PÔRTRAITURE

The modelling of bas-relief portrait buſts in wax brought to the fore a medium that grew to popularity in England and on the Continent in the eighteenth century, and was the mode soon reflected here among people of discernment. In fact, one of the artiſts who made this medium famous in England, was an American, Patience Lovell Wright, of Burlington, New Jersey, who worked here firſt and then eſtablished the vogue in London.

She was followed, in the early part of the nineteenth century by a Dane, John Chriſtian Rauchner, who worked not only in New York and Philadelphia, but wandered all over the country finding sitters. His wax was coloured all the way through in the mediæval ſtyle, and not merely tinted on the surface. When he did a portrait, he firſt made an intaglio mould, and pressed the wax in colour by colour. The form was then removed, and the portrait finished by little touches of real lace or seed pearls, and, finally mounted on glass. When the wax-portrait business was dull, Rauchner worked as a hair-dresser and barber. Which leads us to observe (as we should have done a few paragraphs before) that early artiſts of America were not prone to ſtarve in garrets. Art to them was not only very long, but occasional, and it apparently did not hurt their talent to indulge in some menial craft.

One of the variations of the wax portrait was created by Robert Ball Hughes, who devised a way of keeping the wax from turning yellow. His portraits were mounted on black velvet. New York and New England were the main fields of his endeavours.

Among the miniature painters we find several who were itinerants, although the moſt famous of them was Benjamin Trott (an excellent name for such a vagrant) who rode horseback from Boſton to Charleſton and, in 1805, "visited the weſtern world beyond the mountains"—Ohio and such. He carried the implements of his art in his saddlebags. Although he attempted portraits in oil, Trott's real fame rests on his miniatures which had decided artistic quality. William Dunlap, who wrote "The History of Design in America," was also a wandering painter, and tells of his desperate attempts to stage one-man shows in various parts of the country. Other miniature artists had to adopt speed and salesmanship—in Pennsylvania itinerant miniaturists offered to make a portrait in two hours and would take no pay unless the likeness was right.

In addition to wax portraiture, there used to be quite a thriving little business in life-size wax figures after the Revolution. Many of them were made at East Haven, Connecticut, by Ruben Moulthrop, a portrait painter with an eye to business. So soon as a man became famous Moulthrop modelled his likeness in wax and sent it off to the exhibitions and museums. Often a figure of the worthy's wife was made. Both the men and the women were fully dressed, so that the industry kept quite a number of people busy.

These wax figure exhibitions always included two female figures, a blonde and a brunette, and a placard inscribed "The Beauty of This Place." If the beauty of a town was a blonde, then she wore the sign and vice versa.

SILHOUETTES

The cheapest and most common method of having one's likeness portrayed prior to the coming of the daguerreotype and the photograph was the silhouette, and, in its day, this, too, was raised to a fine art. To a great extent these silhouette cutters were wanderers. The profession even developed its youthful prodigies. So popular became the silhouette that exhibitions of them were common.

Of the numerous itinerant artists in this line three or four are outstanding—Auguste Edouart, William Henry Brown, "Master" Hubbard, and an unfortunate lad by the name of Martin Griffing.

It appears that some time in his twenty-third year Martin fell off a church steeple. What he was doing up there we do not know, but he fell and injured his back. This was his preparation for years of silhouette cutting. Although he could not walk, he did manage to ride a horse, and thus mounted, he went through Vermont, New York and parts of Massachusetts cutting the semblances of the profiles of whomsoever took pity on him. The first year on the road he claims to have cleared $1500. Finally he tired of this art, and settled down to the more sedentary business of making and cobbling shoes. He lived to the relatively old age of seventy-five.

Master Hanks was the *ingénue* of the calling. He not only made money actually cutting silhouettes but gave exhibitions of his skill and charged twenty-five cents admission. His collection of "works" was called a "papyrotamia." He required only a few seconds to snip out of black paper an exact likeness of any person he saw. He was usually considered the successor of Master Hubbard, another silhouette prodigy.

William James, Master Hubbard, was scarcely an itinerant, for most of his work was done in Boston, where he settled when he came from England. He began cutting silhouettes at thirteen, came to America at seventeen, but finally abandoned the art for studying portraiture under Gilbert Stuart. Half a minute was his usual time for cutting a profile and his fee was fifty cents. Some of his silhouettes were gilded and called "Bronze Likenesses."

Auguste Edouart, a Frenchman, fled to England after the Napoleonic disasters and came to this country in 1839. He travelled about doing the silhouettes of all the prominent people of the day. It is said that during his career he cut no less than 50,000 silhouettes. He also wrote a work on his art—"A Treatise on Silhouette Likenesses." He returned to England in 1849. One of his variations on the silhouette portrait was to introduce a background done in wash colour.

The last of the old school of silhouette cutters was William Henry Brown, whose "Portrait Gallery of Distinguished American Citizens" is an invaluable record. Brown was born in Charleston, South Carolina, in 1808 and died in 1883. He was a quick cutter, finishing a silhouette in from one to five minutes. Backgrounds were introduced in many of his works. In 1859 he retired from silhouette cutting. Fifteen years later we find him the author of a book—"The History of the First Locomotive in America." And a strange book it is; for several chapters he discourses on the introduction of steam engines, and then interpolates a chapter called "The Author's Art," in which he tells of some of the remarkable silhouettes he cut. For Brown was famous not only for portraits, but for groups. In Albany, for example, he cut a large silhouette of the entire Burgess' Corps "with staff and band in full parade, in which the likeness of each individual member is presented with an accuracy truly surprising." He also did a profile likeness of the St. Louis Fire Engine Company, the two hose carriages and sixty-five members of that valiant and invincible corps. At Natchez, where he silhouetted in 1844, he did a group of the local fencibles. Others of his works illustrated early engines and trains, some of which are reproduced here.

The black-paper silhouette is not, as some suppose, a very ancient art, although the silhouette form of portraiture is ages old. They were variously called shades and shadowgraphs, and they took the name silhouette from Etienne de Silhouette who in 1757 was made Controleur Generale of France, and immediately instituted such widespread economies that anything cheap was called a silhouette. This bit of argot persisted for years. He died in 1767, but when in 1825, the shadow portrait became famous in England, Silhouette's name was given it.

The silhouettes varied in style. Some were snipped out of black paper and mounted on a white card. Others were outlined on silk, glass, ivory, and metal, and then filled in with

black and sometimes with colour. American itinerant silhouette artists introduced the style of cutting the portrait
out of the centre of the card itself and then pasting black
paper or cloth behind.

PAINTERS OF FRESCOES

Many of the painters of signs, coats of arms, hatchments,
as well as painters of portraits, came to this country from
England, and by the middle of the eighteenth century some of
them had found work here as fresco painters. In such widely
separated areas as Portsmouth, New Hampshire, Quillicote,
Maine, and South Carolina are houses with frescoed walls.
Some of the designs are repeated, and some of the paintings
are non-repeat landscapes. In the Connecticut Valley are a
number of houses with the repeat decorations and all painted
in about the same way, which indicates that they were done
by the same man or group of men. It is said that the artists
were Germans from the Rhine country, as the same designs
and same colour schemes are found on painted chests now
preserved at Perm in Bavaria and other museums abroad.
Between 1820 and 1836 we find record of walls being land-
scaped, as at the home of the late Kate Douglas Wiggin, at
Quillicote, Maine, which was painted by a man, so family
tradition tells, who travelled about on horseback. At Deer-
field, Massachusetts, is a floor elaborately painted in the
Connecticut Valley style of repeat design.

Doubtless quite a number of the men who painted
portraits and were itinerants, were willing to do a wall
or an over-mantel painting for whatever food and lodging
they would fetch.

ITINERANT DECORATORS

Another phase of itinerant art was the decoration of bridal
chests, fireboards, ordinary daily utensils, and the fancy
writing or *fractur* of the Pennsylvania Germans.

Among the collectible items of early American household

furniture are the *Truhe* or dower chests of the Pennsylvania Dutch, which, since these people are not a migratory race, have been handed down through generations. Each young girl was given one at her betrothal or when she arrived at the marriageable age, and, on her death, it would go to her daughter. The styles of these chests are quite distinctive, and, from the designs found definitely in various districts of Pennsylvania, and from the technique of the decorations, they fall into various neighbourhood classes. Thus the Lebanon County chest differs from those of Lehigh and Montgomery Counties. Some have motifs painted on a coloured background and some have sgraffito decorations, the design being scratched into the wood and then filled in with colour. For some time it was thought that these chests were the product of local farm carpenters—each man making his own chest for his own daughter. That may have been true of the actual construction. But closer study of the decorations and the technique of the painting leads us to believe that the final processes were done by journeyman painters who travelled from farmhouse to farmhouse. The work on these dower chests is too elaborate and too well done for any mere amateur hand.

The fireboard, used to fill the fireplace in summer time, was another object of decorative art. Edward Hicks, cousin of the famous Elias Hicks of Jericho, Long Island (who started the Hicksite split in the Society of Friends), was an itinerant artist given to decorating fireboards and painting small pictures of historic scenes. His art was limited to three or four subjects that he painted again and again— Washington Crossing the Delaware and such. Hicks died in 1849, after painting these three or four scenes for half a century.

FRACTUR

Among the arts taught in Pennsylvania by German schoolmasters up to 1840 was *fractur* or illuminated handwriting. And there was also a class of vagrants who wandered about from place to place in the Pennsylvania German areas, and who made their scant living by this art. They carried with them, it is said, a colour box containing goose quill pens, brushes of cat's hair, a varnish of cherry gum and home-made inks of various colours.

Fractur work consists of two kinds—the religious and the secular. The former included illuminated hymns, baptismal and marriage certificates and inscriptions in family Bibles. The secular work covered such articles as the title pages of books, song books and crude allegorical pictures that were framed and hung on the whitewashed walls to relieve their bareness. Crude indeed were the colours—bright reds, blues, yellows, and greens, and the execution was in that style we speak of as peasant. For it was peasant work, and the art was native to these German emigrants. Some of it was done at home by aspiring artists, but much was executed by the itinerant *fractur* painters.

There is a marked Persian influence in the flowers and birds and writing of this *fractur* work. The pages of some of the old hymn books are strongly reminiscent of Persian calligraphy and Indo-Persian painting. How could such a far-away art touch these simple Pennsylvania Dutch wayfaring artists? They came, some of them, from the Rhine country and some from Moravia. Trade from the Levant went first to Venice, thence to Verona and Bolsano and up the Rhine. By the twelfth century, Persian damasks were being reproduced by German block printers in crude forms and colours, and the influence of Persian art was strong. Poland, which is close to Moravia, produced silk rugs of strongly marked Persian style in the fifteenth century, and doubtless the Persian influence crept across the border. This influence, carried across the seas, found its expression in the elaborately penned and decorated *fractur* pieces of the Pennsylvania Germans.

Journeymen painters must also have been responsible for the great quantity of clock faces, mirror panels and other crude paintings on glass and tin that adorned the ordinary home prior to 1850. These, together with samplers, formed the meagre decorations of the walls and shelves. After that, came in the crude lithographs of Currier, and Currier & Ives, for which collectors to-day have such a passion.

CHAPTER X

PEDDLERS OF THE WORD

T HE Boston *Evening Post* in 1744 printed an address to George Whitefield, the itinerant preacher, containing this sentence: "One great reason why we thought you the best minister in the world was because you had persuaded us that most others were good for nothing."

This engaging frankness is characteristic of the times. People spoke their minds in newspapers in those days. It also indicates religious conditions, both of that and of subsequent eras in America.

Religious toleration has never been the dominant characteristic of the American people. There have always been hosts of preachers labouring to persuade their followers that the others were no good. Ecclesiastical competition has bred some of our sorriest hours and, at the same time, raised up some of our most vivid leaders.

Like the huge fold Robinson Crusoe made for his goats, the church has been so far flung and so inclusive that the goats inside have been just as wild as the goats outside. From that wintry day when the Massachusetts Bay fathers persuaded Roger Williams that he was all wrong, and he departed thence to settle Rhode Island—from that day until this year of Fundamentalist grace, the vision of religion in America is not unlike the scenes found at old country fairs. On all sides peddlers bidding against each other. On all sides preachers preaching against each other. Little wonder that the chaos bred an infinity of disagreements! Little wonder that America came to be known as "The Land of Crazy Religions."

Before we reach these peddlers of the Word, however, we have to understand something of the political status of relig-

ion in young America and something of the great waves of
piety that surged through the land and washed up this peculiar type of sanctified hawker.

RELIGION AND THE STATE

There are those who fondly believe that America has
always been the cradle of religious freedom. The facts, however, are very much against so pious a sentiment.

For the first one hundred and fifty years religious liberty
was unknown in this country. In one guise or another limi-
tations were set on what faith a man could lawfully profess or
not profess. Dogmatic disagreements, hair-splitting heresies,
and contentions over fine shades of Scriptural interpretation
entered into the make-up of practically every provincial
government and coloured its life. This was as true of the
South as it was of the North. New England sought to prevent the taint of established orthodoxy or the questioning of
religious authority from reaching the people; the Southern
provinces legislated against the "infection of Puritanism."
Quantities of men and women made it their business to persuade, threaten and bully other people into accepting their
tenets. And such a condition of affairs was not unnatural.

Coming to a primitive country, where safety depended on
solidarity, each religious group was inspired by the same
human instinct to survive, and each combated (save the
Quakers in Pennsylvania)* any ecclesiastical influence, dis-
loyalty or disagreement that might threaten their survival or
safety. Practically all types considered the Church and State
inseparable. Under these conditions toleration soon ceased
to be a virtue or a commonwealth ideal.

When the Union was formed, only two States out of the

---

* However, the Quakers did impose a tax of twenty shillings on each Irish
servant " being Papist, to prevent the growth of popery by the importation of
too great a number of them into the province." They also viewed with alarm
the steady emigration of Presbyterian Scotch-Irish, lest they get control of
affairs. In Virginia the Presbyterians were allowed only on the condition that
they settled as a " buffer " sect, between the Episcopalians and the Indians.

10

thirteen—Rhode Island and Virginia—required no religious qualifications for citizenship or of office-holders. Six insisted on Protestantism, two asked for profession of the Christian religion, four required assent to the divine inspiration of the Scriptures, two demanded belief in Heaven and Hell, and one, belief in the Trinity. In New Hampshire, Massachusetts, Connecticut, Maryland and South Carolina, the Church was a state establishment.

From these restrictions it must not be surmised that at all times religious fervour maintained a white heat either during the Colonial or the Federal period. Quite the opposite. But whenever the fervour dropped below a certain temperature, there immediately appeared numbers of men determined to raise it again. An example of this can be found in the Great Awakening.

THE GREAT AWAKENING

A little over a hundred years after the Pilgrim Fathers landed at Plymouth, Increase Mather wrote *Ichabod or a Discourse Showing What Cause There is to Fear the Glory of the Lord is Departing from New England*. In those one hundred years the heady wine of Puritanism had been diluted by emigrants who were not so fervid as the first settlers. Men were no longer engrossed with church affairs. Ministers realized that their work bore less fruit. One especially felt this— Jonathan Edwards of Connecticut, and his particular points of attack were certain impure books the youth of that day enjoyed, and a custom that the church itself had created. In the early days the Black Sabbath began at sundown on Saturday and lasted the next twenty-four hours, leaving Sunday night free. And the youth of the time, feeling the pious lid lifted, used Sunday night for worldly diversion. The older people were not slow to follow suit. Likewise, by this time the first hard years having passed, women took pride in their appearance and men in their possessions. Quite a worldly little movement began to pulsate up and down the Atlantic seaboard. Then appeared George Whitefield.

GEORGE WHITEFIELD
The famous Evangelist

REV. GILBERT TENNENT
Itinerant Preacher

A METHODIST CAMP-MEETING

FRANCIS ASBURY
The Itinerant Methodist Preacher and Bishop

On May 8, 1738, Whitefield landed at Savannah, and at five o'clock the next morning he started preaching. For a while he remained in that city and founded a home for nearby orphans. Then he headed north. His original intention was to raise funds for his orphanage, for we find him preaching on the Boston Common to 8000 people and collecting £555. His farewell sermon was listened to (if we can believe his figures) by 30,000 devout souls. Having moved Boston to repentance, he started on an itineracy through Connecticut, New York, Pennsylvania, and into the South again, labouring to convert the masses from the worldly habits they had recently acquired. As he dragged his gospel net along the coast, dancing schools were closed, people laid aside their gaudy habiliments, and the sound of repentant weeping was heard in the land.

He attracted many followers. Gilbert Tennent, an Irishman, went about in a girdled great coat and long hair like a monk. He and his brother laboured in New Jersey. Jesse Lee of the Methodists carried on the work in New England. Hosts of others of many persuasions preached up and down the countryside to bring people to their knees.

Seeing this descent upon their folds, the town ministers resented the tearful and paroxysmic ranting of these itinerants. Pulpits were forbidden them. Strife arose in the churches themselves, between those of the Old Lights who were conservative, those of the middle path who were moderate, and those of the New Lights who held to this revivalist preaching.

By 1742 so many preachers were running around that the Assembly of Connecticut passed a law forbidding ministers preaching out of their own parishes without permission, or itinerants exhorting without the express invitation of the local pastor or a major part of the congregation, and completely forbidding the exhortations of illiterate laymen. They were to be treated as common vagrants and banished from the colony. This punishment was actually visited upon two preachers who dared to stray into the confines of Connecticut peddling the Word. Twenty years later Virginia's enactment caught Lewis Craig and his brother Elijah, who were arrested for "preaching the Gospel contrary to the law," and on refusing to desist, these two parsons were thrown into jail where they preached to congregations through the prison bars!

Whitefield died in 1770. A vain, blatant, Calvinistic fanatic he might appear to us, and certainly his journals show him to have been such. But the fire he lighted burned with fierce intensity for many years, and often with disastrous effects.

From this Great Awakening began the habit of revivalist and itinerant preaching, which forms one of the most picturesque chapters in American history.

In the fifty years following the Great Awakening, the minds of the people were concerned more and more with politics and the events leading up to the Revolutionary War. The coming of peace was almost synchronous with the French Revolution which was sympathetically felt in this country. A native brand of skepticism that had gradually evolved, echoed the sentiments of the French masses, and when, after 1790, French refugees and representatives of the French revolutionary party began to appear here, there came a serious wave of Deism and rationalism. This gradually subsided.

By the turn of the century reappears the urge for a religious revival. Not only does it crop out in the lower orders, as among the Kentucky rural folks, but it is carried into the colleges, into Yale and Harvard and Dartmouth. Once more people lusted for salvation. It was this second recurrence of revivals that definitely stamped America as a Protestant country, given to enjoying ecstatic and blatant preachments and the democracy of many and varied sects.

THE INFINITY OF SECTS

Religious intoleration invariably breeds a desire to break away, on the slightest theological or economic provocation, from accepted or orthodox tenets. This country showed no exception. Each man tried to preach the Word in his own tongue and according to his own lights. Consequently the sects began breaking up within a few years after they appeared. The Methodists, the Baptists, the Congregationalists, the Presbyterians, all bore offshoots, some of which survived and are flourishing bodies to-day. The established Church of England suffered the abandoning of their parishes by Tory parsons during the Revolution, and also felt the inroads of Methodism. The Roman Catholic Church in its first years went through a constant wrangling for ecclesiastical control and it had intermittent trouble with priests who broke loose from discipline. Even the Society of Friends eventually experienced the grievous effect of schism and the encroachment of worldliness.

These deflections were accompanied by furious and prolonged doctrinal discussions both by pamphlet and word of mouth. Champions on both sides worked hectically to convert each other and whomsoever came within their hearing. These sons of thunder made a Babel of confusion. The conversion of the native savage to Christianity paled into a minor work beside the conversion of the erring brother and the conviction of members of other sects. "Sheep stealing" was the colloquial term for proselytizing. Benjamin Abbott, a Methodist, complains that once a Baptist parson "stole nine of my sheep and ran them into a mill pond."

This condition of the Church Militant caused the evangelical activities between 1750 and 1850 to fall into two distinct classes: (1) tending and reviving the spiritual fires of those who belonged to the various churches and who settled farther and farther out as the country expanded; and (2) making converts to new phases of the sects. Each religious body was busy strengthening her stakes and lengthening her cords.

And these two forms of activity account for the phenomena with which we are most concerned in this chapter—for the great variety and activity of home missionaries, for the rise of itinerant preachers, for the tireless and courageous circuit riders, and for that vast crowd of men and women who formed an ignorant and unlearned ministry, but who are among the most picturesque of our wayfarers.

WANDERING PREACHERS

The early American home missionary, wayfaring preacher and circuit rider was at once a man of the world and a man withdrawn from it.   Although many of them experienced ecstatic religious conversion, only one can be said to have shown mystical tendencies—John Woolman. They were practical men. They preached the sanctification of human kind. While the Quakers—Woolman, John Churchman, Elias Hicks, Thomas Story, William Savery, John Richardson and their fellows—were austere men, the Methodists, the Baptists and the others came closer to human, everyday contacts. Not that they were worldly, far from it.* The personal sacrifices they made for their calling almost approached monastic discipline and the vows that religious orders take. In the early days of Methodism the marriage of itinerant preachers was discouraged lest family ties and responsibilities should hinder the shepherding of their sheep. Both Bishop Asbury and Bishop McKendree remained unmarried

Since preaching furnished meagre support to wife and children, many of these itinerant preachers had trades at which they worked by day *en route*, preaching at night and on Sundays. Woolman began as a tailor, "but perceiving merchandise to be attended with much cumber," abandoned it and devoted himself to the Word and to his fight against slavery and the exploitation of labour. Samuel Seabury, the first Episcopal bishop, believing the cure of bodies to be as

---

*And yet, according to present-day standards, some of them were pretty rough customers. Prior to 1825, when the Temperance Movement gained strength, many were dram-drinkers and quite a number, heavy chewers of tobacco. It is related of one Indiana circuit preacher that he "spat as often as once in two minutes during his whole sermon, so that the pulpit floor was as filthy as a stable when he finished his discourse."

necessary a part of the missionary's work as the cure of souls, studied medicine. Devereux Jarrett was carpenter and teacher by trade, and doubtless found opportunity to pursue both callings in the twenty-eight Southern counties he served as travelling missionary. David Caldwell was a carpenter, a physician and a teacher, and worked as all three besides preaching the Gospel in North Carolina.

These men knew Holy Poverty as keenly as any monk. Before he was consecrated, Bishop Seabury had less than $250 a year, and even after he was Bishop there were times when he could not afford to keep a horse. The Methodist Conference of 1784 put the itinerant preacher's salary at $64 per annum, with a little extra where there were wife and children—but the collecting of the money was their own responsibility. Later this was raised to the lordly sum of $80 with an allowance of $80 for the wife and $14 for each child. Other than this they were dependent on the voluntary contributions of their scattered flocks, but since the Methodists allowed a preacher to remain on the same circuit only two years, there was little chance of getting his flock into a "giving" frame of mind. Besides, as Timothy Flint, an old colporteur, observed, people believed they had done their duty to a parson when they had listened to his sermons. Peter Cartwright earned the huge sum of $6 for three months' preaching and in one year his total salary amounted to $40. At this time he had a wife and six children. Some of the itinerant preachers did not receive half that sum. One itinerant preacher in Indiana for a year's work received $9 and a pair of trousers. To keep body and soul alive many of them were obliged to quit vagabond preaching and settle down to a "location" where they worked all day and preached in their off hours. The richest and best educated Presbytery in the South in 1853 had twenty-one ministers whose salary did not exceed $25 a year each.

Poverty, celibacy and obedience of sorts these circuit riders exercised, and, like monks, they even had a distinctive dress and tonsure. Homespun clothes—a round-breasted coat, short trousers and long stockings. Some of them wore leather clothes, which resisted briars better than woollen. And whereas the monk was satisfied with an insignificant tonsure the Methodist itinerant preacher had a most pronounced coiffure—the hair was clipped short from the forehead half-way back to the crown and the remainder allowed to grow eight or ten inches long and hang loosely around the shoulders.

Few of these itinerant preachers were educated. While the Episcopalian, Congregational, and Presbyterian preachers usually had some schooling, the lay Methodist itinerant, says Cartwright, "had little or no education; no books and no time to read or study them if we could have had them. We had no colleges nor even a respectable common school within a hundred miles of us. . . . It is true, we could not, many of us, conjugate a verb, or parse a sentence, and murdered the King's English almost every lick. . . . A Methodist preacher in those days, when he felt that God had called him to preach, instead of hunting up a college or a Biblical institute, hunted up a hardy pony, or a horse, and some travelling apparatus, and with his library always at hand, namely Bible, Hymn Book, and Discipline, he started, and with a text that never wore out or grew stale he cried, 'Behold the Lamb of God, that taketh away the sin of the world!' In this way he went through storms of wind, hail, snow, and rain; climbed hills and mountains, traversed valleys, plunged through swamps, swam swollen streams, lay out at night, wet, weary and hungry, held his horse by the bridle all night, or tied him to a limb, slept with his saddle blanket for a bed, his saddle or saddle-bags for his pillow, and his old big coat or blanket, if he had any, for covering. Often he slept in dirty cabins, on earthen floors, before the fire; ate roasting ears for bread, drank buttermilk for coffee, or sage tea for imperial; took, with a hearty zest, deer or bear meat, or wild turkey for breakfast, dinner and supper, if he could get it."

Where there was a congregation and a church the circuit rider's work was relatively simple, but in the country areas he had to go from house to house. He would arrive at a farm-house, hitch his horse, rap on the door and say to the house-wife, "Sister, shall I pray with you?" Almost always he was asked in. Then he gathered the family about him, prayed, exhorted them and sang hymns. For this he was given lodg-ing and entertainment. To homes isolated by great distances, in constant danger from warlike natives, the visits of these wayfaring preachers were a source of great joy and spiritual inspiration.

The zeal for the Word, for service, for making converts carried these weather-beaten peddlers astounding distances. Picture with what fortitude and energy they pursued their calling! And often heavily armed, lest Indians and highway-men attack them.

For thirty years John Woolman was constantly on the road. At first he refused to ride in a carriage or on a horse, and insisted on walking from meeting to meeting. Led by the Spirit he travelled the entire Atlantic seaboard, then to the Bahamas and to England. In the end, in 1772, at York, he died among strangers, his eyes beholding the land that is very far off. William Savery of Philadelphia was another of the tireless travelling Quaker preachers, who gave up his business to carry the Word into all parts of America and to countries abroad.

Although having its missionaries who travelled vast dis-tances, the Roman Catholic Church offers a different type from the circuit-riding preacher. Most of these missionaries were members of religious orders and were under obedience to their superiors; so were the secular clergy in direct contact with their bishops, and they were not afforded the freedom of movement enjoyed by the Methodists and others. But it is a fact worth remarking that even the Protestant circuit-riders had definite areas to which they were assigned, and definite synods and conferences to which they were under obedience and to which they had to report the work accomplished on their long journeys.

It would be difficult to say who proved the best traveller of all these sects. In the eleven years of his episcopate, Bishop Seabury travelled 6000 miles and, in that time, so his journal proudly asserts, he failed to keep only one appointment.

It is said of Bishop Asbury of the Methodist Church that during the forty years of his labours the headquarters of American Methodism were in the saddle. He travelled 270,-000 miles, ordained over 4000 preachers and presided over 230 annual conferences. His counterpart in New England, Jesse Lee, who started preaching Methodism there in 1789, left fifty preachers and 6000 members in that land of Congregationalism as the fruits of eleven years' labour. But the giant of them all was Peter Cartwright, who in fifty-three years of circuit-riding, preached over 14,000 sermons, baptized 12,000, attended 500 funerals, and covered untold distances. Like the others, as we have seen from his own testimony, he was untutored, sought the middle and lower classes, the ecclesiastically neglected, whom he drew to allegiance by the sincerity and fervour of his preaching.

The Methodists early sent out their Peddlers of the Word to all parts. A conference in Philadelphia in 1784 started on their way 104 travelling preachers, and ordained as many local preachers. By 1800 it had 307 itinerant preachers on the road. Due to the efforts of these men and to such giants as Coke, Cartwright and Asbury, by 1850 the Methodists in America totalled something over a million.

THE CAMP MEETING

To Peter Cartwright is generally attributed the credit for the development of the camp meeting, a custom peculiar to this country and, in its heyday, the most potent factor for awakening communities and countrysides to religious consciousness.

The widening frontiers called a miscellaneous people—the intrepid, the ambitious, the long-suffering, the evil. Some were godly folk, some rascals, some malefactors of the worst kidney. To these should be added perfidious Indians ready always to revenge and repel what they considered the invasion of their private lands. Drinking and gambling were the usual vices of these frontier people, together with occasional brigandage, easy murder and a rather loose interpretation of the Seventh Commandment, and of marriage relations generally. They were a rough people, living close to Nature, men and women of all sects and shades of belief, mostly unschooled, and consequently quick to respond to the type of revival appeal offered by these preachers. In the beginning they had no churches worthy of the name, no choirs, no organs, no physical equipment so necessary to church people to-day. Fervid exhorting was their only means of religious excitation. Also, it must be remembered, these people had scarcely any amusements, and the thinly settled countryside no centres of social intercourse.

Into this situation came the camp meeting, fathered by the Methodists, and taken up by the Baptists, Presbyterians, and others. The Methodist camp meeting was the most picturesque, with its bench for mourners.* All of them were attended by enormous crowds that, in moments of repentance and ecstacy, shouted and sang, moaned, wept, sobbed, jerked, jumped, ran, barked, rolled, swayed and swooned in a way that would strike us to-day as simple madness. At Cove Ridge, Kentucky, there was a camp meeting at which at one time, it is said, 3000 men and women who had fainted from religious ecstacy were laid out like so much cord wood.

The year 1801 saw the first of these camp meetings. In 1799–1801 a great religious revival rolled through Kentucky,

---

*Valentine Cook (1765-1820), an erratic and dishevelled itinerant Methodist preacher, added lustre to his biography by instituting this custom of the mourners' bench, set in front of the congregation, where penitents would go to proclaim themselves convicted of sin and be prayed over. Charles Grandison Finney, the Presbyterian missionary ranter, who later founded Oberlin College, gave to the mourners' bench the name of "the anxious seat."

Tennessee, and the Carolinas. The Presbyterians united with the Methodists in a monster sacramental meeting held in Kentucky and protracted for weeks. What happened there set the style for camp meetings thereafter.

Revivals of this sort were held every year. People of the neighbourhood would erect camps with logs or frame them and sometimes even made them permanent with clapboard and shingles. These were the preacher's quarters. They often also built a shed sufficiently large to accommodate several thousand people, roofed in to protect them from wind and rain.

To this centre the people resorted, some coming forty to fifty miles, others farther. They represented many denominations. They came in wagons, on foot, on horseback, in carriages, most of them with food supplies for days. At one camp meeting 1145 wagons were counted and 20,000 people attended. The women slept in the wagons and the men under them. Others were accommodated in the neighbourhood.

Huge bonfires lighted the camp meeting by night and a ghostly sight it must have been when twenty, sometimes thirty ministers of different sects were preaching day and night, four and five days together. As many as seven preachers might be haranguing the people at one time from the different pulpits erected throughout the preaching shed. When one preacher was exhausted, another jumped up to take his place, so that there was never any let-up of the exhorting pressure. Even children would harangue the crowds.

The zeal with which these meetings were conducted, the frenzy and madness to which the people were worked up beggars description. Services went on from dawn until late in the evening, and even after the pious had withdrawn to their wagons and tents they would continue in ecstatic and noisy prayer through a greater part of the night.

The Baptist rallying cry at these meeting was: "Water! Water! Follow your Lord down into the water!" So insistent

AN IMMERSION AMONG THE EARLY BAPTISTS
Courtesy of E. P. Dutton & Co.

PETER CARTWRIGHT, CIRCUIT-PREACHER

THE DOCK-PREACHER

were they on immersion that people began to believe Heaven
an island and you had to swim to it. The Methodists proclaimed their superiority in a giddy little ballad that went:

> "I'll tell you who the Lord likes best—
> It is the shoutin' Methodist!"

Rowdies often attended these camp meetings, and to no
good purpose. They brought along whiskey and tempted the
pious and repentant to take a nip. They stoned the preachers'
tents and made themselves a general nuisance. The chroni-
cles of these rowdy fights offer a pleasant relief to the dry and
pious records of the camp meetings. So, for that matter, do
the continual theological arguments, into which these old
itinerant preachers used to plunge. Their language may have
been Biblical, but is was hardly charitable. Cartwright called
his competing church a "trash trap."* If they couldn't
convert their opponent, they launched forth on a description
of the sort of Hell to which he and his unsanctified friends
were bound to go. Dante at his best is rather pallid beside
some of these "arguefiers". . . . And, when the camp meeting
had dispersed there were left "only a desecrated wood and a
few freshly made graves."

CAMP MEETING RESULTS

Apart from the fact that these sacred saturnalia were pre-
sumably *ad majorem gloriam Dei*, it is natural that we should
ask just how much good—if any—they accomplished. Varied
elements entered into their make-up, the most important of
which was their social value. They were the great social
event of the year among the classes of people who attended
them. Friends met, romances began, laughter and smiles
lightened faces. The going to and coming from them were in

---

*A really masterful piece of ecclesiastical invective was uttered by the Rev.
Gilbert Tennent who described ministers of a competitive sect as "hirelings, cater-
pillars, letter-learned Pharisees, Hypocrites, varlets, Seed of the Serpent, foolish
Builders whom the Devil drives into the ministry, dead dogs that cannot bark,
blind men, dead men, men possessed of the Devil, rebels and enemies of God."

the nature of an annual jaunt. They never were held in times of war or at seasons of the year when people's minds were occupied or the work in the fields pressing. No revivalist would dream of attempting a camp meeting in the planting or harvesting season.

They afforded all manner of diverting excitements, for the religious passion cannot be excited without stirring up a lot of others. Strict regulations were necessary to keep the people in hand. At ten o'clock patrols used to go around the camp to see that all the pious picnickers were in their proper places. Nevertheless men quarrelled and fought and made love to their neighbours' wives, and the youth of the time got highly charged with religiosity and went out and misbehaved itself.

It has been estimated that of the young men who got up these revivals, one in twenty went wrong—not a staggering percentage. No figures are available on the conduct of those who attended them, although it is well known that illegitimate births took a sharp rise after camp meetings and revivals. To the pious this may seem astounding. Yet we must remember that some of our mincing regard for the moral amenities was not found in the early days of America. Even the Puritans of New England accepted the seven-months child and the standard of morality among some of the younger generation makes our contemporary youths and maidens appear as angels of light.

BUNDLING

There was, for example, the custom of "Bundling" ordained, as the "Book of Common Prayer" puts it, "in the time of man's innocency," to save heat and light. It was a winter medium of convenience. There were two phases of it —the entertainment of strangers and the courtship between the young. The stranger would share the extra bed with whomsoever he might find in it, although it might be the wife or the daughter of the house. Young men and maidens went to bed with their clothes on rather than sit up, because candles and heat had to be conserved. This custom continued for a century and a half in New England and in the Dutch colonies. It was found generally among the lower classes. The consequences attendant upon it were not invariably as questionable as one might suppose, although human nature was no different than to-day. As Thomas Campion observes:

> Though love and all his pleasures are but toys,
> They shorten tedious nights.

Moreover, Nature has a way of calmly disregarding a man-made commandment when the increase of the race is threatened. In frontier regions men and women mated naturally without benefit of clergy. Down South the first born was often referred to as "the engagement child." One of the pastoral duties of the itinerant preacher was to solemnize the marriage of these people and sometimes the bride had a child at the breast or at the skirt when the ceremony was performed.

THE ITINERANT PREACHER'S OTHER LABOURS

Apart from their pastoral labours, these wandering preachers definitely influenced the thought of their day and were powerful in politics. Even the least schooled of them was better educated than the average of their flock. They were the leaders of whatever thinking the scattered frontier populace did. The meadow pulpit was the most direct way of reaching rural people. It moulded their opinions and allayed or excited their passions. Certainly in the backwoods these itinerant preachers and circuit riders exerted enormous political and national influence. Down South, until the Abolition Movement began to exert pressure, the spiritual interests of the slaves were neglected. Preachers were then provided for them—some of their own colour, some white. It was the custom of the white preachers to skip lightly over the troubles of this present life and devote most of their efforts to picturing the glories and pleasures of Heaven. This assurance of post-mortem delights may account for the fact that Heaven and what they will do and wear there is the topic of many of the negroes' spirituals.

Many of the missionaries and circuit preachers had definite diplomatic missions assigned them. William Savery aided the United States Commission to make peace with the Indian tribes of the Ohio District. Fr. Peter Gibault was an influential force in holding the Illinois country loyal to the nation in those trying days of 1778–9, a task formally appreciated by the Virginia legislature. In the mid-nineteenth century, Fr. Peter de Smet worked magic in keeping the Indians of the Far West off the war-path and friendly to the government. A great traveller, Fr. de Smet, he covered in his career 180,000 miles, by boat, canoe, dog-sled, wagon, horse, and foot. It is said of him that he was more powerful than an army with banners. In fact, he was a solitary soldier with a banner, for when he went to pacify Sitting Bull he approached that old chieftain through ranks of painted warriors holding a banner of the Virgin in his hand. That one mission brought 50,000 Indians into allegiance with the government.

Among both the located and the itinerant parsons in these beginning days was manifested a rare gift of native oratory. Although they may not have realized it, they set a new style for public speaking both in the pulpit and the forum. The forensic efforts of eighteenth century England were stilted and artificial. These men who faced pioneer congregations were obliged to evolve an easier, more energetic, more persuasive eloquence that, in time, came to influence oratory, although not always for its good. They harangued, acted, declaimed, and uttered absurd and disgusting tautology. These "thundering" preachers,* more than any other

---

*One of these itinerant thunderers had a voice so powerful, his congregation averred, that they could hear his tones pass through their heads and strike the trees behind them. The Rev. Benjamin Abbott was so moving an exhorter that, according to his own statement, when women wept over their sins their tears lay in puddles about their feet.

influence, introduced the habit of fiery, dramatic speaking which attains its dizzy pinnacle in our spread-eagle Fourth of July oration.

THE PARSON AS EMIGRANT LEADER

One of the most romantic figures in the annals of American church history was Demetrius Augustine Galatzin, scion of a noble Russian house, whose name is perpetuated in the town of Gallitzin, Pennsylvania. His parents were Voltairean non-believers, his father, Russian ambassador to the Hague and his mother, daughter of a famous Austrian general. He himself held a commission in the army as a young man, after which he came to America. His travelling companion was a priest, who led him under the influence of Bishop Carroll of Baltimore. Immediately showing signs of a vocation for the priesthood, he was entered at the seminary of St. Sulpice at Baltimore and was ordained in 1795, the first Roman Catholic priest to be educated and take Orders in this country. After serving several small parishes, he was sent into the wilderness beyond the Alleghany Mountains to what is now Cambria County, Pennsylvania, and for forty years he laboured up and down that countryside, spent his own fortune on the people, settled a dozen or more towns, and when he died he left large congregations behind him. He never used his title, preferring to work under the name of Fr. Augustine Smith. His method was to buy up large tracts of land—20,000 acres all told—that he sold to his followers for a nominal sum. In that way he attracted enough Roman Catholics to build up Loretto, Gallitzin, and several other towns. His fortune of $150,000 was completely exhausted in this work. He was an active pamphleteer for his religion and, if contemporary records are to be believed, a headstrong and unmanageable old saint.

Another gentleman of the Cloth who might be classed in this category of real estate parsons was Manasseh Cutler. In 1787, when the Ohio country was thrown open to emigrants,

Cutler, pastor of the church in Ipswich, Massachusetts, inspired a band of his settlers to go out and found Marietta, under General Rufus Putnam. Dr. Cutler followed eighteen months later. Revolutionary veterans were given preference. The Ohio Company controlled a million and a half acres. It then took an option on a tract of from three to five million acres of land adjacent to their grant, originally belonging to La Compagnie du Scioto and sold to French emigrants. The French settlements were a failure, and the people scattered, but Cutler's project succeeded.

COLPORTEURS

There is still another type of peddler of the Word who fitted the title even more exactly than did the itinerant preacher—the colporteur.

The American Tract Society, which was founded for the distribution of religious literature to the churches, gained impetus in 1841 by the employment of Russell B. Cook. In his line he was a "high pressure" executive. To meet the needs of remote communities, he developed the system of American colportage. By 1856 the Society was regularly employing 547 colporteurs with an additional 115 students who worked during their vacations. These men travelled all through the country, by horseback and wagon, by boat and train, distributing and selling Bibles, tracts, religious romances and other pietistic literature. Baxter's "Call or The Saint's Rest" was given away by the thousands, and the tracts bore such names as "Examine Your Hopes for Eternity," "The Swearer's Prayer," "The Lost Soul," "Little Janes the Cottager," "Pike's Persuasives to Early Piety," Nelson's "Anxious Inquirer," and "Pilgrim's Progress." There was even a colporteur boat that plied the western rivers supplying this literature to the pioneers. The number of families visited by these colporteurs is amazing. The Tract Society Report for 1859 states that over 3,000,000 families had been visited by colporteurs, and over 8,000,000 volumes distributed.

For many years these books constituted the only reading matter of rural folks—save almanacs and patent medicine advertisements—until in our generation, mail-order houses relieved the religious tension with their encyclopædic catalogues.

CHAPTER XI

TERPSICHORE PERAMBULANT

MONG the colourful figures of Elizabethan England was one Will Kemp, the player, who danced from London to Norwich in nine days, and was thereafter proclaimed the "hedge-king of English morrice-dancery for ever." He has been glorified in song and story. Alfred Noyes weaves about him in "Tales of the Mermaid Tavern" the romance of a milkmaid who danced with him for a mile. She tucked up her "russet petticoate" and—

> I fitted her with morrice-bells, with treble, bass and tenor bells;
> The fore-bells, as I linked them at her throat, how soft they sang!
> Green linnets in a golden nest, they chirped and trembled on her
>   breast,
> And, faint as elfin blue-bells, at her nut-brown ankles rang.

There may have been other famous dancers but none were so much the itinerant as Will Kemp. And he must always remain the patron of those instructors and masters who, from that time have wandered about teaching people to dance and the joy of life in it. Though the Puritan fathers may never have heard of him, it was the spirit of Will Kemp that descended on them like a divine fire when they took to dancing.

DANCING MASTERS

Now dancing, singing, fencing, and such are scarcely affairs about which the Puritan would much concern himself; we are more apt to expect them in the Cavalier regions of the South. And yet once the pressure of the Puritan regime began to lift ever so little, the minds of the people swung naturally to these relaxations.

The first dancing school in Massachusetts is said to have opened in 1672, and was promptly closed. Later, in Salem we find a Charles Bradshaw venturing to teach the art. The selectmen gave him permission to introduce this worldly diversion so long as he kept order. In 1755 M. Lawrence D'Obleville appears from Paris and teaches dancing and good manners not only to the youth of Salem but to children in surrounding towns. In the same neighbourhood and at about the same time are found two brothers, Robert and George Virat, who took scholars at the equivalent of $2 a quarter to learn dancing, fencing, music, and French. They taught in both Salem and Marblehead.

Thus slowly, Terpsichore finds a place in the people's lives. By 1790 dancing had become the principal indoor sport of New England.

In New Amsterdam the Dutch girls and boys danced quite naturally. Dancing was part of their Christmas merrymaking. Negroes also danced in the public market, to the beat of tom-toms, which is natural, seeing that they were fresh come from their African jungles on the Dutch trading sloops.

Quaker Philadelphia showed no inclination to dance in its early years. Dancing masters visited the city occasionally but not until 1730 did the first dancing school open there. Nine years later John Whitefield passed through Philadelphia and so roused the people against worldliness that he managed not only to stifle the natural desire to dance, but clamped the lid on every other sort of innocent amusement. During the Revolution, Philadelphia regained its laughter. It broke out into a veritable orgy of delights. The winter the British passed in that city and the years during which it was the capital have never been exceeded for social diversions. Ever since, Philadelphia has danced.

As we go South not only does the climate become gentler but the attitude toward these simple pleasures becomes more sane. Merry England was transported to Maryland and Virginia. Dancing assemblies met every fortnight in Charleston before the Revolution, even though in those days Charleston could muster only 5000 to 6000 white residents.

All classes of society of the early days danced and feasted. By 1737 the *Virginia Gazette* was publishing a calendar of sports that included "A Quire of ballads to be sung for by a number of songsters, all of them to have liquor sufficient to clear their Wind Pipes"; "a Violin to be played for by 20 fiddlers," a wrestling match for a pair of silver buckles, and a dancing match at which the prize is a pair of handsome shoes, with an extra inducement of a pair of silk stockings for the prettiest country maiden to appear in the field. This was just about the time the selectmen were softening sufficiently to allow Mr. Bradshaw to teach dancing to the maidens of Salem so long as he kept them in order!

Even in the Cavalier South this business of keeping order at dancing schools seems to have been a problem. Philip Vickers Fithian, tutor to Robert Carter's children, tells of the troubles of Mr. Christian, the dancing master, how he had to rebuke the boys and girls "even in the presence of mothers," the boys for being "insolent and wanton." In one district along the Potomac the master had to slap the girls across the back! Perhaps they were wanton too.

Dancing followed the course of migration westward. In Lexington, Kentucky, a Mr. Terasse taught French and dancing. The recorder of this fact remarks that "in most parts of the United States, teachers of dancing meet with more encouragement than professors of any species of literary science." Mr. Terasse, it appears, opened a dance hall, and a pretty place it was—"a little public garden behind his house which he calls Vauxhall. It has a most luxuriant grape arbour, and two or three summer houses, formed also of grape vines, all of which are illuminated with variegated lamps every Wednesday evening, when the music of two or three decent performers sometimes excites parties to dance on a small boarded platform

AN OLD HOUSE IN LEXINGTON, VIRGINIA, ONCE FAMOUS AS AN EARLY DANCE-HALL

THE DANCING-MASTER

in the middle of the arbour." These delights existed in the
Year of Grace, 1807.

To an extent the dancing master of the South was an
itinerant. Here and there a French indentured servant went
about the immediate neighbourhood teaching the children
on a number of the plantations. Such, for example, was
Stephen Tinoe, a servant on a Virginia estate, who travelled
between Hampton, Yorktown, and Williamsburg holding
classes. There was also another, a Charles Cheate, who
taught dancing in Virginia and was always accompanied by
his servant, a fiddler. In pre-Revolutionary times dancing
classes were held in all the mansions along the Potomac, the
teacher going from house to house. His figures were the
minuet and country dances. He was usually French. Charleston's first dancing master was English, whereas its later
instructors in this art were descendants of French refugees
from St. Domingo. Their assembly halls were known as
"Song Rooms," and here they taught minuets, allemands,
cotillions, hornpipes and other "proper steps for country
dances."

After the Revolution, the teachers of dancing were generally found among the travelling theatrical troupes that went
up and down the Atlantic coast. It is recorded, to his everlasting honour, that a Mr. Russell, of an itinerant stock
company, first introduced to the polite society of Philadelphia the step called "the pigeon wing" in the year 1785. He
was followed by countless others of other companies, but
history is silent on what they contributed to the dithyrambic
gyrations of Philadelphians.

In New York State one itinerant dancing master of the
last century was overtaken by religion in the height of his
career. He used to take rooms in various towns where he held
classes. After his conversion, dancing left a bad taste in
his mouth and he gave it up. Whereupon he was hounded
by tavern keepers and owners of halls to which he had hired
himself as an attraction.

The most picturesque of all these early dancing masters was the one Chateaubriand discovered up near Albany. He had been Rochambeau's cook during the war—at least, he claimed to have been. Chateaubriand discovered him fully dressed and wearing a fastidiously powdered wig, scratching on his fiddle, and teaching a band of yelling, half-naked Indians the latest steps. This funny old French codger took his pay in poultry and bear meat.

L'ELAN FRANÇAIS

At this point and later on, when we come to little itinerant amusements, the reader will note what a large number of the persons concerned were French. The story of just why they came here and how the spirit of light-hearted France infiltrated even the dour soul of New England, comprises one of the most fascinating chapters of our history.

The Huguenots who arrived quite early cannot be said to have added much of the distinctly French spice to our life, although they did give many words to the dialect of the times. They were an easily absorbed people. Occasionally French adventurers drifted this way, but the really strong impress was not marked until La Fayette and his friends took up active support of the American cause in the Revolutionary War. When peace came in 1783 there was left behind at least a deposit of French manners and customs of which people along the Atlantic seaboard had had glimpses. Yet, so concerned were they with the problems of getting the newly born nation on its feet that the French influence cannot be said to have penetrated the national consciousness. In fact, for a few years, the French were not popular among some classes. It was not until 1790 that we can mark the first strong traces of the French ichor. The French Revolution was responsible for it.

The decade between 1790 and 1800 was one of political unrest in this country; the nation was having trouble cutting its teeth. Recriminations, vituperations, and blasphemous back-chat flew from camp to camp by means of pamphlets, broadsides and the press. Philadelphia was the capital at the time, and thither flocked all manner of adventurers. John Fitch, our wandering workman and inventor, started a Deistic Society, but it was soon suppressed. The churches began to feel the inroads of schisms and dissenters against this theological point and that raised up their voices. Atheism and native infidelity grew apace. The ministers got terribly excited about it. Then on the scene appeared the French émigrés. The soil was ready for their sowing.

First, refugees from St. Domingo; then refugees from the French Revolution, then representatives of the revolutionary party, came here and settled in the capital—Genet, Volney and their followers. Many people of Philadelphia became Gallomaniacs, assumed French fashions of thought and of living. The staid Quaker city took on the frivolous air of a French metropolis. It even boasted a cabaret. The papers of the day were filled with advertisements of French dancing schools and dancing masters, French brandy, French pastry, French cosmetics, French shoes and stockings. The notorious Talleyrand used to parade the streets with a mulatto mistress hanging amorously on his arm.

From Philadelphia the influence spread to other states. It cropped out, although in a much diluted form, in New England and in the South. Parents named their children after Genet and Volney. They found their amusements in the itinerant shows that French showmen brought to their towns and cities. And this influence continued, definite and pronounced, until Jefferson was defeated by Adams and the national consciousness began to assume a character of its own.

FENCING MASTERS

Again and again in the records of our towns, prior to 1800 we find the fencing master. He was an itinerant, moved from town to town, staying in one place only so long as the patronage paid him. Such was Richard Kyenall, professor and master of the small sword; such also was John de Florette who taught the broadsword, backsword, spaderoon, and dagger at the Prince of Orange Tavern in Philadelphia. Then in 1824 appears from London William Fuller who gave lessons in the manly art of pugilism. Another pugilist, G. Kensett, also ventured to teach the peaceful Philadelphians "scientific boxing."

SINGING TEACHERS

Save among the Quakers of Pennsylvania and the Jerseys, the early Americans were a singing people.* Even in unyielding New England the rigour of the long services was broken by psalm-singing. The deacon "raised" the tune and the congregation followed, and not with the somnolent hum of present-day self-conscious congregations, but with lusty and open-hearted pæans worthy of a primitive folk. The Dutch of New Amsterdam sang naturally, and so did the Germans of Pennsylvania and the Scotch-Irish, and the men and maidens of the South. In the North, sacred music was first popular and in the South, secular, but in whatever form, the people enjoyed and practised music. Consequently the teaching of singing was no abrupt transition from the early habits of the people in either section. By 1778 William Billings of Boston brings out his "Singing Master's Assistant," and there are soon published any number of books of collected songs.

Again and again in the local histories of towns and in the records left by early travellers, we find accounts of family singing, of singing in the church, and of singing schools and singing masters. Some of the teachers are quaint characters, and about all of them lingers a pathetic reminiscence. There was Mr. Tyles of Pittsburgh, when Pittsburgh was little more than a cross-roads town. As a lad he had been a choris-

---

*The Quakers were counselled against "going to or being in any way concerned in plays, games, lotteries, music and dancing." In fact, Philadelphia did not develop as a music centre until after it ceased being the capital.

ter in a cathedral in England, and his love for singing followed him into the wilderness of Pennsylvania. For a while he taught sacred music in Philadelphia and earned enough to make the first payment on a farm; then he came westward and for two winters went about the countryside near Pittsburgh teaching his beloved art. How different it must have been from those days in that glorious English cathedral where his voice rose up like a lark's to the vaulted canopy!

The itinerant singing master started in this way—he came to a town, announced in school or church that he was willing to take on a few pupils, then went around and obtained signatures and subsequently organized a class. This usually met once a week at night in the schoolhouse or the church. When the class began to fall off, he would move on to another town. Sometimes he played the flute, the violin, or the spinnet and could give lessons on these instruments. Of course, he could always sing himself, and in order to prove his qualifications he gave concerts in private homes for the delectation of the natives.

We read of one such in New England during pre-Civil War days—a Mr. Solomon Huntington, a portly, sociable gentleman "who had seen the world." He had a great compass of voice, and when he played on his viol and represented a thunder storm, a conflagration, the Judgment Day, the Battle of Trafalgar, and several other catastrophies, his hearers were constrained to acknowledge that music in that town had hitherto not reached its grand diapason! There was another singing teacher who, about 1840, drove around the environs of Cambridge, Massachusetts, in a covered wagon, and who used to bring gold fish as rewards to those who paid attention to his teaching!

The singing teacher was a stern master to his pupils. He criticised their method of breathing and gave demonstrations of how they ought to sing that would fill the schoolhouse, as one describes it, with "sparkling scintillations." He would ridicule their singing manners and whine through his nose until he had set his self-conscious pupils at their ease. Let us repeat what followed one of these demonstrations in a small country town class. "It was soon evident that there were two opinions about opening the mouth. Some kept their mouths shut closer than ever; these were mostly the older singers. Others expanded their jaws to a most astonishing capacity. . . .The matter was discussed at parties and on sleigh rides. Mercy Bettis said that when she saw the Scrapewell girls sing she could think of nothing but a trap door. At the next party Emily Scrapewell, in one of the 'awful pauses' in conversation, accosted Mercy Bettis on the opposite side of the room with an inquiry as to her health, and said she understood she had been threatened with lockjaw." And so that town became divided into two parties— the trapdoors and the lockjaws, afterward abbreviated to the "traps" and the "locks."

These singing teachers left their mark on the commonplace life of the countryside people. "The interminable 'tra-la-la' is banished from the kitchen, the wretched hum of a vacant mind tickles or rasps the ears of a suffering family no longer; the dismal 'by-low-by' of cradle song is abolished and the little angel is wafted in dreams to Heaven as the spirits of Mozart and Beethoven breathe sacred airs in the deepening twilight." Thus one sentimental writer observes. But the effect was even more lasting. The custom of singing in classes was responsible for the church choir and for that pleasant domestic diversion which obtained for many years—and may still be found in some sections—of the family gathering around the parlour organ or piano and singing hymns. We find later manifestations of it in community singing and in the strange custom some business men have at their club luncheons of singing between courses.

All of this can be traced back to these portly and pleasant gentlemen of the world, who wandered up and down the

American countryside teaching the young to pitch and throw its voice into melodious numbers.

From this custom of singing may have come also the appreciation of concert music, which manifested itself before the Revolution and grew in volume through the years after it, in all the larger centres. New York had its public concerts, Charleston its St. Cecilia Society and even such relatively small places in New England as Ipswich enjoyed concerts, although in the last named town one wonders what the music could have been, for the instruments were "two fiddles and a drum" on one occasion. However, seventy people were said to have parted with their good money for that evening of culture.

The public concert is a comparatively modern institution, however. Music was once purely a domestic art, as it was in the household of Councillor Carter who played "a harpsichord, Forte-Piano, Harmonica, Guitar, and German Flute, and was indefatigable in the Practice." It is possible that the popular songs brought to this country were those sung at Vauxhall Gardens or Ranelagh, Marylebone, Sadler's Wells and other English pleasure gardens at which "hits" of the day were given. One American city, at least—New York— had pleasure gardens too—its own Vauxhall, The Indian Queen, Niblo's and Tyler's, all popular in their time.

SCHOOL TEACHERS

The peripatetic school masters—and there were such— were often belligerent Irishmen, unable to satisfy the town fathers, and who wandered on. A school master, of necessity, must stay in one place, but the few who wandered, of which we have mention, seem to have been helpless, disappointed, drink-sodden men. On the other hand, school masters were itinerant in this respect, they might serve a large area and travel about from school to school. In Scituate, Mass., for example, Deacon David was selected to conduct a reading, writing and grammar school, the school to be kept one-third of the year at each end of the town and one-third in the middle. Think of the long holidays the other two-thirds had! Then there was Philemon Robbins who came to Andover, Massachusetts, in 1729 and began his teaching in the south end of the town, went to another section after three months and finally wound up his peripatetic pedagogy in the middle. The same system was used at Hanover, Massachusetts (and, doubtless, many other towns), only the parents of the children in the unschooled quarter of the town had to be watched by the selectmen because they would "sneak" their children into the classes wherever the school was being held. Well, the Yankee always did have a thirst for knowledge!

Some of these masters taught writing at nights—"a legiable joyning hand playne to be read." The pupils provided their own lamp or candle—usually a taper set in a turnip—their own paper and writing quills, and, thus equipped, they acquired the art of chirography.

The great American exponent of the art of writing, and, in his time, the most famous itinerant writing master, was Platt Rogers Spencer, who gave his name to the florid style of penmanship. At the early age of fourteen, while he was a pupil in a log school at Conneaut, Ohio, he manifested an insatiable desire to teach his fellow pupils fancy writing. In subsequent years he was an itinerant writing master, held a chair of penmanship in an obscure Ohio college, and was influential in founding business colleges in various cities. As a young man, he wandered through Ohio gathering pupils in farmhouses and towns. His posters, which were tacked up conspicuously in stores and other public places were executed in his own grand manner. Thus heralded, he was always sure of a large class. His copy books, first published in 1848, for years were the ideals set before rebellious and ambitious school children in this country. His flourishing pen was finally laid down in May 16, 1864, but his style has followed him. In many respects it was not unlike the *fractur* work of the itinerant Pennsylvania Dutch writing masters.

There appears to have been another class of restless-footed teachers—some of the instructors in the early medical schools of this country. In Sir William Osler's biography they are compared to the Sophists of Greece who went from town to town, staying only a short while in each.

RECITATIONS AND LECTURES

The recitation is, perhaps, the mildest form of the mimic art, and it is not surprising to find people giving them even before the Revolution when, in the small towns, diversions were few and far between. They used to read plays and between the acts sing the airs from an opera. This was a favourite amusement and we find it appearing in most of the chief towns in the country. Then there would be moral and satirical lectures written by famous persons and delivered by a reciter. One such appeared in Salem, Massachusetts, in 1792. His subject was *Human Hearts* and he advertised his diversion as concluding "with a hornpipe." The reading and recitation of standard British authors was another way of improving the mind; it saved its hearers the bother of reading these authors!

A lecture is also a painless method of mental improvement although after a course of diversified lectures one's mind is apt to be a sterile chaos. However, no such chaos was possible for the men and women of the years prior to and immediately after the Revolution because lectures were rare, even in intellectual New England. The audience had a chance to think them over between times. After 1800 they increased in number until by 1830–40 the Lyceum spread across the fertile fields of the Atlantic seaboard like a spring rain over a newly planted meadow. Popular lecturers would return to towns in which they had been generously received and extended courses were common.

There was one pre-Revolutionary speaker whose topic

was *Heads, Coats of Arms, Wigs and Ladies*—evidently a
humourous talk. Many of the early lectures were merely propaganda. From 1790 on up to the Civil War we find numerous Quaker ladies and gentlemen and others of other persuasions travelling about the North and West talking on the
evils of slavery. Temperance, too, was a favourite topic
among fanatics. One such lecturer was Dr. Charles Jewett of
Rhode Island who forsook the care of the sick and devoted
forty years of his life to lecturing on temperance in various
parts of the country. Science in its many manifestations
always seemed to bring a big "house," especially in New
England. There we find lectures on pneumatics, on electricity (then very little understood), chemistry, botany,
economics and astronomy. One favourite lecturer advanced
his pet theory that the earth was hollow. Another talked on
geology, another on dietetics, on physiology, and on animal
magnetism. Zerah Colburn, the mathematical prodigy,
paraded the whole seaboard doing sums! For some time
Samuel Colt of Hartford, Connecticut, lectured on chemistry
under the name of Dr. Coult. With the money he made he
was able to perfect his models of the Colt revolver. Then
came lectures on the Holy Lands and on other countries
abroad and on the Indians of our Southwest.

We feel rather sorry, though, for one lecturer who
attempted valiantly before the Civil War to elevate the
cuisine of America. M. Pierre Blot was his name. His efforts
to introduce French cookery methods met with a cold and
stony reception. Americans refused stoutly to surrender the
frying pan. Whatever the topic, these lectures were intended
to teach something, and in that spirit they were generously
patronized.

Their popularity marks a decided transition. Once on a
time the pulpit was the centre of the town's intelligent life;
the minister was its oracle. Gradually he was supplanted by
the schoolmaster and certainly the parson's hold on the youth
of the town was threatened when the dancing, singing, and

fencing masters began to appear with their inducements toward worldliness. His final congé was given by the lecturer. From the moral director of the lives of his townspeople and as the leader of thought, he was relegated to second or third place when the occasional travelling lecturer appeared. And since the lecturer was a stranger to most of his audiences, there was no familiarity to breed contempt.

CHAPTER XII

THE PURITAN BEGINS TO SMILE

Y THE Puritan mind—whether it be in the Southern Provinces or in New England—amusement is looked upon with suspicion. So universal in early American history is this fact that one naturally wonders what fun the Puritans found in life. How did the Spartan habits and blunt conversation of these people gradually melt before the desire to smile?

The early Puritans of New England were a witty people —of sorts. Even the most pious of their ministers was not above puns in his writings. In their dealings with one another they used what Sidney George Fisher calls "sarcastic chaffing and a dry, sharp sort of humour." Outwitting each other and strangers in a business deal evidently afforded them a great deal of amusement. Some of these traits still persist among New Englanders.

In the beginning, of course, life everywhere on the Atlantic seaboard was repressed and economical. There was little about it to cause laughter. As the settlements grew and prospered and more of the less religiously inclined came to these shores, a lighter spirit began to pervade the life. In the towns the better classes assumed frivolities and luxuries of dress and manner, but the country folk continued dour for a long time after. They were especially insistent on taking their religion neat; they even resented a parson's preaching on the lighter side of life.

During the early 1700's a worldly mood seemed to capture not only New England but the other provinces as well. People were reacting to their previous difficult style of existence. The hair shirt of penance was laid aside. And it was during this period that the first faint smile began to wrinkle the stern Puritan countenance.

Following this initial period of frivolity, as we have seen in Chapter VIII, came the Great Awakening of 1738–40 when George Whitefield and his ranting confréres travelled up and down the Atlantic seaboard reminding people of their sins. However, amusement had gained its foothold. People had not forgotten their first taste of it. After the storm of revivals had quieted, came the still, small voice of laughter.

This laughter began in very simple ways and at things we of to-day would think almost childlike. Truly the period between 1700 and 1850 may be called America's Age of Innocent Amusements!

PUPPET AND PEEP SHOWS

One of the oldest and simplest forms of itinerant amusement is the puppet show. For centuries these shows have been known to Europe, and again and again we have records of their appearing here. Punch and Judy and the other puppet romances were exhibited in the taverns and on village greens and at fairs.

Both the young and the old of New England and Pennsylvania patronized them. At Henniker, New Hampshire, an ambitious puppeteer appeared in 1814 and gave his show in a private house. Each image was two feet high and it was placed on a stand. In front of each was a bell, and the puppet held a hammer with which it struck the bell. A man at the back controlled the actions of the figures by turning a crank, so that tunes could be played and the puppets made to dance. At Lancaster, Pennsylvania, something of the same sort was exhibited, together with waxworks.

One of these strange little shows was encountered by Hawthorne at North Adams, Massachusetts, in 1838. The picture he draws is rather pathetic. "After supper, as the sun was setting, a man passed by the door (of the tavern) with a hand-organ, connected with which was a row of figures, such as dancers, pirouetting and twining, a lady playing on a piano, soldiers, a negro wench dancing and opening and

shutting a huge red mouth—all these keeping time to the
lively or slow tunes of the organ. The man had a pleasant,
but sly, dark face; he carried his whole establishment on his
shoulder, it being fastened to a staff which he rested on the
ground when he performed. . . He had come over the high,
solitary mountains where for miles there could hardly be a
soul to hear his music."

The peep show was another early form of itinerant amusement, and, like the puppets, it, too, has a lineage. In 1748,
so the New York *Post Boy* states, there appeared an itinerant with a "Philosophical Optical Machine" that showed
perspectives including "English prospects." This, of course,
was a panorama into which one peeped. As late as 1862 a New
York humourous journal, *Yankee Notions*, printed a cartoon
of a peep show. In it Brother Jonathan acted as showman
and Jeff Davis peered in terror at the scenes of horror dis-
closed within. These shows seem to have been very popular
on lower Broadway before the Civil War.

While neither puppets nor peeps, the deaf and dumb seem
to have added their little contribution to the joy of our forebears. The first institution for these unfortunates was established in Hartford in 1812. Shortly thereafter groups of the
inmates were taken on the road to give performances of their
skill. They sat on a platform with blackboards, and questions
were asked by the audience, which were transmitted in the
sign language and the answers written down. Such marvels
apparently delighted the people of small country towns.

In the back country of Pennsylvania appeared a variation
of the puppet show in an exhibition of automatons. These
were two life-size figures, representing an Aristocrat and a
Sans Culotte. There were springs in their bodies, and the
marvel of the performance was that no one touched them and
they touched only a bar of iron to which they hung by the
arms. They played various pranks on each other and the
Aristocrat would refuse to dance to a Republican air. This
travelling show was produced by a M. Blanchard. Another

LAMBERT, Holding *Four Perfons*, at Arm's Length.

On a bet of 20 *Guineas*: He weighed 739 pounds, and is faid to be the largeft and heavieft Man, ever known in any part of the world. His wife is a very fmall woman, and weighed but 89 pounds. Lambert meafures round his body 10 feet 4 inches; round the leg, 3 feet 1 inch; and is 6 feet 2 inches tall. And is a wonderful production of *Nature*.

The *Museum* has lately received a a great variety of *New* and *valuable Additions*; and fuch as are pleaf- ing, and gratify- ing to the eye, as well as thofe that are interefting, and amufe- ing, to the in- habitants of this *Town*, as well as for the *Strangers*.

Mrs. Ann Moore, The very extraordinary perfon, who has fulfilled al- moft *Six-Years*, without ei- ther Eating or Drinking, in the leaft degree, any thing, whatever; fhe even con- fented to be removed from her home, to the houfes of many Gentlemen in *London*, and a conftant guard fet over her for many months to- gether, untill they were per- fectly fatisfied for themfelves. And they were conftrained to confefs the fact, and have fubfcribed their names to the Narrative, of *Mrs. Moor*. No perfon that has read the account can reasonably any longer doubt the fact; for it is certified by 130 of the moft refpectable people in *London*, who affirm that fhe fubfifts entirely on *AIR*.

Juft Added an excellent Likenefs in Wax of the Indian PROPHET, who headed the whole Indian Forces, at the battle of *Tippacanoe*, againft Col. Boyd, and the American Army. This Savage Warrior is dreffed in an emblematical drefs, to the one, which he ufually appears in, which was profefs'd by Gen. Brock. The Likenefs is very much approved, by all thofe who have feen the PROPHET; and is recommended as worthy the attention of the Public, in general.

Boston Museum,

In the red Building, *Five Stories High*, oppofite the North fide of the old *Market-House*---Bofton.

CONTAINS A GREAT VARIETY OF
Natural And Artificial Curiofities,

Large and Elegant Paintings, *Prints, Statues, Bufts, Birds, Beafts, Infects, Reptiles, &c. &c.* Which are too numerous to particularize in a Catalogue of this defcription; but it is faid to contain more than TWENTY THOUSAND RARE CURIOSITIES, many of which are not to be found in any other *Collection of Curiofities*, in the United States.

A Monftrous, and *Extraordinary* Large SERPENT, Which was lately brought from the Coaft of *Africa*, and meafures nearly 25 Feet long. Juft added to the MUSEUM, an excellent *Likenefs* (in Wax) of BONAPARTE, and the Ruffian Envoy to *Paris*; the Envoy is producing the Credentials of his miffion to Bonaparte. *The Likeneffes were executed in France*, and are done in a ftyle, fuperior to any *Wax-Figures*, ever yet exhibited in America. In addition to the former apartments, which contained the MUSEUM; there is now opened,

another NEW and Elegant HALL.

Alfo, Ghofts, Witches, Devils, Coblers and Monfters.

Which are curioufly conftructed upon a *Mechanical Plan*; fo as to have the *Ghoft* arife from the Tomb; The *Cobler*, will work, fpeak, &c. And the DEVILS will appear from their abodes of darknefs, &c. &c. *The Mufeum is open every Day and Evening, with Mufic on different Organs, and feveral other Inftruments.* Admittance, to the *Mufeum*, 25 cents; to converfe with the *Invifible Lady*, and fee the *Mufeum*, 37.

PHILIP WOOD'S BOSTON MUSEUM, eftablished 1804, oppofite Faneuil Hall Market.
Discontinued 1822. This poster about 1813. Found in Shirley, 1915.

BILLBOARD POSTER OF THE BOSTON MUSEUM

THE FORERUNNER OF THE CIRCUS

showman, Obed M. Coleman, invented and exhibited his Automaton Lady Minstrel and Singing Bird, which did amazing tricks.

Travelling waxworks were still another subterfuge for the wicked theatre. In Boston and Philadelphia were to be found more or less permanent shows of marvels in which waxworks set in realistic poses depicted historic and lurid events. A Joseph Stewart advertises his Hartford waxworks in the *Connecticut Courant* for January, 1801. P. T. Barnum had a waxworks show in New York before he took seriously to the circus business. They were a source of public amusement up to the 90's. From time to time special features were added by the temporary employment of a freak or two. Thus, the billboard of the Boston Museum, illustrated here, tells of a newly arrived feature—Lambert, who could hold four persons at arm's length. His waist measurement was 10 feet, 4 inches. He weighed 839 pounds and his wife only 89. He is advertised as a "wonderful production of Nature." On the same bill was Mrs. Anna Moore, who is said to have subsisted almost six years without eating or drinking. These were the specialities for the year 1813. After showing at Boston, they moved on to another museum in another city—Hartford, New York, Philadelphia, and so on down the coast.

PETTY FAKERS

The taverns of the early American country towns were the favourite places for the performances of all sorts of petty fakers and for the exhibition of small and amusing inventions and skill. Tavernkeepers encouraged these showmen—gave them part of the stables or an outbuilding—because the crowd they drew would patronize the tavern bar.

When electricity first flashed into public ken, electrical machines were carried about and shown for the amazement of those collected in the taproom of the "ordinary." Fortune tellers, exhibits of dwarfs, musical clocks, waxworks; truly the number and variety of these petty fakers is legion.

One of the most valuable commentaries we have on early New England amusements is found in the "Annals of Salem" by Joseph B. Felt; valuable in that the dates are significant, and because we find some of these attractions appearing in other parts of the country, indicating that they were itinerants.

The first notice of feats of horsemanship appears in an advertisement in the *Essex Gazette* of Salem for November 18, 1771:—

> John Sharp, High Rider and Performer in Horsemanship, late from England, but last from Boston, where he has been performing for some time past, intends to ride for the entertainment of the people of Salem, etc., in the Street by the Upper Burying Ground near the Alms-House this day if the weather will permit; if not, he will perform To-morrow. He rides two Horses standing upon the Tops of the saddles with one foot upon each in full Speed; Also three Horses, standing with one foot upon each of the outside ones and in full Speed; Likewise one Horse, and dismounts and mounts many times when in full Speed.

Some of the Salem attractions that followed John Sharp were:

1790, a balloon eighteen feet high and fifty-four feet in circumference, followed by balloon ascensions in 1795 and 1838.

1791, wax images, including likenesses of General Washington and Mrs. Washington.

1795, Mr. Perrette, a machinist from Paris, exhibited a self-moving carriage.

1796, Signor Blitz, magician, visited Salem several times —he also went to Waterbury, Connecticut.

1802, Mr. Rannie, and in 1821, 1822 and 1824 three others, gave entertainments of ventriloquism. Later Signor Blitz added this to his entertainment.

1804, the Acoustic Temple, with its "Invisible Lady" was shown.

1807, an exhibition of phantasmagoria apparatus.

1809, an exhibition of fencing.

1817, a panorama, "The Temple of Industry," containing thirty-six figures each engaged at his particular occupation.

1818, a kaleidoscope exhibition.

1821, a daily show of glass blowing.

1825, the Anfroides, "images so formed and regulated as to bring any article of fruit desired by a spectator."

By no means do these Salem dates represent the earliest performances in this country. There was, for example, a funambulist or slack wire artist, Dugee, who performed at Van Dernberg's Garden in New York City in 1732 and in other cities. Before him appeared in Philadelphia a boy of seven who "dances and capers upon the strait roap and a woman who dances a corant and a jigg with baskets on her feet and iron fetters on her legs." In August, 1801, Mr. Wooley notified the palpitating public of Philadelphia that he would eat fire and walk on red hot iron in his naked feet at the sign of the Castle and Grapes. Mrs. Eleanor Harvey, fortune teller, also perambulated as did John Ramie, professor of legerdemain and ventriloquism. There was a display of fireworks at Williamsburg, New York, as early as 1702.

PANORAMAS AND BALLOONS

On the Salem list of amusements we note the panorama and the balloon. The former was very popular before the Civil War. It usually consisted of a large box with a row of candles placed in front to illuminate the scenes, which were on rollers and were passed from one side to the other. War pictures and battle scenes were accompanied by realistic musketry made on a drum by the showman. "The Burning of Moscow" was a favourite. Then there were travel scenes from foreign lands that were quite popular.

Among the itinerant panoramists was John Vanderlyn who exhibited in New York, New Orleans, and Havana.

Nathaniel Hawthorne meets with one of these showmen at the top of Hoosic Mountain. "We left our horse in the shed, and, entering a little unpainted barroom, we heard a voice in a strange, outlandish accent, exclaiming, 'Diorama.' It was an old man, with a full, gray-bearded countenance, and Mr. Leach exclaimed, 'Ah, here's the old Dutchman'— though, by the way, he is a German and travels the country with this diorama in a wagon. . . .We looked through the glass orifice of his machine, while he exhibited a succession of the very worst scratches and daubings that can be imagined—worn out too, and full of cracks and wrinkles, dimmed with tobacco smoke and every other wise dilapidated. There were none in a later fashion than thirty years since, except some figures that had been cut from tailors' show bills. There were views of cities and edifices in Europe, of Napoleon's battles and Nelson's sea fights, in the midst of which would be seen a gigantic, brown hairy hand (the hand of Destiny) pointing at the principal points of the conflict, while the old Dutchman explained. . . .When the last picture had been shown, he caused a country boor, who stood gaping beside the machine to put his head into it, and thrust out his tongue. The head becoming gigantic, a singular effect was produced."

William Dunlap, itinerant artist and playright, exploited a new scenic device called the Eidophusicon or Moving Diorama. In rapid succession it displayed a series of scenes, producing the illusion that is now found in the modern cinema. Dunlap's scenes formed a travelogue of the Hudson Valley. No less than 250,000 square feet of canvas were required to produce these views. New York and other cities went wild over this show in 1828.

Shortly after they were invented, balloons became a source of public attraction and amusement. The same M. Blanchard who ran the automaton show in Lancaster, Pennsylvania, and who was advertised as "known to the World for his Airy Flights and Balloon Expeditions," appeared in Salem, where he sold 400 tickets to witness his ascension, at three shillings each. Later, in Philadelphia, he took in $100 a night! His ascent was preceded by the firing of a cannon. The village green in front of the tavern was the favourite starting place for the balloon ascension.

Captive balloons often took up passengers. These were given fantastic names—Archimideal Phaetons, Vertical Aerial Coaches and such. And the proprietors of them, after the manner of showmen the world over, attributed to flights in their balloons all manner of wonderful therapeutic properties. They not only amused and caused wonder, but a flight in them was said to cure certain "humours." Witness the advertisement of Mr. John Graham in the *Connecticut Courant* for June 9, 1801:

JOHN GRAHAM

Having obtained a deed of the exclusive right for the county of Hartford of the Archimideal Phaeton, Vertical Aerial Coach or Patent Foederal Balloon Begs leave to inform the Public that the Machine erected near Mr. John Lee's is now strengthened and supported in all its parts—rendered perfectly safe and secure, and elegantly painted and redecorated—system and regularity established, so that voyagers may be treated with slow and steady or more rapid movements as they may order; so that persons of a timid cast will enter with assurance and be much delighted; others may progress 500 yards per minute. Attendance daily from 3 o'clock till dark. Parties of 2, 4, 8 or more will be waited on at their call at any hour of the day. . .

A popular English song of the day immortalized these balloons—

> Tho Miracles cease
> Yet wonders increase,
> Imposition plays up her old tune,
> Our old Gallic Neighbours,
> Scientifical labours,
> Have invented the Air Balloon.

> This puff'd up Machine
> Most Frenchmen have seen,
> And perhaps as a very great boon;
> Our wide gaping isle, Sir
> May expect in short while, Sir
> The wonderful Air Balloon.
>
> A Man and a Hog
> A Sheep and a Dog,
> It will carry aloft very soon;
> You may view all the Nations,
> Particular Stations,
> If you ride with the Air Balloon.

Some people did dare to ride with it; whether their "humours" were cured or not, history fails to record, but it does record a tremendous enthusiasm for balloons. In the *Massachusetts Centinel* for July 14, 1784, we find this remark: "The taste for Air Balloon matters has grown to such an extraordinary pitch, that nothing can pretend to have any intrinsic value in it, unless it has this name as an appendage. The gentlemen and ladies upon *bonton* are not the only objects that can boast of the aerial bombastic insignia to their ornaments; as a countryman was heard to say one day last week—'Fine Balloon String Beans.'"

MAGICAL ENTERTAINMENTS AND GIFT SHOWS

In the Salem list was named a Signor Blitz, magician, who became famous in his day. In 1872 he published his reminiscences—"Fifty Years in The Magic Circle." It was precisely the sort of book a magician would write.

"Magical Entertainments" increased in popularity with the years. In 1791 at Danbury, Connecticut, was displayed this advertisement of a Magical Show:

TO THE CURIOUS

On Wednesday and Thursday evenings next will be exhibited at the house of Major Frederic F. Whitney, by a gentleman from New York, a number of devious and entertaining performances by slight of hand, each being of a nature so surprising that they cannot fail of giving general satisfaction to the spectators. At the same time will be exhibited a most surprising feat, by cutting off a man's head and laying it a yard from his body in the presence of the spectators; afterwards putting it on again and restoring him to life.

The exhibition will begin at candle lighting. Tickets may be had at the place of performance. Price one shilling.

Macallister, the magician, was a favourite for a long time and in the 1850's the Davenport Brothers, who did trick rope-tying in the dark, added spiritualistic stunts to their act and advertised themselves as "Spirit Mediums." The father Davenport managed the troupe and delivered a lecture on spiritualism. They toured the country in 1855.

It was also in the 1850's that there appeared a form of entertainment called the "Gift Show." On the opening night, instead of paying admission, each member of the audience brought a present. Tickets taken at the door the following evenings, entitled the holder to a sealed envelope in which was a numbered slip. At the close of the performance, numbered slips were drawn from a box and those who held the duplicates won the prizes. One Yankee conjurer by the name of Allyne even gave away sets of furniture, barrels of flour, coal, and other expensive gifts.

The gift show trick of attracting an audience was often worked with minstrels. Sam Sharpley's Troupe, famous in its day, used this as an attraction, together with a magician by the name of Logrenia, who showed trained birds, cats, and mice.

MINSTREL AND CONCERT TROUPES

The negro minstrel show started as a frank imitation, and oddly enough, in New York State. Negroes sang in the New York City streets years before the Revolution, and they used to sing to banjos in the Philadelphia streets early in the nineteenth century. They soon became a favourite form of peripatetic city entertainment. But no one thought to imitate them until George Washington Dixon, a small-part comedian playing in Albany in 1830, blacked up his face, put on an exaggerated wing collar and came out before the footlights with a banjo. The first "negro" minstrel! In this character he toured all the cities. His two favourite songs were "The Coal Black Rose" and "Zip Coon." Dixon died in penury at New Orleans in 1861. Exactly contemporaneous with him was Thomas D. Rice—born in 1808—who raised negro minstrelsy to a genteel amusement. He, too, died in poverty in 1860.

After Dixon's character began to make a hit, he was imitated by many minstrel troupes and the "cork op'ry" grew to be a favourite. Edwin P. Christy formed Christy's Minstrels at Buffalo in 1842. He, poor fellow, killed himself by jumping from a New York window. In 1845 the Virginia Serenaders were a popular company. At one of their performances in Philadelphia in that year Jim Sanford—to his everlasting glory—introduced that lovely ballad "Carry Me Back To Old Virginny."

Around 1820 we run across the trail of a group of musical prodigies—the four children of a Mr. Lewis of England, who travelled about giving exhibitions of their musical skill. The youngest was three years old and the eldest nine. They performed on the "pedal harp, piano-forte, violin, and violoncello"—quite a gifted little group of offspring.

Twenty years later we hear of the Ranier Family or Tyrolese Minstrels giving entertainments. They were followed by the Hutchinson Family, from New Hampshire. These names are all forgotten now, but once on a day they were magic in the minds of amusement-hungry people.

Another early concert troupe was the Peak Family—man, wife, and son William—who were members of a church choir in Bedford, Massachusetts. In 1829 they joined forces with John B. Gough, the famous temperance-mountebank of his day—and gave a musical entertainment that preceded Gough's arid exhortation. They played the organ, harp, guitar, and banjo, and, by their popular entertainments, managed to make the temperance talk attract a crowd. Later they bought a set of bells and did the bell-ringing stunt. They were the first of all the bell-ringing troupes to tour the country. When their popularity increased, the family divided the workable areas of the States—the son taking the territory West and South, and the old gentleman appearing only in the district east of Rochester, New York. By this time they had managed to get along without Gough—or Gough without them. Later the elder Peak annexed a family of juvenile musicians by the name of Berger.

These Berger Children, in time, also became famous. They gave their first concert at York, Pennsylvania, for the benefit of sick and wounded Union soldiers. The next year they travelled with a dramatic company, furnishing the orchestra and playing and singing between the acts. In 1864 they joined forces with the Carter Zouaves, a band of twenty children, who drilled, played music, and did vaudeville specialities. In short, the first "pony" ballet.

The Hutchinson Family mentioned as appearing in Salem, Massachusetts, consisted of Abby, Asa, John, and Judson Hutchinson, and they came from New Hampshire. Their specialty was temperance and spiritualistic songs.

TRAINED ANIMALS AND FREAKS

The organ grinder with the monkey and the man with the trained bear, still occasionally to be met going through the country or on city streets, are both lineal descendants of an itinerant known to Americans shortly after the Revolution. This solitary petty showman with one trained animal was often a foreigner, and he was carrying on a trade that he doubtless had pursued along the highways of his native land. How he eventually gave rise to the circus, we shall see later on.

A lion was exhibited in the Jerseys, New York, and in Connecticut as early as 1729, and horses and dogs that performed tricks were known long before the Revolution. Our old literary friend "The Annals of Salem" gives us a list of their attractions in this and kindred lines. The uncommon animal and the freak human have always proved an attraction. Thus, Salem paid to see the following strange sights— 1789, two camels, male and female, from Arabia; 1793, a great ox, 2044 pounds in weight, brought from Rye, New Hampshire, and slaughtered at Newburyport after being exhibited; 1795, an African lion; 1797, an elephant, at 25 cents for each adult; and a bison from Arabia, 9d per person; 1805, a great tunny-fish, found stranded; 1808, a 60-foot whale found dead at Marblehead, was towed to New Salem where it was visited by many and was then towed to Boston to be shown; 1816, an elephant in April, and a royal tiger in July; 1820, a buffalo of great size came in January, a caravan consisting of a lion, a llama, an ocelot and an ichneumon in July, and two camels in November; 1831, an ourang outang, and a unicorn with other animals; 1839, a giraffe "reputed to be the tallest animal in the world" and an ibex. So much for the uncommon animals.

Of freaks, Salem enjoyed the following:—In 1809, Miss Honeywell, "a young woman born without hands and with only three toes on one foot," who gave exhibitions in which she "embroidered flowers and cut watch papers and other fancy pieces"; in 1818 an albino woman "with silky white hair and pink eyes"; in 1824, a mermaid "the lower part a codskin stuffed and neatly connected with the breast and head of a baboon"; also a mummy from ancient Thebes; 1831, the Siamese Twins; 1836, Master S. K. G. Nellis, "born without arms, was exceedingly skilful with his toes—he cut paper likenesses and executed fancy pieces in writing, drawing, shooting with the bow and arrow and in playing the violoncello"; 1840, M. Bihin, a giant from Belgium; 1843, a lad named Tom Thumb, Jr., eleven years old, twenty-five inches in height and fifteen pounds in weight; and in the same year "a girl from the West" who, though seven years old, and four feet, seven inches high, weighed (poor child) 240 pounds! The list ends with O'Clancy, the Irish Giant, who stood seven feet, two inches in his stocking feet.

Philadelphia and other towns enjoyed "Spottie," the learned African horse, with a tail like an elephant and an amazing acquaintance with arithmetic; a cat with eight legs and two tails, and a learned pig who could tell colours and count.

Mr. Felt, the author of the "Annals" apparently had his doubts about the unicorn. We wonder what he and his fellows thought of the "Pygarg" from Russia that was exhibited in various parts of the country. It "had the likeness of a camel, bear, and common bullock." And by this description would they have recognized the moose—"a face like a mouse, ears like an ass, neck and back like a camel, hind-parts like a horse, tail like a rabbit, and feet like a heifer"?

However, he does record one interesting fact as happening in the year 1834. He had already spoken of a caravan of animals—the strange assortment of a lion, a llama, an ocelot and an ichneumon arriving in 1820. Fourteen years later he speaks of a June day when all Salem rushed to its windows to see a large company of animals, "twenty wagons drawn by sixty horses. A great India elephant, ten feet high and of 10,000 pounds weight, brought a band of musicians on his back."

This was the circus!

CHAPTER XIII

CIRCUS AND THEATRE START ON TOUR

 MAN with a dog drifts into the tap-room of a tavern. He plays a fiddle or a flute, and to its tune the dog does its tricks. Then the hat is passed around among the denizens of the bar. The Boniface ſtakes the solitary showman to a drink and a snack. Finally he goes out, to show his dog on the village common or wherever he can attraĉt a crowd.

From this simple, primitive and pitiable figure comes the circus of to-day, with its adjeĉtival press agents, its menagerie of ſtrange and rare animals, its gaudily uniformed bands, clowns, parades, acrobats, special trains, and luxurious winter quarters.

As we have seen in the previous chapter, the solitary showman with one or two trained or uncommon animals, was followed by the man with a caravan of numerous animals, for there was money to be made ſhowing them to people in isolated towns where the current of amusement ran slowly. At the same time there were men who gave exhibitions of horsemanship and acrobatic skill and prowess. These two were quite separate kinds of attraĉtions at firſt. Not until a relatively late date—1851—were both shown together for one price of admission. But that is getting ahead of the ſtory.

THE INITIAL ELEPHANT

The cities that claim Homer's birth are few compared with the years that claim to have seen the firſt elephant brought to this country. Controversy has long raged around this initial pachyderm.

It appears that the firſt elephant was landed at New York in April 1796, a faĉt recorded by the *New York Journal* of that date and further corroborated by John Davis, an English traveller here between 1798 and 1802, who, at Asheepo,

THE SOLITARY SHOWMAN

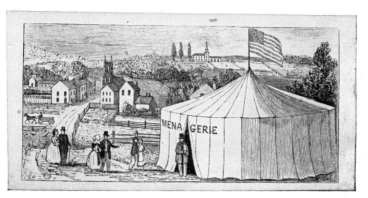

THE MENAGERIE

INSIDE THE MENAGERIE

THE COMING OF THE CIRCUS

South Carolina, encountered an elephant and its master on the road. They were headed for Savannah. The man also had a monkey.

Nineteen years later the famous "Old Bet" arrived. This elephant is often erroneously stated by some to have been the first. Like all strange animals brought to this country up to 1830, she was the speculation of a sea captain. She was sold to Hachaliah Bailey, who lived in Somers, Westchester County, New York. The year was 1815. At first he exhibited her in a barn at Somers. The War of 1812 being over, and the people having settled down to enjoy peace once more, Bailey believed they would be willing to pay money to see his elephant. So he began to tour the neighbourhood with her, travelling only at night time and with the beast heavily blanketed lest the country people catch a free glimpse. It must have been pretty slow going, for these show elephants make only about four miles an hour. Tavern sheds and barns served as exhibition halls, and either an admission was charged or Bailey passed the hat.

Bailey's success with "Old Bet" prompted some of his neighbours to go into the menagerie business, and this part of Westchester County and the township of Southeast in Putnam County became the home of the American circus.

The names of the first showmen include Gerard and Thaddeus Crane, Nathan A. Howes, Aaron Turner, John June, Lewis Titus, Chauncey Weeks, Purdy & Welch, Raymond Angevine, Quick, Buckley & Wick, and John Robinson. In pre-Civil War days these names spelled wonder to the populace. And each of them contributed something to the evolution of the circus.

EARLY CIRCUSES

John Robinson, who hailed from Little Falls, New York, launched his show in 1824, and, it is claimed, took the first tented circus across the Alleghanies. He had three wagons, five horses, and a 70-foot canvas top. His show ran for twenty-

13

three years, one season of which it travelled on its own
Steamer and did the riverway circuit.

Nathan Howes and Aaron Turner, in 1826, organized the
first American troupe of acrobats and fancy horse riders to
appear under canvas. Hitherto acrobats had performed in
theatres and behind side canvas open to the sky, set up in
tavern yards. This was, indeed, a great advance from the
acrobats of a century previous—the show of slack and tight
ropedancing that appeared in New York in 1724 and included
men and women performers.

The two Cranes and Nathan Howes crossed the Alleghanies in 1831 and toured with their menagerie as far South
as Mobile. The Cranes eventually amalgamated their interests with those of John June, Lewis Titus and Isaac Van
Amburgh, the last a celebrated lion tamer. June and Titus
are reputed to have been the first showmen to import animals
especially for the menagerie business, instead of depending
on what ship captains brought. P. T. Barnum was a partner
with S. B. Howes in importing to this country from Ceylon
the first elephant herd consisting of ten animals.

What magic that name Barnum has! What romances he
lived! Here's a Connecticut Yankee (he was born at Bethel,
Connecticut, July 5, 1810) starting in as a peddler of molasses
candy, gingerbread and cherry rum at Training Days and
then becoming a showman at twenty-five by buying Joyce
Heth, a coloured woman, said to have been the nurse of
Washington and 161 years old! The next year he joins Aaron
Turner's travelling circus on its southern trip, the following
year organizes a new company, goes West with it and reaches
the Mississippi where he buys a steamer, and takes his circus
to the river towns all the way down to New Orleans. Three
years later he is touring the West with a minstrel troupe,
returning to New York in 1841, to buy the American
Museum. The following year he secures General Tom Thumb
and in 1844 sails for the other side with his company of wonders. In 1850 he brings in Jenny Lind and tours with her for

a year. In 1858 he is going through the British Isles with Tom Thumb and lecturing on "The Art of Making Money." His "Greatest Show on Earth" was not organized until 1870, although his "Great Asiatic* Caravan, Museum and Menagerie" had been started in 1855, by which time, of course, railroads made the going relatively easy.

As we have seen, quite a number of menageries penetrated the Middle West before Barnum's. There was Chauncey Week's circus which toured from 1833 to 1836 and covered in that time not only the Atlantic seaboard but penetrated Canada as well. In 1847 a circus run by Lewis Jones gave Chicago, then a mere frontier village, its first sight of the "Big Top." In 1856 Spaulding and Rogers took the first circus touring by railroad in their own cars. Three years later this same aggregation toured the rivers of the West in a "Floating Palace" or show boat.

Thus we can trace the evolution of the circus not only by the character of the show itself, but the manner in which it travelled. The first men were foot-goers; then came the caravans or wagon shows, and finally the railroad circus.

By 1820 so fast had grown the circus business that it is estimated more than thirty shows were touring the States. The middle period—the wagon shows, from about 1817 to 1860—was the most picturesque of all.

THE FIRST PERFORMANCES

In the beginning these gave very primitive performances —half a dozen horses, a couple of wagons, and a band of acrobats including a clown and a trick mule. The music usually consisted of a fiddle or two. In old John Robinson's first shows, John himself furnished the music, and he used to sit in the middle of the ring scraping his fiddle. There might also be one or two songs.

---

*The "Asiatic" touch to these menageries and circuses is found relatively early—Chang and Eng, the Siamese twins, landed in America in 1829 and were exhibited here for twenty-five years. The first troupe of Japanese acrobats were brought to this country in 1848 by Richard Risley Carlisle.

These circuses were shown behind side canvases fastened to six-foot poles to form a ring, open to the elements. The performances, of course, had to be held in day time. A few boards made a platform for the tumblers and dancers. No seats were provided except a few dragged in for the ladies, and sometimes the crowd would mount the tops of the wagons. If the circus could attract 250 at 25 cents a head it was considered a big house.

The show started with the usual grand entry, after which the trapeze artists would perform, then the clown cracked his jokes and made appropriate and complimentary flings at the local characters, merchants, and hotel proprietors upon whom the show was dependent for hospitality. Finally he would try to ride his trick mule.

Even in those early days the picturesque publicity methods of the circus had begun. Travelling a few days ahead of the show, a man on horseback or muleback appeared with a couple of weeks' supply of posters in his saddle bags. These he tacked (for this was before the age of paste) on available barns and trees. When the circus itself arrived in town, the clown would ride onto the village green and proclaim the wonders of the show. When he had attracted sufficient of a crowd, he would lead them, Pied-Piper-of-Hamelin-like, to the edge of town where the canvas was pitched.

From these simple beginnings, the circus started to grow, both in variety of entertainment and in its equipment. Benches were added for the spectators, and some companies ventured evening performances by the light of hundreds of candles stuck in wooden chandeliers. By 1828 Buckley & Wick's circus had 40 horses, eight wagons and thirty-five people and carried a tent accommodating 800. Minstrels were added to the attractions, but for many years the main part of the programme was devoted to acrobatic stunts, dancing and an occasional negro song. To this primitive music was eventually added a band.

Much the same methods were employed by the itinerant menagerie. It, too, grew in size and equipment with the passing of the years. All manner of strange animals were added— hyenas, anacondas (playfully handled by their keeper), white bear, elephants, two-headed calves, and other monstrosities, or a blind horse that could waltz, and monkeys and camels. By 1830, the "Great Caravan" boasted among its other interesting exhibits, a white-tailed gnu, an elephant, two tigers, a leopard, a Canadian lynx, a puma, and a cage of monkeys. Giraffes first appeared in 1836.

By 1851 these two shows, the menagerie, and the circus, were united into one attraction, and from the one-ring show it grew to two, and from two to the grand three-ring "Aggregation of World's Wonders" that completely impoverishes the vocabularies of press agents to-day. The "Wild West" show comes much later, in 1883 when Buffalo Bill Cody, an erstwhile Pony Express rider, organized his company.

THE WAGON SHOW *EN ROUTE*

However picturesque it may have been, wayfaring with these wagon shows was no easy life. The show usually started on the road in April. Each man "doubled up" on half a dozen jobs—keeper of animals, mule driver, canvas man, or clown. The runs between stops were not more than twenty miles at most. The elephant went first because he was the slowest of the beasts. The start was usually made at three in the morning, the manager leading the cavalcade in a buggy and carrying a torch; other torches were held along the line. And thus the sleepy caravan lumbered along the rutted country roads. Sometimes they lost the way, sometimes they were stuck in the mud. Now and then a farmer would rouse from innocent slumber to find an elephant swaying in his front yard, an elephant whose driver had missed the right turning. What picturesque migrations these must have been!

The big parade was an early feature for attracting spectators. The caravan stopped outside the town, and while the canvas men went ahead to put up the tents, the company would wash the wagons and dress for the parade.

THE CLERGY PROTEST

Here we encounter another phase of the duel between the haranguers of the town and the amusement hawkers of the rolling road. The clergy, always quick to combat worldly influences that might reduce congregations, did not receive the circus and the menagerie with open arms. The ministerial attitude may be represented by this comment from the Rev. Frederic Denison, historian of Westerly, Rhode Island, in 1867. "Various wandering companies, bands, troupes, mostly comic and vulgarly theatrical, are often flaunting their handbills on the streets and seducing vulgar crowds to attend on their mimicries. Usually the characters of the actors comport with the scenes. Such coarse buffoonery, set off by stale songs and monkey dances, only degrades and corrupts the spectators."

In order to circumvent trouble, the circus was never advertised as a "show" or a "diversion" but as a "Great Moral and Education Exhibition." On the sides of the animal wagons were painted Biblical scenes, a quaint concession to the pious brethren. The troupe also usually presented itself at church on Sundays. P. T. Barnum became famous for his familiarity with the Scriptures and the ease with which he could discuss theology.

There was ample reason for this pious and humble attitude. In its early days the circus did not attract a highly moral class of men. The visit of the circus to a town usually meant fisticuffs with the natives, bad debts and "a train of low and dissipated memories." Having become very sick, the Devil a monk would be. To this day it is not unusual to find these pietistic touches about the circus. Still it must be said, to their everlasting credit, that the charity and straightforward humanity of circus folk would put to shame many people in other walks of life.

THE MEDICINE SHOW

In a later chapter we will consider the waterway circuses which once were famous on the Mississippi, the Ohio and other rivers of the awakening West. At this point we reach the medicine show.

This form of entertainment adopted circus methods but had nothing to do with the evolution of the circus as we know it. True, the early circus gathered in its train the candy-seller, the gingerbread man and the vendor of pinchbeck jewellery, but the hawker of patent medicines who gave a show is an older manifestation than even the early menageries of this country. It was a transplantation of Continental fair methods, where a tumbler was used to attract a crowd so that a hawker might sell them his wares. An early form of advertising, in fact.

We all can remember the Indian medicine shows and some have vivid recollections of Dr. Morgan's burlesque aggregation that travelled through New York State, but few people realize that these medical mountebanks existed before the Revolution. Evidence of this we find in 1773 when Connecticut, that land of steady habits and strange legislation, passed its famous Act for the Suppression of Mountebanks. This quaint old act is worth recording in full:

"Whereas the practice of mountebanks in dealing out and administering physick and medicine of unknown composition indiscriminately to any persons whom they can by fair words induce to purchase and receive them without duly consulting, or opportunity of duly consulting, and considering the nature and symptoms of the disorder for which, and the constitution and circumstances of the patient or receiver to whom they administer, has a tendency to injure and destroy the health, constitution and lives of those who receive and use such medicines: And whereas the practice of mountebanks in publickly advertising and giving notice of their skill and

ability to cure diseases, and the erecting publick stages
and places from whence to declaim to and harangue the
people on the virtue and efficacy of their medicines, or
to exhibit by themselves or their dependents any plays,
tricks, juggling or unprofitable feats of uncommon dex-
terity and agility of body, tends to draw together great
numbers of people, to the corruption of manners, pro-
moting of idleness, and the detriment of good order and
religion, as well as to tempt and ensnare them to
purchase such unwholesome and oftentimes dangerous drugs:

"Be it therefore enacted by the Governor, Council
and Representatives, in General Court assembled, and
by the authority of the same, That no mountebank, or
person whatsoever under him, shall exhibit or cause to
be exhibited on any publick stage or place whatsoever
within this Colony, any games, tricks, plays, jugling
or feats of uncommon decsterity and agility of body,
tending to no good and useful purposes, but tending to
collect together numbers of spectators and gratify vain
or useless curiosity. Nor shall any mountebank, or person whatsoever under him, at or on any such stage or
place offer, vend or otherwise dispose of, or invite any
persons so collected to purchase or receive any physick,
drugs, or medicines, commended to be efficacious and
useful in various disorders."

To be an "attraction" in a medicine show is scarcely the
sort of thing a man would boast about in his autobiography,
and yet one famous and well-beloved American found a
colourful youth in this and other forms of itineracy, James
Whitcomb Riley. His taste for the road was honestly inherited; his father rode the circuit from court to court and the
youngster went along on these legal peregrinations. His fond
parent had visions of the boy taking up law, but James had
other plans. He became a nomad sign painter. For a time he
even had the effrontery to advertise himself as a blind sign
painter! A small boy led him from job to job and crowds used

to collect and marvel at the skill of this sightless artist. On one of these wanderings he met up with a medicine man who became struck with young Riley's nerve. By this time the people must have caught on to his tricks, for James was only too happy to offer himself as an attraction. For a time he travelled with the show, singing songs and accompanying himself on the banjo. His theatrical appetite whetted, he later joined a band of barnstormers, and for them improvised songs and adapted plays. On these wanderings Riley picked up the Hoosier dialect that he later used so effectively in his poems.

THE FIRST THESPIANS

People of seventeenth century England considered play-acting non-conducive to morals. Not until the Stuart dynasty was restored did the theatre enjoy the popular favour it once had known. Wherever it was, the Puritan temperament carried on this prejudice. In Virginia in 1612 a prayer refers to actors as "scums and dregs of the earth"; the Quakers of Philadelphia proclaim them as "inlets of vice." In 1686 we find Increase Mather writing (and somewhat with the dread of an impending cataclysm) "There is much discourse of beginning Stage Plays in New England." What he referred to were innocent little amusements called drolls and interludes performed in tavern parlours and coffee houses. "Pickle Herring" and "The Adventures of Harlequin and Scaramouch" appear to have been the favourites.

By this time Governor Andros had arrived in America and the persecuting ardour of the New England Puritans was being checked by this representative of the crown. But it is many years after this that we encounter the first play. Two Englishmen, assisted by some frivolous inhabitants of Boston, dared public wrath by performing Otway's "Orphans" at the British Coffee House. Promptly the Boston City Fathers set their faces against such a display of extravagant gaiety. So shocked were they that the General Court—the year was 1750—passed an act to prevent further manifestations of

play-acting. The very essence of Yankee Puritanism is crys-
tallized in the reasons given for this act: "To prevent and
avoid the many mischiefs, which arise from public stage
plays, interludes, and other theatrical entertainments, which
not only occasion great and unnecessary expense, and dis-
courage industry and frugality, but likewise tend greatly to
increase immorality, impiety and contempt of religion."
Protesting clergymen of Philadelphia in 1793 gave this same
excuse of monetary waste for their objection against the
theatre. The New England prohibition was repealed in 1793,
however. Down South, where life was lived a little more
kindly, we find Charleston opening its first theatre in 1737.

The Revolution over, staid Salem, Massachusetts, enjoys
three troupes of actors within a short time. One of them was
accompanied by a band. With scarcely a struggle Boston
succumbed to the lure of the footlights, although here and
there some of the more straight-laced held out unyieldingly.
The manager of a hall in Boston almost begged for martyrdom by stating that he would sooner burn down the place
than to suffer it to be used for plays. Even that early did
Boston have its potential membership for a Watch and
Ward Society.

In Salem in 1828 a theatre was built by a venturesome
soul from New York, but the attempt to entertain the Salem-
ites met with failure, and four years later the building was
converted—the irony of it!—into a church. "From that
time on," says the local chronicler (writing in 1849, and with
grim satisfaction), "our citizens have found it a much more
profitable mode of spending their time and money, to hear
lectures on interesting and useful subjects than to listen to
actors." By 1838 we find the historian of Rochester, New
York, giving public thanks that "neither theatre nor circus
can now be found in Rochester."

Turning southward, New Yorkers were enjoying an actor,
an Englishman, Tony Ashton, in 1701. He apparently was
the first professional Thespian to tread the American boards.

He visited New York, the two Jerseys (East and West, as they were known in those days), Maryland, Virginia, the two Carolinas, South Florida, the Bahamas and Hispaniola. Quite a blade was Tony! In New York he meets up with his old pal Jack Charlton, fencing master, and says that "after acting, writing, courting, and fighting that winter," he sailed to Virginia. He returned to England in 1731.

England furnished practically all the actors of this initial American stage. Lewis and William Hallam landed at York-town, Virginia, and on the fifth of September, 1752, the first play was performed by a regular company. "The Merchant of Venice" was the presentment. At Annapolis in September, 1753, Hallam opened the first American theatre; the curtain went up at six and three performances were given each week. This was the first serious penetration of America by the legitimate stage. Hallam called his troupe the American Company.

Evidently knowing the antipathy of New England, Hallam toured the South first; we find him appearing in cities as far south as Savannah. In Charleston there was "a genteel playhouse where a very tolerable set of actors called 'The American Company' of comedians" frequently played. Lewis Hallam died, and David Douglas, who maintained a company here for fifteen years, married his widow. Douglas brought a troupe over from London and one up from the Bahamas, to appear in Charleston, as we learn by a broadside published in that city in 1765.

The path of the Thespian was not rosy in those days. Philadelphia passed a Blue Law in 1759 (later to be set aside by the King) exacting a fine of £500 lawful money from those who dared play-act, and six years later we read the angry protest of a Philadelphian who claims that "these vagrant and sturdy beggars" travel through America "propagating vice and immorality." In 1761 worthy and pious citizens of New York protested against plays, and five years later an angry mob wrecked the Chapel Street theatre. Even in sweet old Charleston did one voice raise itself to call the theatre "the Devil's Synagogue." Vulgar and hostile interruption from the audience was a commonplace.

In the face of such persecution, Hallam and his associates were obliged to make concessions to popular prejudice. He gave "lectures" ending with a pantomine. In Philadelphia, David Douglas gave a benefit "for improving youth in the divine art of psalmody and church music." Both Hallam and Douglas, in the proverbially generous style of the theatre, constantly gave benefits for the poor, and now and then they produced a benefit performance for some actor or actress who came over as an indentured servant and wished to buy off his or her time.

Lancaster, Pennsylvania, contributes an unusual page to this history of the early American stage. There in 1730 and up to 1742, strolling players gave performances, and during the Revolutionary War, British prisoners and their wives essayed Shakespeare. While the British were in New York the military did the same, but none of these could, strictly speaking, be called itinerants.

Great impetus to the American stage was given by the arrival in 1791 of John Bernard the comedian and in 1810 by Cooke. Bernard played in Philadelphia, Boston, New York, Albany, and in 1816 started a tour of the country as far south as Charleston, west to the Ohio and into Canada. Cooke opened up in New York with "Richard III" and proved a big success.

The taste for theatricals began to spread. A traveller through Ohio in 1821–23 speaks of them having been given by itinerant companies for some time, and he says that "a society of young people in Cincinnati have lately erected a playhouse, in which they themselves perform." The first of the "Little Theatres."

The frontier territory contiguous to the Ohio and Mississippi seems to have been fertile ground for the theatre. Sol Smith, who wrote his recollections of theatrical management

Eng'd by W.G. Jackman, from a Daguerreotype by J. Burney

SOL SMITH, ITINERANT ACTOR

in the West and South previous to the Civil War, spins many picturesque yarns of these regions and how the stage came to them. His first engagement, for which he was paid the lordly stipend of $6 a week, was with a company of four men and two women who ventured to play "Pizarro." The cast shows how this minute company managed.

Pizarro, the Spanish general Ataliba, King of Quito	Mr. S. Drake
Rolla, the Peruvian leader Las Casas, a Spanish priest	Mr. Fisher
Alonzo, joined with the Peruvians Orozembo, an old cacique	Mr. A. Drake
High Priest of the Sun Almagro, a Spanish officer Blind Man Sentinel Valverde, secretary Guards	Mr. Sol Smith
Peruvian boy	Miss Fisher
Elvira Priestess of the Sun	Mrs. Fisher
Cora	Mrs. Mongin
Child	Miss A. Fisher

"Thus Sam Drake (as Pizarro), after planning an attack on the unoffending Peruvians while engaged in worship at their ungodly altars, and assigning his generals (me) their several posts, in the next act is seen (as Ataliba) leading the Indian warriors to battle. He is victorious, and goes to offer up thanks to the gods therefor—when, presto! on comes the same man again (as Pizarro) smarting under the stings of defeat!

"Fisher (as Las Casas) calls down a curse on the heads of the Spaniards; throws off his cloak, drops his cross, doffs his gray wig, and appears in the next scene as the gallant Rolla, inciting his brave associates to deeds of valour. Alexander

Drake, as Orozembo, gives in the first scene an excellent character to the youth Alonzo, proclaiming him to be a "nation's benefactor"; he is then stuck under fifth rib by a Spanish soldier (that's me, again), and is carried off by his slayer; he then slips off his shirt and skull-cap, claps on a touch of red paint, and behold, in the next scene, he is the blooming Alonzo, engaged in a quiet tête-a-tête with his Indian spouse.

"For my own part, I was the Spanish army entire! but my services were not confined to that part. Between whiles I had to officiate as High Priest of the Sun; then, as the Blind Man feel my way, guided by a little boy (one of the Fisher children) through the heat of battle to tell the audience what was going on behind the scenes; afterward, my black cloak being dropped, I was placed as sentinel over Alonzo. Besides I had to find the sleeping child, fight with Rolla, fire off three guns at him while crossing the bridge, beat the alarm drum, and do at least two-thirds of the shouting. But, being a novice, all my exertions were as nothing in comparison with those of the Drakes, particularly Sam, who frequently played three or four parts in one play, and, after being killed in the last scene, was obliged to fall far enough off-stage to play the slow music as the curtain descended.

"Our stage was only ten feet wide and eight feet deep. When we played pieces that required bridges and mountains, we had not much room to spare; indeed, I might say that we were somewhat crowded. . . .The season lasted about eight weeks. The company proceeded to Louisville, and I footed it back to Cincinnati, having declined the offers of the Drake family for a permanent engagement. . . ."

All manner of strange experiences befell actors like Sol Smith. There was, for example, the night the people of Wellsburg, Virginia, to a man, refused to come to the play until the price of admission had been lowered. We might try that on present-day managers. Then there was the rich experience at the town that didn't exist. Smith and his company were floating down the Allegheny River on two skiffs. The first boat went ahead with the understanding that if they found a likely town, they were to leave a flag flying on the bank, as a signal that arrangements had been made for a performance. Sure enough, one day they discovered a white handkerchief on a pole at a point where there was not a single house to be seen. Finally a voice hailed them from the bank, "Oh, you're looking for the houses," it remarked. "Bless ye, they are not built up yet; but we shall have some splendid buildings shortly."

Smith goes on to describe the play—"We found our party very comfortably situated in a double log cabin, which was literally covered with playbills announcing that Mr. Sol Smith and his dramatic company would perform that evening. . . . Upstairs had been fitted up pretty neatly. The room was twelve by sixteen, with the scenery and curtain at one end— while three large benches represented the boxes and the pit. . . . Dinner over; the audience began to assemble from every direction—the men and women all coming on horseback. An unexpected difficulty now presented itself—there was not a candle in the town—that is, in the house! Night was coming on; we could not act in the dark; that was certain. The landlord hit upon an expedient at least. He tore up some linen, of which he made wicks, and, rolling them in tallow, soon had six decent candles. He thereupon took half a dozen large potatoes, and, boring holes in them, converted them into candlesticks, placing them on the floor in front of the curtain for footlights. In our narrow quarters, a change of dress was not to be thought of. So Norah and Lenora, being played by the same person, wore the same dress—and so with the other characters. . . At length, one by one the lights went out, and we were in danger of being left in total darkness! Observing this, I hurriedly brought the farce to a close, cutting the Lovers' Quarrels short, and reconciling the parties in the middle of the piece, and speaking the 'tag.' Down came the curtain just as the last candle burned out; and the spectators made their way downstairs in the darkness as best they could, highly delighted with their entertainment. . . ."

Sometimes, in the Indian districts of the South, Smith would hire natives for supers, paying them fifty cents and a glass of whiskey. On one occasion the Indians acted so realistically, or the firewater acted so potently, that they completely demolished the show by staging their own song and war dance.

On another occasion Smith found that he and his company were billed for an entertainment in a room only fourteen feet square, and the room was filled to overflowing with the audience. So they set a table outside the window and each member mounted this for his songs and recitations. That "house" brought in $40.

The manner in which Smith's troupe travelled was simplicity itself—the company went in barouches and the baggage was sent in a large Conestoga wagon.

Many of the early troupes travelled by these wagons, especially some of the first companies to play "Uncle Tom's Cabin," or "Tom" shows, as they were commonly called. To this day, "Tomming the Tanks" means, in the argot of the theatre, playing "Uncle Tom's Cabin" in small towns.

The first performance of this play was given in 1852, and from that date up to the late 80's it was a headliner with every barnstorming company on the road. No other play has ever had so many productions.

CHAPTER XIV

QUEER CUSTOMERS

N ADDITION to the fairly well-defined call-ings considered in previous chapters were numerous "queer customers" who tramped our roads and whose lives and romances played a part, albeit small, in the colour of the countryside and the excitement of the isolated town. Some of them are to our history what the "cagers," rogues, "bigors," "priggers of pracers" (horse thieves), and "rufflers" (high-waymen) were to mediæval England and the Continent. Some were feared. Some were laughed at. Being rascals and ruffians, most of them enjoyed the paternal surveillance of the police or the military. Homeless, many of them, the forest leaves thatched the only house they knew, the roadside fire was their hearth and the soft fern their bed. Others, being better circumstanced, enjoyed the accommodation of wagons or horseback and the relative comfort of inns.

In this category we have placed the tramp, the Romany folk, the strange local itinerant characters, the wandering religio-maniacs, and some others who, though just as colour-ful, were hardly to be distinguished for piety.

THE APPEARANCE OF THE TRAMP

It was only natural that the tides of itinerant workmen, peddlers, actors, preachers, third-rate artists, pack-train men, and medical fakers, which surged up and down our early country roads, should sweep along a number of people who took to the highway without any evident means of support or any special purpose. Laziness, the easiest way, the short cut, are human traits that function at all times. So also is the lure of the rolling road a temptation to which human nature can readily succumb. And, these two influences, together with cer-tain economic factors, caused to appear on our roads, during the latter half of the nineteenth century, great quantities of tramps who loathed honest labour and despised lawful trade.

Among certain levels of society vagrancy got to be a habit. Generations of journeymen tramping about in search of work bred other generations which also tramped, but worked only when necessary. From a class habit, created by physical and economic conditions, arose a class habit pursued from choice.

The tramp is usually the product of sudden changes in the employment of capital. Thus, when capital used for the pursuit of a war is suddenly turned again to the pursuits of peace, this restless element almost invariably appears. Human beings do not adjust themselves so abruptly. On the other hand, mere economic reasons are not always the cause, for the tramp usually has the kind of mentality that avoids responsibility, restraint and the mental concentration required by regular employment. Drink may have a lot to do with this. Tramps usually start on their careers when young, when the lure of vagabonding overcomes ambition.

Although tramps seem to have existed in all ages and countries, we do not find the class conspicuous here until after this country had well passed its primitive state. Following the Revolution there was plenty of work for common labourers in building the turnpikes and digging canals. Quantities of ex-Revolutionary soldiers also trailed after Manasseh Cutler into the frontiers of the Ohio district. Following the War of 1812, restlessness could be gratified by pushing out with the tide going to settle the Middle West areas. The war with Mexico opened up the Southwest for those whose foot was uneasy. But the aftermath of the Civil War was the growth of a hectic industrialism that herded men into factories. Those who rebelled against this, took to the highway. So it may be said that, although their ancestors go back to the earliest days, the tramp is a figure which does not appear prominently on our country roads until after the War of the Rebellion.

THE GYPSIES

The Romany folk are the original and universal vagrants of the world. And it is not surprising to find traces of them in this country quite early. Some of the families have been here for a long time; in fact, they have a Colonial heritage.

We encounter an early colony of them on Biloxi Bay, Louisiana, brought over by the French. They were French Romanies, spoke a French patois, but, so far as can be discovered, they lost their distinctive habits, settled down and were assimilated. There is also record of Spanish Gypsies having been introduced into Louisiana during the Spanish occupation. They married mostly with mulattoes.

When England swept up her social outcasts and shipped them to Maryland and the other Colonial Provinces, it was not unlikely that many Gypsies were caught in the net, since in England at this time they were a proscribed race. During the Revolution they were also caught by the press gangs that collected soldiers for England's thinning ranks, and they were forced into regiments being transported to America. Many of them deserted on reaching shore. Some accepted the bounty merely to obtain passage here. Others mutilated themselves so that they were no longer fit for military service. The Gypsy never makes a good soldier. Some found Gypsy wives among earlier bands transported here.

In those early days when the Gypsies met camps of equally nomadic Indians, they had the same sort of surprise that used to strike our negro troops in France when they encountered a regiment of equally black Singalese. However, there never was any *sympathie* between the Gypsy and the Indian.

Before the Civil War, Walter Simpson, a Gypsy historian, found English, Scotch, German, Irish, and Hungarian clans in various parts of the East. They often were squatters on unclaimed land in thinly settled districts, taking to their native trades of tinkering, peddling, horse-dealing, tavern-keeping, broom-making and the mechanical trades. Not a few of the Yankee peddlers encountered on the roads previous to the Civil War were, in reality, Gypsies and descendants of Gypsies. So, too, were some of the showmen, exhibitors, wandering doctors, nomad fortune tellers, horse dealers and mechanical workers. In the South they flourished for a long time, and on the lonely frontiers their patteran was set beside many a solitary Indian trail.

Mr. Henry Shoemaker of Pennsylvania, a well-known Gypsy scholar, has found traces of Romanies in that state as early as 1750. She-keners, they were called. They were from the Palatinate, Germany, and had attempted to join the early bands of emigrants from that country, but were refused passports. So anxious were they to come to America that they chartered a vessel for themselves at Rotterdam. This attempt also was frustrated, for they were caught, driven off the ship and some were hanged by the angry mob. The survivors of this brave band (surely the Pilgrim Fathers never suffered worse!) finally sold themselves as redemptioners, were transported to this country by the Dutch slave traders, and, when they landed here, bought their freedom, finally settling in Lancaster, Pennsylvania, about 1760. Some settled in York, some in Lebanon, Reading, and Pittsburgh. From these points they began their seasonal journeys, starting, tradition says, about 1763, following the course of the rivers and along the Indian trails. At first they travelled afoot or on horses and donkeys; later they took to wagons. To-day they ride in automobiles! Up to seventy years ago these Pennsylvania German Gypsies are said still to have maintained their individuality; their men were expert metalworkers, their women told fortunes and made baskets, lace, and other objects for sale along the road.

Some German and Hungarian Gypsies were also found in Maryland. They were often farmers, but when the summer came, took to their tents, leaving the farm work in hired hands. In New York City before the Civil War, Gypsies conducted tin-ware and basket stores. Some were musicians and organ-grinders. Their women, as always, told the fortunes of susceptible *Gaji*.

QUEER CUSTOMERS

In a quite different class would come those strange and unaccountable wandering figures that are woven into the tapestry of almost every countryside in early America. Some are merely legendary, others actually existed. Some were recluses, dwelling in forests and caves, some were fugitives from justice, some were men "under a cloud," as the Scotch gently speak of the weak-minded, some were good lusty brigands compelled to keep moving.

In the forties of the last century, the town of Westerly, Rhode Island, had a character typical of this class, a David Wilbur, who dwelt in the forests without house or home. The local historian describes him: "Seemingly gifted, but wholly uneducated, extremely eccentric, afraid of all human kind, even of children, he was commonly called 'the wild man.' Having studied the stars and the clouds and winds he was proverbially weatherwise, and was popularly named 'the astronomer.' In the summer he lived chiefly on berries and fruits, and slept in the swamp by the side of a large rock. In winter he fed on nuts, roots, such grains as he had stored, and such game as he could entrap. . . . Though he traversed quite a region, he seldom allowed himself to be seen. In passing through the fields of the farmers he displayed a singular penchant for scratching numbers, signs, and figures on the pumpkins!"

Philadelphia had "Whistling Harry," an itinerant negro who carried a tin kettle on his arm. Put a cent in his kettle and Harry spelt "Constantinople," between each two syllables smacking his lips with a report like a pistol, and then winding up the performance with a prolonged whistle that could be heard a city block.

The most ancient of our college graduates may still have

dim recollections of Daniel Pratt, a "touched" vagrant of pronounced individualism. Daniel saw the light of day first in Chelsea, Massachusetts, in 1809. For a while he worked as a carpenter. His mind fading, he took to the road and lived on charity. Only, he was a specialist. He considered himself a man of great erudition and, in this rôle of the wandering savant, he made regular rounds of the New England colleges. His appearance on the campus was the signal for the college body to assemble. A meeting was arranged, and old Daniel was given the chair of honour and solemnly addressed the gathering. He had a rapturous way of using big words and mouthing bombastic sentences which the collegiates of those days received with frantic applause. For years on end this poor old fellow plodded from campus to campus, playing the buffoon to merciless students and sublimely happy in the delusion that they believed what he told them.

JOHNNIE APPLESEED

Among the strange figures known to the trails and waterways of the Middle West in the beginning of the last century was Johnnie Appleseed, a rare soul. Poets have extolled him, and the legends gather so thick about his figure that it is difficult to unravel the false from the true. He may have had some Indian blood in him, but he was a harmless enough person.

Jonathan Chapman was his Christian name, and he burned with a beautiful zeal to plant frontier apple orchards so that the settlers would have something else to eat besides meat and fish. He was born near Springfield, Massachusetts, in 1775. The first orchard he planted was in Licking County, Ohio. He appeared in that part of the country in 1801 with sacks of apple seeds collected at cider mills in New York and Pennsylvania, and set them in favourable spots. In 1806 he drifted down the Ohio River with two canoe-loads of apple seeds lashed together, making for what was then the western frontier. Everywhere the Indians treated him with respect;

and during the War of 1812, while other white settlers were being slaughtered by these native allies of the British, Johnnie Appleseed passed unmolested. He was a religious man after the Swedenborgian persuasion, and in addition to apple seeds he carried Bibles, and preached to the Indians and settlers *en route* and distributed the Word. Occasionally he would retrace his old trail to cultivate the trees that had sprung from his seeds.

He was not exactly a prepossessing person, from all accounts. A man of medium height with light blue eyes and long, light brown hair, he wore scarcely any clothes—sometimes merely a coffee sack with holes cut out for legs and arms; sometimes he traded apple trees for old clothes. Winter and summer he went barefoot. And on his head, in lieu of a cap or hat, he wore a tin pan in which, when it was not otherwise used, he cooked his food.

What it was that drove him forth, we do not know. Maybe (such things are possible) the desire to do good with his apple trees and his Bibles. It was estimated that by 1838 the seed he planted had grown into trees bearing fruit over an area of 100,000 square miles. On this peculiar mission he spent forty-six years of his life, travelling by foot, by boat, and on horseback.

Death came to him soft-footed and kind. One dusk, in 1847, having tramped twenty miles, he reached the home of a friend near Fort Wayne, Indiana. He sat down wearily on the doorstep, and the people brought him bread and milk. Having relished these courtesies, he read aloud the Beatitudes to his kind hosts, and then stretched out on the floor to sleep. And during the night he died.

BOWLES, THE ADVENTURER

Of a quite different kidney was William Augustus Bowles. A man with such a name should have been a writer or the parson of a fashionable church and the ecclesiastical delight of the ladies. Not so! Listen to the story of his adventures.

Born the son of an English schoolmaster in Frederick County, Maryland, in 1763, he decided, at the tender age of thirteen to leave home. This he did, and made his way to Philadelphia where he managed to join the British army. As a mere stripling, he was given a commission and sent to Pensacola, a British outpost then. Here he neglected his duties. His military career was ended by dismissal. He then took up with the Creek Indians and married a woman of the tribe—or perhaps the woman came first. In any event, here he is, apparently gone "native." But being an industrious person he set about to justify his existence by instigating the Creeks to annoy the settlers of Georgia. When the Spaniards captured Pensacola, in 1781, Bowles led the Creek Indians to the assistance of the British; for which service he regained his commission in the British Army. By this time, he had attained the lordly age of eighteen!

At eighteen no man is sure of the career he will eventually adopt, so it is not unnatural to find this adolescent adventurer trying his hand at a number of things. He came to New York and joined a troupe of players. When the company went to the Bahamas he went along. There he added to his avocations the pleasant business of painting portraits. How he learned to be an actor or how he learned to paint, and whether or not his Creek wife was along on this theatrical and artistic foray we do not know.

The next we hear about him is his appointment as trading agent for the Creek Indians by Governor Dunmore of Virginia. He built a house on the Chattahooche and apparently was ready to settle down, but McGillivray* the Creek Indian chieftain, made it so uncomfortable for him that he had to retire from the scene.

Later we find him back in the Creek country as com-

---

*Alexander McGillivray, by the way, was one of the most picturesque figures of his time. His father was Scotch and his mother a half-caste Creek princess whose father was a French officer of Spanish descent! He became autocrat of the Creeks and commander of their forces and of their allies, the Seminoles and Chickamaugas. His reputation as a warrior almost equalled his reputation as a liar.

WILLIAM AUGUSTUS BOWLES
The Adventurer

JOHN B. GOUGH
Itinerant Temperance Advocate

The Morning of Life is gone—

We're Journeying to that Land
LORENZO DOW—Aged 39—(1816.)

The Evening shades appear!

From whence there's no return!
PEGGY DOW—Aged 35.

Lorenzo Dow was a famous itinerant preacher. His wife Peggy always accompanied him on his pious peregrinations

mander-in-chief of their warring bands. He so annoyed the Spaniards that they put a price on his head. And when he was not annoying the Spaniard he was making life miserable for the pioneers and government of Georgia which was then trying to settle its differences with the Indians. Finally the Spaniards captured him and he was sent as prisoner first to Madrid and then to Manila. This was in 1795. On the pretense of going to Europe where he would settle and behave himself, he obtained his release. But his word was not his bond, for he straightway headed back to his beloved Creek country. In 1804 he was betrayed into the hands of the Spaniard again, confined in Morro Castle, Havana, and there he died on the 23rd of December, 1805.

It has been said of him that through all these years, Bowles was really an agent of the British government, a statement the Foreign Ministry was prompt to deny. In his memoirs he is called "Ambassador of the United Nations of Creeks and Cherokees." Or could it have been the love of his Indian maid that again and again lured this wanderer back to the primitive huts of her tribesmen?

VENUS PEDESTRIS

Although extremely difficult, it might be possible to trace the wanderings of those women who, from time immemorial, have haunted towns when fairs were going on, or courts sitting, or the legislature in session. *Venus Pedestris* is a vagrant with which society has always had to contend and probably always will. Early America was no exception, although we do not encounter many of the commercially amorous in the strictly pioneer days.

As a profession this type of vagrancy was not pronounced. In primitive New England the laws regarding adultery were rigid and only one penalty was known—death. Later, the votary was obliged to wear the Scarlet Letter. As a consequence of this strict ruling, we find, among the annals of New England which are not printed for popular consumption, some of the worst cases of sex perversion imaginable. The private diaries of some of the early Fathers and pious New England clergy would have made Rabelais white with envy. Truly, they were Impuritans! Later the Puritan mind seemed to relent. If a brother and sister of the faith so forgot themselves as to yield to illicit pleasures, they were hailed before the congregation for public confession and remonstrance, and that, apparently, was all there was done about it. The Quakers of Pennsylvania and New Jersey, so some of the old meeting records show, pursued the same course and were immensely charitable about it. Behind closed doors, Sister So-and-So may have been an adulterous daughter of Satan, but outside in the world no Friend would ever acknowledge her as such.

The prostitute was a common figure among the convicts sentenced to Maryland and other Southern provinces. In "Moll Flanders" and "Colonel Jack," De Foe gives a lively picture of these unfortunates. New Orleans also had its quota of prostitutes sent over from Paris together with vagrants. Once landed, they were immediately married off, given land and expected to turn instantly into good farmwives. But Destiny was against the scheme. Many died of want, some of misery, and a fortunate few managed to make their way back to France. Imagine what they had to say of this country (and the way they said it!) when, once more, they were seated back in their bordelloes.*

Early New York City used to sentence her ladies of the evening to the stocks, or banish them. Twenty-two of these "frail ladies," as the record calls them, were sent out of the city at one time. Writing to his wife about Gray's garden in New York, Oliver Wolcott reports, "We have Eves in plenty, of all nations, tongues, and colours." In later times James Silk Buckingham, an acute English observer who was here

---

*Lola Montez, the adventuress and Adah Isaacs Menken, the actress, both could add pleasant chapters to this record of those women whose names were only whispered. But we shall be content with having merely mentioned them.

from 1837 to 1840, comments on the fact that prostitution did not obtrude itself in the New York of his day, and remarks that, after being in the city four months and visiting every part of it at all hours, he did not encounter as many prostitutes as he would find in London on a morning's stroll from Charing Cross to Cornhill. However, conditions were not so ideal as Buckingham thinks. In 1837 and 1857 the City suffered panics, many people were thrown out of work and the prostitute appeared on the street in quantities. Unfortunates of this kind are almost invariably the product of economic pressure.

With the early armies there were doubtless *vivandieres*—since army nurses were not heard of until the Civil War—lusty little wenches who, with equal ease, comforted the sick, fed the hungry, solaced the solitary, bound up the wounded, and followed the uncertain course of Venus through many a campaign. Their names, alas, are writ in water. . .

And ever since we read of her, we have been curious to learn (which we never shall) what became of the baronet's daughter, that light-fingered and lovely damsel, shipped to America as an incorrigible, and who, *en route*, ransacked the luggage of William Byrd! . . . And the two maidens of lenient virtue, disguised as Quakeresses, who invaded the stage coach in which John Davis was riding to Philadelphia. They seemed full of pretty tricks. . . . And likewise, what was the end of Margery Ruggs, the perambulating temptress who, in Barnstead, Massachusetts, led a youth, one George Palmer, to commit folly; for which she bared her back to twenty lashes!

THE PIOUSLY DELUDED

In a previous chapter, Peddlers of the Word, we considered the Church Itinerant, the authorized and representative types of circuit riders and other travelling religious agents. Beside these were any number of the piously deluded who preached and ranted from town to town, and who **are** remembered to-day more as picturesque and faintly amusing figures than as leaders of religion. They were self-appointed prophets. Many of them belonged to the "lunatic fringe" of society. Some of them went off with a handful of followers and tried a communistic or monastic scheme of living.* Others stayed on the road until a merciful Providence relieved the world and them.

Out of a large number we have selected four—Robert Matthews, Lorenzo Dow, the notorious Stephen Burroughs, and the deluded girl of whom Le Marquis de Chastellux tells who believed herself to be the reincarnation of the Christ.

Street preaching in the towns and cities was found in the earliest times† and grew common in the days preceding the Civil War, and for certain obvious reasons. Few of these wild exhorters could afford a hall and certainly their chances to speak from the pulpit of a church were slim. The respectable parson would have none of them. Among those who used the curb for his pulpit was Lorenzo Dow, a mighty man in his day, although this generation would consider him just a little mad.

LORENZO DOW

As his portrait shows him, Lorenzo Dow was no creeping Christian. A fearsome person, tall, dishevelled, with long black hair that cascaded over his shoulders in the current Methodist style of coiffure, and, if we can believe contemporary accounts, not intimately acquainted with soap and water. A Yankee, he was born at Coventry, Connecticut, in 1777, and caught the urge for preaching the Methodist persuasion from Jesse Lee, a Wesleyan itinerant exhorter. Dow hungered to attain the ministry at one leap by the mere act

---

*It has been estimated that between 1607 and 1894 this country saw the start of more than two hundred of these communities.

†In 1657 two zealous Quaker maidens were put in irons and banished from New Amsterdam for street preaching and at Gravesend, eight travelling preachers were accorded the same treatment. Boston lashed them at intervals as they were driven about the suburbs, tied at the tail of a cart.

of going out and preaching, but it was denied him; so at eighteen he started out on his own hook without benefit of ecclesiastical sanction. His first preaching tour took him 4000 miles, lasted eight months and he preached from ten to fifteen times each week. His favourite device in country towns was to assemble a congregation inside the schoolhouse, and then put his back against the door and preach. Having no way to get out, the congregation simply had to sit there until he finished his fiery discourse, which sometimes lasted four hours. At other times he encountered active opposition from the church parsons whose congregations he drew away. In the course of his self-appointed ministry he appeared in practically every State of the Union and in England and Ireland. For a time he had a large following. Whenever he appeared on the streets, he was sure of attracting a big crowd of sanctified shouters and curious idlers.

His writings and the samples of the sermons he left behind show him to have been a man of prodigious conceit, fiery temper, and an enormous flow of words. The last was the sort of thing that impressed people in those days: what a preacher said was immaterial just so he said it for a long time and with enough violent gestures, wit, irony, and quick repartee. Dow's especial trick was to "adjust himself to adventitious circumstances . . . a sudden storm might be the forerunner of God's immediate wrath; a change of elements might betoken Paradise restored." He was a pastmaster at exhorting and shouting. This sort of thing went awfully well at camp meetings.

Still, there must have been some attractive personal quality attaching to old Lorenzo which the world never saw, for his lovely little wife Peggy went along with him wherever he travelled on his gospel perambulations. That she listened to all his ranting sermons is scarcely to be conceived, but her fidelity to him is at least worth a nomination for a martyr's crown.

In this respect Dow was more fortunate than a fellow-ranter of the Middle West—the Rev. Moses Crume, whose wife accompanied him on his circuit and insisted on smoking a pipe, much to the horror of the sanctified.

MATTHIAS, THE IMPOSTOR

About 1820 there drifted to New York City from up country, a young carpenter by the name of Robert Matthews. He was a good carpenter, and his chances for steady employment were promising, but, somehow, New York disagreed with him and he went to Albany. There he developed a peculiarly annoying habit. In the midst of work, he would suddenly stop and harangue his fellow labourers in a boisterous way on the evils of their lives and on the great benefits of salvation. So much time was lost by these pious distractions that Matthews was dismissed. This gave him abundant leisure, and he began street preaching in earnest, exhorting crowds of people at the street corners. He converted a fellow workman who accompanied him carrying a large white banner inscribed "Rally Round the Standard of Truth." Matthews allowed his beard to grow to a formidable length, put on grotesque attire, and adopted the name of Matthias. The city simply wouldn't rally around the standard of his incoherent harangues. After the manner of prophets from the beginning of time, he declared that Albany would soon be destroyed, and evidently not wishing to be caught in the cataclysm, he shook the dust of that city off his feet. His immediate objective was the conversion of the world.

This grand apostolic tour led him through the Western States, through forest and over prairies, until he had covered Arkansas, thence southeast to Mississippi and Tennessee and, penetrating the Cherokee country in Georgia, he began preaching to the Indians. But the Cherokees were not a people to be stirred up, and the Georgia authorities descended on this minor John the Baptist and clapped him into prison. Martyrdom, of course, was pleasant to such a pious soul, but it limited his congregation. He promised to be good, and was released on the condition that he leave the State. Finally, having passed through Washington, where his mouthings seemed to be of no avail, he appeared again in New York. Mounted on an ancient and half-Starved horse, himself grotesquely and meanly clad, he went about the Streets proclaiming the evil times, the sins of intemperance and all the other venial and major misdemeanors of mankind. He grew to be a city character, this Strange gaunt Street preacher, and crowds of small boys followed him around terrorized by his fierce looks and prodigious geStures.

From the legions of queer ranting creatures who once wandered the roads and Streets it is difficult to choose which were the moSt picturesque. Quiet-voiced but determined Quakers preached Abolition, loud-voiced but equally determined men and women preached temperance, and unnumbered queer souls preached whatever came into their heads. And the attractions ranged all the way from John Bartholomew Gough who arose from a protracted case of delirium tremens to become the foremoSt actor-temperance advocate of his day, to the notorious rascal Stephen Burroughs, and the quaint little woman of whom Chastellux wrote.

Chastellux, who travelled here in 1780–82 remarks, "A very comely young woman is, or pretends to be, impressed with the belief that she is in her own person the Saviour of the world revived, and travels from place to place attended by twelve young men, whom she calls her apoStles; and who, if the general assertion be credited, have literally followed the precept of 'making eunuchs of themselves for ChriSt's sake.' General Gates told me that he heard her preach at Rhode Island, and I made an attempt to hear her at Philadelphia in October, 1782, but the crowd was so turbulent (very uncommon in America) that it was impossible to get near the place of worship." Later accounts say that she bore a child during her tour, but this may have only been a canard perpetrated by some evil-minded and envious gossip.

This young woman was none other than Ann Lee, in her

time one of the most vivid personalities among the piously
deluded.   A native of Watervliet, New York, she married
when very young, bore and lost four children, and at 22 left
her husband and went to England where she became a
"Shaking Quaker," given to strange pietistic extravagances
and claiming to have Divine revelations that she was the
reincarnation of Christ.   One of her pet points of attack was
marriage, and she carried on such a loud and persistent war-
fare against the connubial estate that the authorities were
obliged to clap her into jail.   In 1774 she arrived in America
and, returning to her native district of Albany, carried on her
religious activities.   She was accused of witchcraft, of being
a spy for the British Army (for this she was held in jail for
a year), but by 1780 she began to have quite a following
among those who flocked to hear revival preachers and
ranters.   She founded a religious society, "The Church
of Christ's Second Appearing," and in 1781 started on an
extensive preaching mission, accompanied by her "elders."
Chastellux's report of her attests the popularity with which
her fanatical preachments were received.

Women on pietistic crusades are apt to do some strangely
unaccountable things.   New York City in 1821 saw the
appearance of a female of the Presbyterian persuasion who
became gloomy and ascetic over what she considered to be
the immodesty of women's dress.   Together with a coterie of
satellites, she instituted a crusade which worked as follows:
Under various pretenses, committees of two would make
their way into a private house, kneel down, pray for the conversion of the women of that household and start to harangue
them on the extravagance of their clothes.   They were joined
in this knight-errantry by an itinerant preacher.   For two
years or more respectable people never knew when they would
find these praying women in their front hall.   The movement
finally died when the preacher departed for what is commonly
called his "rest."   Fashionable women were immensely
relieved by this intervention of Providence.

STEPHEN BURROUGHS

Were there time and space we might speak of those splendid ruffians, the card-sharps and con-men who travelled the river and coastwise boats and early trains. One such was George H. Devol, for forty years a gambling itinerant on the Mississippi; another was Jonathan H. Green, who after gambling for twelve years and serving several jail sentences, turned from his evil ways and went about the country lecturing on the vice of gambling. Or we might elaborate on the highway careers of such bandits as Jesse James, or J. G. Clarke, the Worcester gambler, who travelled on the river boats, or Joseph Eisell who terrorized the countryside of West Virginia, or the life and adventures of David Lewis, robber and counterfeiter, who, in his day was the Robin Hood of the historic Cumberland Valley in Pennsylvania. But the end must be made somewhere, and we will stop with Stephen Burroughs.

Parsons' sons, so the adage goes, are especially prone to the naughtiness of this wicked world and the sinful lusts of the flesh. Stephen Burroughs probably made his first mistake by being born a parson's son—a New Hampshire parson's son at that. By ten he had acquired a reputation as the town's naughty boy. Several times he ran away and had to be hauled back by his forgiving parents. When he went to preparatory school, this reputation grew, and by the time he matriculated in Dartmouth, he had become a pronounced limb of Satan. The restrictions of college life irked him, and he broke loose once too often. His collegiate career came to a dismal end.

Taking his destiny in his own hands, he travelled to the coast, to Newburyport, and there convinced a captain that he knew medicine and could be accepted as the ship's physician. His persuasive talk was always irresistible. He went aboard and for several months served in this capacity. Back on land once more, he visited his family, and while there

15

stole ten of his father's favourite sermons. He had an idea
back of his mind, had Stephen. He went to Pelham, Connecticut, where he found a congregation needing a pastor. With
his father's sermons to start him off, this young scamp made
a place for himself as the local dominie, and, despite a few
doubting Thomases, he managed to bluff his way through
several months of preaching. He used the alias of Davis.
Then appeared the usual old college chum, who called him by
his right name, and the game was up. His departure from
the ministry was precipitate.

During his wanderings he had met up with one Glazier
Wheeler who claimed to be able to transmute base metals
into gold. In his memoirs Burroughs professes to have
believed this—but a man must tell his story. He soon found
that he was a counterfeiter, and for a moment he had qualms.
But a circumstance arose—a chivalrous circumstance that
involved a lady who needed medicine—in which it was
necessary for Burroughs to pass one of Wheeler's counterfeit
bills. Springfield, Massachusetts, was the town. He was
seized. Instantly someone from Pelham recognized him as
their erstwhile pseudo-parson. He was found guilty, clapped
into jail, and the papers printed a yarn to the effect that while
he was preaching he had made off with another parson's
clothes and left a note that read, in true Scriptural form,
"You shall seek me early, but shall not find me." Burroughs
denied ever taking the clothes, or writing such a note, but
what a gorgeous person he would have been had he possessed
such a sense of humour!

The third or penal phase of his life was one of amazing
experiences. He was held in jail at Northampton. From the
first he was a bad prisoner. Constantly he tried to break out,
and constantly he was thrown in the dungeon in irons. Finally his reputation as an incorrigible grew so Titanic that he
was taken to the government jail on Castle Island in Boston
Harbour. Scarcely there, he began to dig his way out, and
did succeed in getting off the island with a band of his fellow

prisoners. They were captured the next day, and Burroughs was brought back to face severe punishment. But even that did not break his spirit. He played possum for a time, won the good graces of his jailers, and then sprang a revolt on them. Once again he was overcome, and he finally subsided until his sentence was up.

And that brings him to his fourth or domestic phase. In this, he marries and begins to acquire children. He has only the barest means of subsistence, but his wife stands by him through great poverty. He really is trying to go straight. He starts a school. The school is successful. But Fate is on his trail. Without the slightest evidence, he is accused of having assaulted three young girls. He is brought to trial. His enemies bear false witness against him. He sees jail yawning ahead. There is only one way out—he flees the jurisdiction of the court.

We next find him at Bridgehampton on Long Island, where he starts teaching again. Remember, the man has a wife and children. He loves them. He sincerely wants to go straight. And lest there happen to him in Bridgehampton a recurrence of what happened before, he goes to the local minister and tells him the whole story of his life. The parson listens, counsels him, agrees to tell no one, and says that he will support him in his work. Heartened by this, Burroughs throws himself into the development of his school. He brings his wife over to Long Island and once more they look forward hopefully to their available future.

Among the ideals he has for Bridgehampton is the establishment of a library. The leading citizens of the town rally to his support. The money is subscribed. Then the question arises as to who will choose the books. The parson selects his, and the judge his, and Burroughs his. Immediately there is a clash of minds. The disagreement resolves into bitterness. Burroughs and the parson become open enemies. His opponents in the district hold meetings to consider his case. They take into counsel with them a notorious woman. In a few weeks, without the slightest shred of evidence, this woman accuses Burroughs of criminal assault. Crash goes another ideal! Down comes another effort to climb back into respectability! Burroughs is obliged to flee again.

The story of the persecution of this man is one of the bitterest commentaries we can offer on the hypocrisy of the times. It is a long story (his memoirs cover 360 pages) and it need not be recounted.

The end brings a pleasanter picture. Legend says that he went to live in the little town of Three Rivers, which lies between Montreal and Quebec, and there, surrounded by books and by scholars who loved him, he passed on into a peaceful dotage. And so eventually, this crime-crusted old mariner reached the harbour where he would be.

CHAPTER XV

ℒℴℭℯℒ VENDORS AND STREET CRIES

CARCELY a section of the country but still has its local vendors and its memory of legions of men who, in one guise or another, swelled the ranks of the itinerant army. This book, for example, is being written in a Connecticut valley through which to-day pass a ladder peddler, an itinerant butcher, and an oil vendor who is also a barber and who cuts the shaggy locks of the farmers and even ventures to bob and shingle the heads of one or two of the more advanced farm women. A few miles from the house dwell the sons of an erstwhile candle peddler, and almost everyone here can remember the itinerant vendors of Indian specifics who regularly passed through the valley.

So it is true of almost every section that can boast more than fifty years of permanent settlement. From one restricted area in Massachusetts come recollections of a stoneware peddler who exchanged his wares for paper rags: any quantity of tinware peddlers; the ice cream, the hulled corn and hominy men; the fisherman with his horn selling Connecticut River shad and the fruit man vending watermelons and early Delaware peaches; the yeast man who kept his precious fluid—barm, it was called locally—in a jar in front of him in his cart; and the soft soap seller who exchanged his slimy mess for suet and beef and pork drippings.

Without the regular visits of these local vendors country life would have been very dull indeed. They had their local names, and picturesque names they often were. "Dewdrop" Herrington of one New York State section was so called because at all seasons of the year he had a dewdrop pendant from the tip of his nose; others were called "Leather Breeches," Jim or Tom, because they were clothed in these

ancient and hardy habiliments. One tea vendor was rightly
known as "Johnnie Cup O' Tea."

In his wanderings, Hawthorne even met up with a nut
vendor—"an old man, selling the meats of butternuts. . .
He was dressed in a dark, thin coat, ribbed velvet pantaloons
and a sort of moccasins or shoes, appended to the legs of
woollen stockings. . . . His nuts were contained in a square
tin box having two compartments, one for the nuts and
another for maple sugar, which he sells in small cakes. . . .
He said that butternuts did not sell so well as walnuts, which
are not yet in season; that he might to-day have sold fifty
cents' worth; of walnuts, never less than a dollar's worth,
often more; and when he went around with a caravan, he had
sold fifteen dollars' worth per day, and once as much as
twenty dollars' worth." Truly a prosperous merchant in
little things, this nut vendor!

SPECIALIZED VENDING

Likewise we could encounter, on these early American
roads, all manner of specialized vending to one or two trades
in a restricted district—cotton yarns for those who wove rag
carpet at home; wooden screws turned out of hickory and
sold to cabinet-makers in towns around the maker's neighbourhood; blacksmiths who specialized on making nails and
sold them through the countryside. There were also those
who farmed out work, such as the controlling agents of the
farmer-cobblers or farmer-weavers or even of the wives of
farmers who made shirts—took the cut goods from the travelling agents, sewed them, laundered them and then were paid
by the agent when he came around for his stock.

The most cunning figure of all these specialists was the
itinerant seller of locks who hailed from Bridgeport, one
Alfred C. Hobbs, representing the firm of Day & Newell. He
specialized in bank locks, did Alfred, and it was his duty to
convince bankers that the locks they were using were worthless. Mr. Hobbs acquired a suspicious set of implements, and

a stock of Day & Newell's locks, and thus equipped, he set forth upon the unsuspecting financial world. His first call was at a bank in Stamford, where he challenged the directors. They accepted his challenge and promised that if he could open the outside door of the bank and get into the vault in two hours without injuring the locks, they would consider his wares. Mr. Hobbs examined the keyholes, took a few instruments from his bag, and within twenty-three minutes he had picked the outside lock and the three locks on the vault. The year of this great feat was 1847 and the month January. From that time on Mr. Hobbs devoted his entire time and energies to travelling about the country, picking bank locks and selling bankers his special brand of locks to supplant them.

The train hawkers, with which we are all familiar, seem to have found their opportunity as soon as trains began to run. Newsboys were evident on trains in districts where schoolmasters were a curiosity. They sold newspapers, books, apples, biscuits, and such, and were so skilled that they could figure to the exact minute when the train began to pick up speed and they had to jump off. On his visit to America in 1849, Sir Charles Lyell tells of one of them calling out "in the midst of the pine barren between Columbus and Chehaw, 'A novel by Paul de Kock, the Bulwer of France, for twenty-five cents! All the Go! More popular than The Wandering Jew.'"

CITY VENDORS

Since the coming of the automobile the character of city streets has changed radically. To-day they are arteries for the passing of swift traffic; once on a time they were also the avenues of street vending of all sorts. It was the custom of merchants to live above their shops, so there was no sharp distinction between the residential and business districts. Wherever the huckster went he found trade.

Because there were so many complaints from inhabitants

who had been imposed upon by hucksters or "shinners," as they were often called, early town authorities established the public market.

In many Colonial cities and towns this weekly or semi-weekly fair or market was a fixed institution. To them the farmers brought their produce. To them also, they drove their "show" beef, fat cattle, decorated with flowers and garlands and ribbons, and preceded by a trumpeter or fiddler who led the procession to the slaughtering.

Housewives, basket on arm, or trailed by servants carrying baskets, went to market. The market knew no social distinctions. New York, for example, had five markets by 1766 and every day was market day save Sunday. Weights and measures were sealed, and an eye was kept on the condition of meats and butter sold. In Philadelphia, on Tuesday and Friday evenings before the market day, the bells of Christ Church were pealed. They came to be known as "Butter Bells."

The remains of these markets can be seen in Boston, Philadelphia, Baltimore, as well as New York, and in Baltimore it is still *en règle* for the housewife to carry her basket to the stalls. As to-day, so in the years between 1700 and 1850, all manner of wares were found at the market—garden truck, meats, fish, cheeses, groceries, shoes, clothing, piece goods and articles of household manufacture.

Another form of collective street selling in pre-Revolutionary days was the vendue or auction sale. Goods were sold cheap; and often, as an inducement, rum would be passed out by the auctioneers, who were mostly peddlers—or "merchant peddlers," as they were referred to in Pennsylvania where they were especially active. The peddler Hawthorne describes on a preceding page, was holding a vendue. In 1726 we find the established merchants of Philadelphia agitating against these peddlers. Their haunts were said to be the resorts of idlers and their sales, frauds. The governor refused to sign the bill because the market and the auction

"CHERRIES"

"PEACHES"

"CHARCOAL"

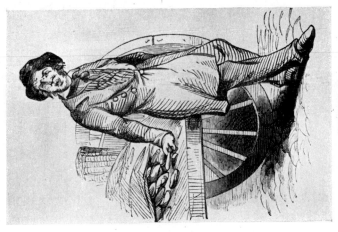

"CLAMS"

THE
NEW-YORK CRIES,
IN RHYME.

Stereotyped by James Conner, New-York.

NEW-YORK:
PRINTED & SOLD BY MAHLON DAY,
AT THE NEW JUVENILE BOOK-
STORE, NO. 376, PEARL-
STREET.

HOT - CORN !

" Here's your nice Hot Corn!
" Smoking hot! piping hot!
" O what beauties I have got!"

Here's smoking Hot Corn,
  With salt that is nigh,
Only two pence an ear,—
  O pass me not by !

SCISSORS to GRIND !

Jingle, Jingle, goes the Bell.

Any Razors or Scissors,
  Or Penknives to grind ?
I'll engage that my work
  Shall be done to your mind.

LOCKS OR KEYS.

" Any Locks to repair ? Or
Keys to be fitted ?"

Do you want any Locks
  Put in goodly repair ?
Or any Keys fitted,
  To turn true as a hair?
THE END.

PAGES FROM "THE NEW YORK CRIES"
Courtesy of Brooks Bros.

afforded buying opportunities for the poor, whereas the stores of the established merchants served only the rich and aristocratic.

In the same manner was the business of the huckster protested against in many cities and towns. The trade of the established market found unfair competition coming from itinerant hucksters who, by peddling through the streets, or by appearing at the stalls of the markets before the local merchants and farmers could set up their goods, would forestall profitable trade. Many cities passed ordinances against them. In Marblehead, Massachusetts, before the Revolution the market was open on Tuesdays and Thursdays till one o'clock and on Saturdays till sunset, but no huckster was allowed to sell provisions of any kind until after one o'clock, i.e., until after the market had done its business. Pennsylvania threatened an equally strict regulation against these vagrant traders. In New York City, as early as 1691, a city ordinance forbade hucksters selling their wares until the market had been open for two hours. In 1707 all street hawking was forbidden, on penalty of twenty shillings for each offense, half of which fine went to the informer, and half to the city poor. By 1738 the *New York Gazette* was publishing the "Act to Restrict Hawkers and Pedlars" by which a £5 import tax was exacted and £5 for each horse and three shillings for the license. This law, however, did not apply to persons selling fish, fruit, or victuals, or to those who were selling "wares of his or their own manufacturing . . . nor any Tinker, Glasier, Cooper, Plummer, Taylor or other person usually trading in mending or making of Cloaths, Kettles, Tubs or Hoashould goods." In 1740 New York also passed a city ordinance forbidding negroes, Indians, and mulattoes from selling boiled Indian corn, peas, peaches, etc., in the streets, lest they spread infectious diseases. Offenders were to be publicly whipped.

From this legislation we can deduce two facts—that street peddling in New York City, at least prior to the

Revolution, was not so common as is generally supposed; and that it really developed only after the turn of the nineteenth century.

Pushcart peddling, such as we find to-day in New York, Chicago, Boston, and other cities, is an outgrowth of the huckstering that arose after 1800, only to-day it is mainly in the hands of Jews and Italians.

Despite his bad name, the huckster served a useful purpose in that he brought his wares to the housewife's door, and that he served the poorer classes. He was a true itinerant, although his field of wandering was limited to the city and its immediate environs. Moreover he was a picturesque figure, for he called his wares, and his street cries were among the pleasant (or unpleasant) noises of our early cities and towns.

STREET CRIES

Nowadays city people know that spring has come when they see the flower vendor's cart, spilling red geraniums, trundled down the street and hear his unflowery and raucous solicitation. They rush to their doors, to their windows—and somehow, life takes on a happier aspect. Imagine how the housewife of a century ago used to listen for the tinkling bell of the muffin boy or the horn of the grimy man selling charcoal! The streets at times were a veritable Babeldom in their confusion of tongues. Vociferous and importunate newsboys shouted as loudly then as they do now—and some of the papers were just as scandalous as our own. The charcoal man went around with his cart and sold charcoal for lighting fires at thirty-five cents a barrel (that was the Philadelphia price of 1850). His was a long narrow wagon and, although he was a sadly besmirched cadger, he sometimes sported a blue and white checked apron. Up to 1835 in Philadelphia he used to blow a horn, but this so unnerved the more sensitive souls of that somnolent city that a city ordinance was passed to silence him. So he used a handbell and sang a song, almost as noisily as he had blown his horn, that went this way:—

> Charcoal by the bushel,
> Charcoal by the peck,
> Charcoal by the frying pan
> Or any way you lek!

In autumn the woodman would appear. His cry was, "Wud! Wud! Wud! Wud! Wud!" uttered staccato. The song of the soft soap man went, "Sam! Sam! The soap fat man!" Brick-dust vendors—usually a negro woman with a tub carried on the head—sold fine, pounded, salmon-brick dust for scouring knives. Sand men* used the cry, "Sand your kitchens! Sand your floors!" or "Want any Sand? Want Sandy?" Also there was the milkman—still with us—who used to utter blood-curdling cries early in the morning. Likewise a great variety of vendors of food.

The local fish dealers in early times first carried their wares in panniers on horseback, or in pushcarts. Later, in New England, they took to a two-wheeled vehicle covered with white canvas, the vendor sitting on the shafts, his feet dangling. In Philadelphia and the South the pushcart was used till quite lately. Various cries had this peddler—"Fresh fish fit for the pan," or in shad season, "Shad! Buy any shad!" and in some cities was heard this deathless lyric:—

> Here comes the fishman!
> Bring out your dishpan,
> Porgies at five cents a pound!

Sometimes these fish hucksters blew horns and the tin horn came to be called in some districts, a "fish-horn."

In Philadelphia and the South the crab man was a regular figure—commonly a negro pushing a wheelbarrow of live crabs. "Crabs! Crabs! Alive!" went his song, or

> Fresh, fresh crabs,
> Fresh Baltimore crabs;
> Put them in the pot
> With the lid on top;
> Fresh Baltimore crabs!

---

* Before the Revolution in houses that lacked carpets, this sand was spread on the floor and drawn into fanciful figures with the sweep of the broom.

The Philadelphia and Baltimore oyster vendors were an accommodating lot: they had a pushcart with a table attached, equipped with tin plates, forks, vinegar cruet, salts and peppers, and you stepped up to the oysterman's cart and as he opened his wares, ate them from the half shell *al fresco*. In the autumn, honeycomb vendors appeared—men in white jackets and aprons with white linen cap, and carrying a large wooden tray of honeycomb balanced skilfully on the head.

Women were the special vendors of fruit and vegetables before the descent of Greeks, Armenians, and Italians. Sometimes they went about with a tray on the head and cried their wares through the streets. Wilmington, Delaware, had a picturesque and rotund lassie known as "Dutch Molly," who peddled vegetables, and is said to have had quite a past. She also possessed a meek little husband whose trade was tailoring and, when his viking wife wasn't around, told fortunes! In late summer came peaches, and the cry for these was, "Peaches, Oh, here dey go!" Watermelons also appeared and were called "Watermelyuns" in the itinerant vernacular, together with apropos remarks as to their ripeness.

The most musical of all the cries was that of the hominy seller. At first hominy was a negro delicacy but after 1828, white folks began to enjoy it, and you find hominy hucksters on the streets of New York, Philadelphia, and Baltimore. Their cry went "Hominy! Beautiful hominy!" or they sang this refrain:—

> Hominy man is on his way
> To sell his good hominy.

Pepper pot is a dish that can be relished only by those who hail from that Mecca of gastronomic delights, Philadelphia. In that city were found negro women pushing carts on which were round kettles of pepper pot kept warm over charcoal, some pretty blue striped bowls and spoons. They chanted this inducement:—

> All hot! All hot!
> Makee back strong!
> Makee live long!
> Come buy my pepper pot!

The sweet potato man of Philadelphia in the first half of the last century was a bard of no mean calibre. His street song went:—

> My hoss is blind and he's got no tail,
> When he's put in prison I'll go his bail.
> Yed-dy go, sweet potatoes, oh!
> Fif-en-ny bit a half peck!

Beside these were to be seen chimney sweeps—usually small negro boys led by a parent, who announced his offspring's vocation with a sort of Tyrolean yodeling song, "Sweep-ho! Sweep-ho! Sweep-ho!" the song the sweep would sing when he issued from the chimney. Chimneys had to be swept once a month and forty shillings was the fine if your chimney took fire in consequence of neglect.

Women and girls selling hot corn were not uncommon. And their song was a delight to the ear:—

> Hot corn! Hot corn!
> 'Ere's yer lily-white hot corn!

One hot corn girl especially seems to have captured public imagination. She sold in the streets of New York. Her name was Clio, a quadroon fair to look upon, of about twenty summers, daughter of a fugitive slave. Her slow chanting voice was one to throw the passer-by into raptures. Stephen C. Foster tried to make a song of her cry. "There's a wild, wooing tone in her voice," he said, "that I cannot catch." So the song was never written.

Pastry boys carried rolls, muffins, and sweets on trays on their heads. They were subsequently supplanted by the muffin man, who appeared late in the afternoon carrying a basket and tinkling a bell. Wilmington, Delaware, had a well-known pastry seller, a Michael Wolf, who carried a cake-board on his head piled high with hot gingerbread, iced cakes and sweet rusks. A worthy fellow, old Michael, and for his services to the sweet tooth of men and children, a kindly Providence permitted him to live to the ripe old age of eighty-nine. He died in 1825.

Revolutionary Philadelphia also boasted its gingerbread man, and a great person he was—Christopher Ludwick. He came to Philadelphia from Germany in 1753 and set up as a gingerbread-baker and confectioner. From this trade he amassed a fortune. During the Revolution he gave freely of his funds to the cause and even served in the ranks, where he got into contact with Hessian troops among the British and persuaded great numbers of them to desert. He was appointed Baker-General to the Continental Army—perhaps the first man and the last ever to have held such a post. When the hideous yellow fever epidemic struck Philadelphia, Ludwick laboured with his own hands baking bread which he gave to the destitute. He died in 1801, and all his money was left to the poor children of Philadelphia. And so his gingerbread was really a Living Bread that came down from Heaven, whereof, if a man eats, he shall live forevermore.

A less elegant figure—usually a darky—was the garbage man, but he did not lack his song, which went this way:—

> Bring out yer slops to feed me pigs
> To buy some meat fer me niggers to eat.

The glazier went about the streets and his proclamation, "Glass put in!" was transformed to "Glash t' p't eene." Umbrella menders, tinkers, rag men and purchasers of old clothes had their individual street utterances. The organ grinder was a common sight, both those who had monkeys and those who carried miniature panoramas. Also the scissors grinder went around tinkling a little bell, as he does to-day. He was found in practically every city and town.

Occasionally you encountered an ambitious scissors grinder who proclaimed his potential services by blasts on an old army bugle.

Another type of bell ringer has passed entirely save in one or two New England towns where he is still preserved as a picturesque figure. The town crier had to read proclamations to the populace, announce runaway servants and apprentices, and sometimes he served as night watchman. In the last rôle it was his duty to patrol the streets, "to give notice of ye time of night, what weather, etc., according to custom . . . and to continue ye said perambulation until break of day." In Philadelphia the night watchmen carried rattles, doubtless to warn conscientious burglars of their coming! This archaic type of policeman disappeared from the City of Brotherly Love about 1848. Our early policeman had some strange tasks. In Albany before the Revolution they were required to correct children found playing on the Sabbath, and they were often seen entering a front yard and administering physical chastisement to naughty, Sabbath-breaking boys!

SOUTHERN VENDORS

In Charleston some of the street vending was conducted by negroes who spoke Gullah, the quacking patois of the littoral and sea islands between Charleston and Savannah. Thus a negro would come along the street crying his chickens:

"Here one, here murrer, here two pun tapa 'turrer here tree wid e two leg tie to garra." (Here is one, here is another, here are two on top of each other, here are three with their two legs tied together).

Also, the Charleston vendor of porgies would proclaim to the populace how human these fish really are, as he discovers when he tries to catch them off Black Fish Shoals:—

> Porgy walk and porgy talk
> And porgy eat with knife and fork,
> Get yer nice por-gy!

Another poetical huckster was heard to shout:—

> Mullet! Mullet! Mullet!
> Flounder and Black Fish!
> Shark steaks for dem what likes 'em;
> Sword Fish for dem what fights 'em;
> Fish-ee! Fish-ee!

When travellers reached New Orleans, they heard street cries in the Creole argot—*marchandes* from the St. Mary market or the environs of Carrollton crying, "Belle des Figues! Belle des Figues!" "Bons petites calas! Tout chauds! Tout chauds!" "Confitures coco!" "Pralines, Pistache, Pralines, Pacanes!" The bayou peddlers, who went about the waterways near the city, were negroes mostly. They sang trist little songs of very few notes, doubtless what we now call "blues."

However not always was the vending so musical. The levees of New Orleans were commercial and racial beehives, especially when boats were leaving for up-river. About them swarmed "little boats filled with pedlary," as one traveller in '51 describes them. "The Jew was there with his hundred-blade pen knives, sponges and metallic tablets; the Yankee with his curious knick-knacks brought from every auction mart in the town; nondescripts with oranges, bananas and conch shells, which latter, now and then were blown with sounds resembling the bray of a mule when touched with colic." Here too, was a colourful melange of peoples— French, Spaniards, Americans, Creoles, quadroons, mulattoes, Mexicans, and negroes.

We have noted the plaster cast sellers from Lucca who tramped our city streets and country byways. His fellow Italians went about with organs and monkeys or with harps, prior to the Civil War. In Philadelphia the street music consisted mainly of negroes singing, and occasionally an old Scotch-Irishman with Irish bag-pipes. Italian children used to sell flowers on the streets of New York, and, in a later day, their little brothers took to bootblacking, thereupon supplanting the negroes, who were the first bootblacks in New York. In New Orleans, the Italian having passed above this trade, bootblacking fell again into the hands of negroes. Later the itinerant selling of fruit through the New York streets was controlled by Italians—Genoese and Sicilians mostly.

FOREIGN LANGUAGE ITINERANTS

Although many of the Yankee peddlers travelled great distances to distribute their wares, there were groups of itinerants in restricted areas who devoted their energies to serving the needs of their own people and speaking their own tongue. We find this among the bayou peddlers of the district around New Orleans, who spoke a Creole patois—French and Indian mixed—and among the Pennsylvania Dutch, whose dialect was a fusion of virgin Indian words, German, Huguenot French, Welsh, English, Swedish, Hollandish, and Scotch-Irish solecisms.

The cross-section of Pennsylvania prior to and immediately after the Revolution offers interesting sectional divisions—a predominance of English-speaking Quakers in the east, a layer of Germans in the middle, in what are now Berks, Lebanon, Lancaster, and Lehigh Counties, and a fringe of Scotch-Irish in what were then the wild frontiers of the state. The Scotch-Irish were wanderers—they drifted down the valleys to Georgia and out the Ohio until they were scattered over the face of the country, and left their mark wherever they went. But the Pennsylvania Dutch were clannish and settled folk. An agricultural people, they resented the idea of moving about. We do not find them migrating but we do find a distinct race of itinerants who spoke their tongue and who served them.

In the vernacular of these Pennsylvania Dutch all itinerants were known collectively as *fusgaengers*, foot-goers, and included the *kramera*, or business men, the *pokmon*, or ped-

16

dlers who sold *klanichkada*, or knick-knacks, and *herdsing* or
house-furnishings; *krout-brondrela*, or *blousmon*, vendors of
herbs; *shoonmachera*, cobblers, *Zinkera*, *shpengler* or *kessel-
flickers*, tinkers or pewter-menders; *Shreinera*, cabinet-
makers; *blechmon*, tinware dealers; *wevera*, weavers; *letter-
orsha*, chimney-sweepers; *safemon*, soap-maker; *lichtermon*,
candle-makers; *pictarmon*, artists; *foosgeigera*, wandering
fiddlers; *glofamon*, harpsichord teachers; *geikmon*, violin
instructors; *donsamon*, jig dancers; *gasharmon*, harness
makers; *predichera*, or *pora*, preachers; *lamarar* or *Aw-bay-
tzamen*, teachers; and *gloferer*, piano or melodeon men, music
teachers who carried a small collapsible organ strapped to
their backs.

These nomads were generally of German descent. Honest
fellows and observant, none knew the by-roads better than
they. In return for their talents and work they were housed
and fed. Besides selling their wares and plying their trades,
they served as messengers, carrying all manner of missives—
love, business, gossip. A few expounded the Gospel on Sundays. It was quite common to find one or two of them
scholarly men, possessing a remarkable knowledge of the
classics and of literature. This type, however, were usually
seeking solace in peddling, from past love affairs and disap-
pointments.

Going farther west in colonial Pennsylvania, we find the
Scotch-Irish. And while they did not produce their own distinctive race of itinerants, they had one or two types that
wandered locally—the ballad singer and the musician.
Whereas the Germans brought the violin or fiddle to Pennsylvania, and the Huguenots the dulcimer, the Scotch-Irish
introduced the bag-pipe and the cruit or harp. In the early
days old men used to wander from settlement to settlement
and sing the songs of Jacobite times and the Scotch Border.
Pipers used to go about, too, showing up at local fairs,
horse races and other gatherings. The fiddler attended backwoods dances.

CHAPTER XVI

COMMERCIAL WANDERERS OF WATERWAYS

S SOON as the Revolutionary War was over, began the serious and persistent pushing forward of the frontiers. In the seventeen years between the Peace of Paris and the turn of the nineteenth century, more than half a million people left their original homes forever and migrated to Western New York and the hinterlands of Virginia, Tennessee, and Kentucky. Many of them were New Englanders, for New England was a nursery of men, whence were annually transplanted into other parts of the United States thousands of its natives. By 1816 the Ohio Valley was filling up. The Ordinance of 1787 had opened that territory to settlement. The Ohio Company, with the Rev. Manasseh Cutler of Ipswich, Massachusetts, as one of its leaders, lured many old Revolutionary soldiers and their descendants to the fertile banks of this valley. By 1840 the cotton states of the Southwest were witnessing the arrival of a steady stream of new families. Illinois and Indiana received great quotas of settlers. Georgia enjoyed a veritable land boom. By 1860 the Mississippi Valley was hectic with *gauche* towns and squatters. Eleven years before this the discovery of gold in California served as a magnet to draw vast hordes of new people to the Pacific Coast. The California and Oregon trails became beaten paths and their camps echoed to the refrain of "Oh Susanna" and "The Days of 49."

In each of these advancements, rivers afforded the principal means of transportation. Fourteen states can be said to have been settled by this river migration—Arkansas, Illinois, Indiana, Iowa, Kansas, Kentucky, Louisiana, Michigan, Minnesota, Mississippi, Missouri, Ohio, Tennessee, and Wisconsin. It is a dependable axiom that if you would seek old houses and old settlements, you must look first along the watercourses.

Settlements established, an active and picturesque river traffic sprang up. From conveyors of people the boats became conveyors of goods. The waterway itinerant of the rivers and canals grew to the status of a commonplace figure.

There is scarcely an early description of the Ohio, Mississippi or any other river-drained valley but has its record of the various kinds of transporting, merchandising, and working boats along these rivers. English visitors especially were intrigued by them.

THE VARIETY OF RIVER CRAFT

The simplest form of cargo craft was the pole boat, which originated on the Delaware and Connecticut Rivers. Ranging from twenty to thirty feet long and from three to five feet wide, and with a flat bottom and pointed ends, it was poled along by the crew. Four to six men would manage such a craft, each man equipped with a long ash or hickory pole shod with an iron spike. They would jam the pole in the mud of the bottom and walk along the boat toward the stern on narrow runways. Since this kind of craft drew less than a foot of water, it was easily speeded along. Sometimes these pole boats were twice the size and carried twice the crew, and were equipped with masts and sails.

Another crude transport was the log raft or timber float— hundreds of logs fastened together with chains and with a cabin for the men who worked the sweeps. When they reached their destination the float was broken up and the timber sold. *En route* they used to shed logs or "sawyers" which made the going perilous for other river craft.

The ark, or flatboat, was built of heavy timber bolted together, and originated on the Susquehanna and Delaware Rivers. It would range from seventy-five to one hundred feet long and fifteen to twenty wide, and it was steered by a sweep that was sometimes forty feet long. Five or six men

WESTERN END OF THE GREAT ERIE CANAL.

Sketched with the Camera Lucida by Capt. B. Hall R.N.

Engraved by W.H. Lizars.

BAKER'S FERRY

A MISSISSIPPI RIVER STEAMBOAT

These boats were "coaled" from stacks of wood on shore, the work being done by the crew and "deck" passengers, who were usually riverway itinerants returning from New Orleans

could navigate an ark, since it was floated with the current and rarely run upstream. It had a draft of from three to five feet. At night the ark was moored to the bank. There was a cabin for the crew or family at one end and at the other an enclosure for live stock. These arks carried emigrants and all manner of stores. They were floated from the headwaters and tributaries of the Mississippi down to New Orleans where they were sold for their timber after the cargo had been disposed of.

The crew made their way back to their homes as best they could—just as the early tinware peddlers used to dispose of their wagons at the end of their journeys, and return to Connecticut. At first these boatmen were obliged to trek back through the forests or take a skiff and row upstream against the current. Sometimes they were away from home three to nine months on these voyages. Later they made their way back on the river steamers that by 1828 were leaving New Orleans daily for the upper reaches of the Mississippi and were "deck passengers" working out their passage by helping to "coal" the boat—loading on fuel wood from the stacks on the river bank, a daily task *en route*.

The flatboat, which was the one most used for family migration, was sometimes called an Ohio or Kentucky boat, since it was used for this type of migrations in the Ohio and Mississippi Rivers from 1788 to 1840. It was entirely enclosed. From twenty to sixty feet long and from ten to twenty wide were its dimensions. When loaded it drew from one to two feet of water. As it was made of heavy planks and was so enclosed, it could serve as a fort, which was necessary in the early days. The walls were often slit with loopholes for rifles. Of course this type of boat was at the mercy of the current, and its only means of steering was the sweep extending over the stern.

Other types of boats seen on the rivers in early days were: log canoes, pirogues, or large Indian canoes; skiffs, flat-bottom affairs of heavy planks, manned by two or three men and used for long trips; the batteau, a big skiff that would accommodate a family, and was guided downstream by a sweep and poled upstream; the keel boat, a development of the batteau, which had a heavy log keel with which to meet the onslaught of submerged obstructions—these ran forty to seventy-five feet long and from seven to nine wide, and had masts and sails: from them was evolved the canal boat. Then there were the barge and the packet boat. The packet boat was a large barge or keel boat equipped with masts and sails, and carrying passengers and freight. From 1794 on, these ran regularly between Cincinnati and Pittsburgh. The barge was the speed boat of these early rivers. It had masts, sails and rudder and could make four to five miles per hour with the current, and, when it was poled upstream, two miles. It ranged from thirty to seventy feet long and seven to twelve wide, and it had a covered cabin for the passengers. Then came the steamboat, which was introduced on the Mississippi and Ohio in 1817.

All types of boats were used by various waterway peddlers, but the store boat, shanty boat, or ark was the most common. Once the settlements were established, the people had to have supplies, and these were the mediums by which they were brought.

RIVERWAY PEDDLING

Comparable to the general store of the country town was the general merchandising boat that plied up and down the navigable rivers of the South and Middle West. Some of them were quite roomy, having a cabin for the families of the crew and accommodations for the store, with shelves around the sides and a counter with scales. They stocked everything necessary for a general retail trade, from bandanna handkerchiefs to hardware. There was a pleasant dry-goodsy smell about these floating stores and an air of congeniality about their keepers, who served to please their customers. The manner of attracting trade was unique. The boat would fly a flag

DECK-HANDS

Great sweeps guided the early river boats which carried cargo and passengers down the rivers of the opening
West. These two illustrations were made by Captain Basil Hall

that designated the kind of stores it carried, red for groceries and yellow for drygoods. Then—but let the good old Quaker merchant, Robert Sutcliffe describe it. He journeyed through the country in 1804-6 and was quite observant. "As they sail along the river (this happened to be the Ohio) on coming to a plantation they blow a horn or conch shell, to give notice of their arrival; when the planters with their wives and daughters repair to these floating shops and select such things as they are in want of; and make payment in the produce of their plantations, such as grain, flour, cotton, tobacco, dried venison, the skins of wild animals. The shopkeeper, having disposed of his goods in this way, returns home with the produce he has collected and again renews his stock and proceeds on another voyage." It wasn't unusual for four or five of these floating stores to pass by every day.

Sometimes the boats were owned and controlled by merchants in the cities. The firm of Baynton, Wharton & Morgan of Philadelphia for example, ran a line of merchandise boats between Pittsburgh and New Orleans and had $150,000 invested in the venture—a large sum for 1767. They employed 300 boatmen. About 1800 another Philadelphia firm, Bryant & Morrison, also controlled a line of boats. Other firms in the river ports also owned lines. These store boats were not cheap either to equip or to operate. A merchant would sometimes invest $10,000 to $15,000, in a single boat. The big boats would range as heavy as twenty-five tons, whereas the smaller ones, as we have seen, were mere rafts with a cabin, covered deck, and sails.

Like the ark, they were operated in the simplest fashion—floated down with the current and then poled back. Later they were operated under their own power. The cheaper grade of free-lance dealer would float his boat down the Ohio and then the Mississippi to New Orleans, and there sell it.

Among the natives and the owners of plantations bordering on the rivers these store-boat owners bore anything but an enviable reputation. They were commonly called "Chicken

Thieves," because of their illicit traffic with thieving negroes. It was necessary in some regions to obtain permits to trade with the negro. Lacking these, and lacking common honesty, the owner or captain of the boat would anchor her at the stern and, under cover of night, the darkies would come aboard at the bow. Only a few of them were allowed on board at one time. The storekeeper sold them everything their money could buy and would barter for the cotton, sugar, chickens, and equipment they stole from the plantations. By morning, when the robberies were discovered, the boat and its dishonest "fence" were out of sight downstream.

Some of the boats were equipped with copper stills for making peach and apple brandy and rye whiskey, and they conducted a lively trade in this illicit liquor among the negroes and the poorer populace.*

The crew of the store-boat usually consisted of two men (and their families), sometimes partners who were both boatmen and merchants. Like the first tinware peddlers who filled the triple role of manufacturer, agent, and salesmen all in one, these men served the dual rôles of navigators and shopkeepers. They would turn from the rough handling of a sweep to the more delicate work of snipping off lengths of dress goods from a bolt, or weighing out rice and sugar.

Occasionally they took on a passenger, especially in the more thinly settled districts, as on the Arkansas River, where means of water travel were limited.

Eighteen to twenty miles a day was about all these boats were capable of making. When they went downstream they were steered by long sweeps, and in going upstream the sweeps were used as oars and when shallows were reached, long pushing poles were called into service. Sometimes the boats were towed by a long cable or "cordelle" carried by men trudging along the river bank. This was called "bushwhacking."

---

* Stephen Girard, who became one of the great shipping princes of his day, began as a riverway peddler of bottled cider and claret on the Delaware.

The nationality of the riverway peddlers was mixed—some were sharp Yankees, others, especially in the southern reaches of the Mississippi, French and Spanish. While most of the French *habitans* of the Mississippi Valley were agriculturists, the more ambitious of them became traders, some having stores of goods in their houses, and some trading by boat up the western tributaries of the river—the Red, the Platte, and such. They also often served as *engagés* of the American Fur Company, and bartered their coarse cloths, beads, vermilion, kettles, knives, guns, powder, and illicit liquor with the Indians in return for horses, mules, furs and the like.

Often the store-boat was the method by which a family would make its way into a new territory. A Down-east farmer would sell his land (or abandon it), trek or ride in a Conestoga wagon to Pittsburgh and there buy and equip an ark. Thus loaded with goods, his household gear, a pig or two, chickens, family and other impedimenta, he set forth. *En route* he peddled merchandise until he reached his point of settlement, when the ark was sold for whatever it would fetch.

This mode of commerce was not without its dangers in the early days. There were the spring freshets, the sudden shifting of the channels, the perilous mud banks that appeared overnight, the stray logs that drifted off from the timber floats to become "sawyers" and ripped holes in the hulls of the crafts. And there were also Indians and outlaws who would swoop down on a solitary ark, or a group of them, and plunder at will. A famous gang of river outlaws on the Ohio near Shawneetown used to watch for boats caught on the flats, board them, kill the occupants and take the boat on down to New Orleans. In some neighbourhoods these store-boats—as were the earlier migration boats—were obliged to become floating forts, and their merchant-navigators had to be as agile with the gun as they were with sweep and scissors.

A hardy, picturesque crew of ruffians, these Mississippi

peddling boatmen, a lanky, sleepy lot who were slow to speech but quick to action, and, once under way, managed to acquit themselves with honour. They usually wore bright red flannel shirts, a loose blue jerkin or short coat, and rough brown linsey-woolsey trousers. Moccasins were on their feet; at their belts hung the ubiquitous hunting knife and tobacco pouch, and they invariably wore a cap of untanned fur—coon skin usually—with the fur side out.

RIVERWAY WORKMEN

When it began to pay them to travel by water—when the settlements were well established and not too far apart—all manner of trades were represented among the floating population of those rivers that served for avenues of national advancement. On the Ohio the floating grist-mill was a common sight—a mill supported by two boats, the wheel moving between them. The boat was moored in the current, where there was an effective head of water of about twenty inches, and the stream turned the millwheel, about twelve feet in diameter, which revolved the millstones. Sometimes the current would spin this wheel at the dizzy rate of 120 revolutions a minute. To this floating establishment farmers brought their grain.

Blacksmiths had their own crafts, which they moored close to the shore and did whatever work the neighborhood needed. There were also travelling sawyers, who worked up the logs that were washed ashore from the timber floats. In later years, the craftsmen became varied and numerous— cabinet-makers, upholsterers, daguerreotypers, photographers, circus and theatre companies.

THE THEATRE AFLOAT

Since the time of the Civil War is the elected terminus of this book we cannot go into the more picturesque manifestations of the floating theatre found in the late seventies and early eighties of the last century, but we can show

how these waterway Thespians brought amusement to the people who first made their homes along the rivers of the Middle West.

In the chapter on the circus we have seen Barnum in 1836 purchasing a steamer on the Missouri River and going with his travelling circus to New Orleans, and how before the Civil War both the John Robinson and the Spaulding & Rogers shows toured the rivers of the West with their "Floating Palaces" or show boats. But the first floating theatre brought joy to river dwellers even before that.

Sol Smith tells of an N. M. Ludlow who crossed the Blue Ridge Mountains to the headwaters of the Cumberland in 1817, and there built a sheltered keel boat on which he ran a show that gave performances along the Cumberland, the Ohio, and the Mississippi. This competition roused Sol Smith to get him a floating theatre, and for several years Ludlow and Sol Smith ran competitive shows.

In 1827, ten years after Ludlow launched his first "opera boat," there came to Pittsburgh an English actor, William Chapman, with his family which consisted of six, all actors. There he launched a show boat which, with his family, became famous on the Middle West rivers.

For some years before the Civil War show boats gained a bad reputation as dens of gamblers and prostitutes, and were driven off the river by irate citizens. Not until 1878 did they appear again, when Captain A. B. French started the modern show boat business that still flourishes.

MARITIME PEDDLING

Much of the life of the coast towns and cities of Massachusetts and Connecticut was dependent on the sea. Whereas Connecticut developed its domestic industries earlier than Massachusetts, and whereas both of them supplied many of the goods that went into the packs and carts of the earlier peddlers, still shipping and things concerned with shipping and the sea have always been the staple livelihood

of the coast of these two states. From the first trafficking
with the mother country, the ships went to other British
settlements along the Atlantic seaboard and then to the
colonies in the Caribbean. The story of the beginning of
the coastal commerce of this country is not without its
romance, and, incidentally, it had its phases of itinerant
merchandising.

In the beginning, the location of the Dutch at New
Amsterdam cut off New England from the other British
settlements, and the most feasible method of reaching them,
since roads were practically nil, was by boat.

By 1624, the ship carpenter of the Plymouth Bay settlement had built two shallops, one of which was loaded with
corn after the harvest of 1625, and sent to the Kennebec
River where the cargo was bartered for beaver and other
furs. This was the beginning of the New England coastwise
commerce. By 1627 they had opened trade with the Dutch
and in 1631 the first ship built on this side of the Atlantic,
The Blessing of the Bay, was launched by John Winthrop,
and coastal trade was under way. Virginia corn was brought
to Salem, and in 1633, when a pinnace from Virginia loaded
with cattle and salt sailed into New Amsterdam harbour, it
found there a trading boat from Plymouth—the first of the
great shipping of New York! Three years later at Marblehead is built a ship of 120 tons, *The Dove;* Connecticut builds
a boat called *The Blessing* (quaint names these old fellows
gave their boats!). In the same year Bermuda potatoes
appear in the market. Intercourse with the West Indies
began, and grew apace. Indigo, sugar and salt came up from
these islands, then cotton, tobacco and wine. Before the
Revolution this West Indies trade totalled $18,000,000
a year. Commercial relations began to be extended to
Spain and quite regularly packet ships went to England.
The Barbadoes and Jamaica commerce became the most
profitable trade of the New England colonies. By 1790
Boston was the chief shipping port of the Union. Massachu-

setts was said to have one vessel to every hundred of inhabitants. The Yankee skipper was well known on the high seas.

By the beginning of the eighteenth century the coasting trade was well established not only between the ports of New England, but with the ports of the Southern Provinces. To Virginia and Maryland went salted beef, pork, cod, mackerel, flour, malt, rum, molasses, salt, wine, sugar, the boats bringing back foodstuffs, tar, pitch, and other naval stores. This intercourse served to bind the provinces together, and in later days, when manufacturing reached a prosperous stage, served to carry goods from one section of the seaboard to another.

Trade with the Southern colonies began as early as 1732. In winter, when the ketches and shallops were not being used for fishing, they were headed south by their owners. No wages were paid on these trips, for each man aboard was allowed to carry along and bring home an allotted quantity of cargo. The cargoes ranged all the way from rum, sugar, and molasses that had been brought to New England by boats from the West Indies, to woodenware, iron, hats, caps, stockings and other articles of both domestic and imported manufacture.

These light-draft ships would go up every inhabited inlet and bay of Virginia, Maryland, and South Carolina, drop anchor before a town, and there the members of the crew would barter their individual cargoes for the local products— corn, beans, bacon, hogs, and such. These vessels navigated without orders, since the skipper was usually his own factor, agent, and trader.

And once again we encounter the Yankee peddler's reputation cropping up among these "hucksters of the sea" that went down to the deep on their unlawful occasions. Often the owners of the boats as well as the crew would carry on an illicit barter with plantation slaves for stolen goods, and time and again, misrepresentations were made

and questionable swapping engineered by the sharp Yankees. They would claim to have several grades of rum
for sale, to quote one example, but all the grades would come
out of the same cask. Finally the practice got so flagrant that
the authorities, supported by the complaints of local trades-
men, enacted restrictions that brought this sort of coastal
peddling to an end. In New England restrictions held down
profit on coasting trade to three pence in the shilling, but
once outside the jurisdiction of this law, the Yankee coastal
peddler took all that his wily salesmanship could squeeze out
of a buyer or seller.

One of the Yankee maritime peddling tricks was this:
The New England crew would buy corn of the plantation
owners. The grain was measured on the quarter deck near
the centre. When the measuring commenced, one of the
crew began playing a jig on a violin, and all the spare hands
started dancing vehemently. As the deck was springy, some
of the corn would spill into the scuppers. The percentage of
corn gained by this operation was considerable.

A Virginia statute compelled ships to stop at Jamestown
or other ports before starting to peddle at private river landings. Having passed that inspection and paid the local nominal customs—for trade between the early provinces was
equivalent to trade with a foreign country—the ship could
proceed to its selling. And just as the later store-boats on the
Susquehanna, the Ohio, and the Mississippi would cause a
flutter among the inhabitants, so did these coasting ships
when they neared the landing of a plantation. Some of them
carried mail, and many had implements for the farm and
finery for the women.

It must be remembered that these coastwise boats—both
cargo boats and peddlers—were the means by which manufactured goods were distributed in quantity. Up in Danbury,
Connecticut, old Zadoc Benedict (who fathered the hat industry in that town) would take a cartload of hats down to
Norwalk, where they would go aboard a vessel and be distrib-

uted to merchants all along the coast. Or Richard Wistar of
Alloway, New Jersey, would move a shipment of his glass to
Delaware Bay where a coastwise boat would start its distri-
bution. So Danbury hats would appear in Charleston and
New Jersey glass in Connecticut.

CHAPTER XVII

CARRIERS OF GOODS AND THE MAIL

SO VERY much are we dependent on the mail that we cannot conceive of living for months and literally years without receiving a letter. Yet that is precisely what hundreds and thousands of isolated people did in the beginning years of this country. Nor was the absence of mail any great hardship. Quantities of people could neither read nor write; of what value were letters to them? And, besides, they weren't accustomed to receiving or even expecting letters. They may have been concerned with what went on in their immediate neighbourhood or in neighbouring towns, but curiosity did not lead their interest further. Not until after the War of 1812 did a national consciousness appear in this country, and even then it affected the scattered country folk very little. What news they received came by the occasional paper or by the lips and hands of travellers and wandering traders.

But, say you were a love-lorn maiden, the delight of whose eyes dwelt twenty or thirty miles down the valley; or, say you were a farmer with a granary full of wheat ready to sell, and desirous of finding out the current prices in the nearest centre; how would those personal, individual messages get back and forth? They would be carried by travellers going that way, or, in case of necessity, by a special messenger, who was given food and lodging for his services. Every one who went upon the road bore messages. When a traveller packed his saddle-bags or a peddler his pack, he put in the missives entrusted to him. And you could rest assured, if you lived in those primitive frontier days, that they would be delivered.

Important state documents and the correspondence of influential city merchants were dispatched by special messenger. Thus in Maryland official papers were entrusted to the sheriff of one county who carried them to the sheriff of the next, and so on until they reached their final destination. Letters marked "For the Publique Service" were carried from one plantation to another, being re-directed by each recipient. He who failed to play his part in this chain was fined one hogshead of tobacco for each default. In 1661 a Virginia law required that "when there is any person in the family where the letter comes, as can write, such person is required to endorse the day and houre he received them, that the neglect or contempt of any person stopping them may be better known and punished accordingly." Even at this early date the mail had assumed a sacrosanct air.

The first postmaster general of whom we have record was Thomas Neale, in 1693, appointed not only for Virginia but for all other parts of North America. Rather an ambitious field! His position was established by royal patent and the House of Burgesses further supported him by stating that he should receive three pence for every letter not exceeding one sheet and not directed to or from a place exceeding four score English miles away. By 1706 the mail was forwarded eight times a year from Philadelphia to the Potomac, but the post rider never left Philadelphia until he had enough letters to cover the expenses of his journey.

In Massachusetts the General Court in 1639 appointed Richard Fairbanks of Boston the local postmaster. Letters were deposited with him and he dispatched them by travellers. His pay for this service was one penny per letter. By 1674 post riders appeared, and were granted three pence per mile for their services. Moreover, no innkeeper could charge them more than two shillings a bushel for oats and four pence for hay, whether they reached the inn by day or in the dead of night. While most of these early carriers bore the mail in saddle bags, there were some who kept it in a little tin box. January 1, 1673, saw the first regular mail between Boston and New York. The rider carried two "port mantles" filled with letters and small packages.

17

Mail was very expensive in those early days, which may account for the fact that few of the ordinary people used it. Over £2 per letter was the rate from Boston to Portland, Maine. No wonder the first mail carried between these two towns totalled only five letters! By 1775 the rates had dropped from the luxury class to something nearer the average pocketbook—5¼d for sixty miles, 8d for sixty to 100, 10½d for 100 to 200, and one shilling, one penny for 200 to 300 miles.

Some of these riders covered great distances, and at a time when roads offered scarcely any going at all. Forty miles a day in summer, and into the final town on the dot of the hour! In autumn or winter, when the roads were bad, no such schedule could be maintained—if the rider did twenty miles he was lucky. In the north he was often obliged to cover his route on snow shoes.

By 1787 many of these riders began using wagons or post-chaises, thereby permitting them to carry more mail and to take along a passenger who added to their profits. By 1820 a regular mail coach appeared on New England roads.

The General Congress of 1775 appointed Benjamin Franklin Postmaster General, and decreed that a line of posts should be established from Falmouth, Maine, to Savannah, Georgia. By August 30, 1776, we find Congress requiring that "there be employed on the public post roads, a rider for every twenty-five or thirty miles, whose business it shall be to proceed through his stage three times in every week." If a town happened to be on a post road, then mail came regularly and under government supervision; if it was off the road, then the mail was brought by a carrier supported by the townsfolk. In September, 1786, the Postmaster General was ordered to contract "for the conveyance of the mails by stage carriages." Thus public transportation was first used for carrying the mail, just as the railroads are used to-day.

By 1780 not only were letters carried by the post riders,

HEADING FROM "THE BOSTON WEEKLY POST-BOY"
First printed in October, 1734, by Ellis Huske
Postmaster of Boston

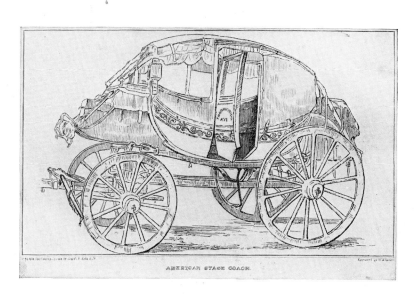

AMERICAN STAGE COACH.

THE MAIL COACH

The Fliers of the Past

but newspapers also began to appear in his sack. And thereby hangs an interesting sidelight on the early postmasters in cities. The job was especially sought after by printers and owners of newspapers. Mail riders were literally newsboys and subscription agents. Two Boston papers frankly called themselves the *Post-Boy and Advertiser* and *The Boston Weekly Post-Boy*. The latter was founded in 1734 by Ellis Huske who had just been appointed postmaster of Boston. In 1719 when William Brooke was appointed postmaster he started publishing the *Boston-Gazette*, and four Boston postmasters in succession were proprietors of this newspaper. Also consider this advertisement in the *Independent Chronicle* of Boston in February 17, 1780:—

> "Samuel Bean, Post Rider from Boston to London-derry, informs his customers that the time for which he engaged to ride expires the last week in this month. He purposes to ride another Quarter, which will begin the first week in March. The price will be Sixteen Dollars in Cash or half a bushel of Rye or three Pecks of Indian Corn for three months, which is as cheap as they were before the war. As there are about a Hundred, exclusive of those who agreed to pay him in Grain who had the paper the last quarter and have not yet paid him, he hopes they will settle the same immediately. He would also inform them that if they aren't more punctural in Payment he must quit riding at the end of the ensuing Quarter. As it is uncertain what numbers of Papers to be engaged for with the Printer, he hopes all who intend to become Subscribers will immediately give in their names."

Before 1833 newspapers were delivered to subscribers. Not until after that date did street vending of them become common.

These pre-Revolutionary post riders were a fine, picturesque lot. When they entered a town they awoke the inhabitants with long blasts of a horn, and some riders, realizing the importance of their position, used to shout "Open the gate for the King's Post." They also seem to have been an especially long-lived crew. Some kept on their routes forty or fifty years, with never a break, winter or summer, through mud and over mountains, through raging torrents and desolate forests. They were obliged to take a tremendous oath, swearing "by the Everlasting God" to carry the mail safely. Their fidelity to the mail they carried was evidently the foundation for that respect the American people have always had for the mail until the banditry of the past few years lessened our reverence.

In Virginia and the Carolinas negroes were not entrusted with the mail, so they took along a white child—usually a small boy—who rode in the cart and who was the nominal guard of the mail bags. In parts of Connecticut the deputy sheriff was the postmaster, and he conveyed letters, packages and prisoners, and served his neighbours with household supplies as cheerily as he served them with warrants.

THE PONY EXPRESS

The recent disregard for the sanctity of the mail was by no means the first attack made upon it, for in the days of the Pony Express, Indians had no compunction about halting the riders, killing them and rifling the pouches.

There was a time when the youth of America used to thrill at tales of the Pony Express, and fine thrills they were too. This mail service between St. Joseph, Missouri, and San Francisco was begun in 1860, and it had for competitors three other mail lines carried by stage coaches across the continent, although the bulk of the mail went by way of Panama and took twenty-two days to reach Frisco. To speed delivery, a private concern, the Overland California and Pike's Peak Express Company, started riders, first weekly, then semi-weekly, with the mail and soon cut down the time between St. Joseph, Missouri, and Frisco to eight days.

The route ran from St. Joseph, which was the western

terminus of the railroad, to Fort Kearney, up the Platte River to Julesburg, to Fort Laramie and Fort Bridger, to Salt Lake City, via Camp Floyd, Ruby Valley, the Humboldt, Carson City, Placerville, and Folsom to Sacramento, and to San Francisco by boat. Every twenty-five miles along this route was a station with a fresh pony or a fresh rider to mount and carry on the mail that a previous rider flung to him. Only two minutes was allowed for the exchange. Each rider covered seventy-five miles a day. He was lightly clad in a hunting shirt, cloth trousers tucked in high boots, and a slouch hat, and he was armed with a brace of army revolvers. In all there were eighty of these riders, paid $100 to $125 a month, and along the route were scattered 500 horses, mostly half-breed California mustangs.

Only ten to fifteen pounds of mail was carried. This was placed in a *mochilla*, a leather saddle cover that could easily be slung from one pony to another. The *mochilla* had four pockets into which the mail, wrapped in oiled silk, was locked. One pocket was left unlocked for *en route* distribution, the others could not be unlocked until an army post or Salt Lake City was reached. Eastern papers used to print special Pony Express editions on tissue paper. In the beginning the charge was $5 for half an ounce besides government postage; later this was reduced to $2.50. The shortest time made by the express was in carrying President Lincoln's inaugural address from St. Joseph to the coast—seven days and seventeen hours.

While many of the riders were pursued and some killed by Indians, their greatest danger came from emigrants who, mistaking them for Indians, shot them out of hand as they streaked by. Indians often attacked and destroyed the exchange posts.

This valiant race of mail carriers was thrown into the discard by October, 1861, when the Pacific Telegraph Company completed stringing its wires across the continent. Meantime the feelers of the railroad started creeping east and west toward each other. Finally the distance was spanned.

CARRIERS OF GOODS

In the story of Pennsylvania's industrial awakening we find references to Juniata iron, and to an iron king of his day —commercial forebear of our Carnegies and Schwabs— Phillip Bumer, who, in 1794, erected a forge at Bellefonte and helped lay the foundation of what is now one of Pennsylvania's chief industries. But between Bellefonte and Pittsburgh, where this iron would reach the headwaters of the Ohio and an easier avenue of transportation, lay a long stretch of rough country. The roads at that time were mere trails. Carts were out of the question. So this Juniata iron went by pack horse.

The rôle these pack horses played in the first overland movements of commerce was vastly important. Usually they went in strings of from ten to twenty, and often several strings at a time, for protection. One driver rode the lead horse, and the others trailed in single file with a rider at the end. Like the cat of the Mother Goose story, the horses wore bells on their collars. At night when the pack train bivouacked, they were turned loose, hobbled with withes, and when time came to corral them in the morning, the bells jangled accommodatingly.

Salt, iron, sugar and other necessities were carried to the scattered settlements of the widening frontiers by these pack trains. On the return trip furs were "packed" back. Sturdy horses these, each carried about 200 pounds. The rate was $3 per hundred.

Though rivalry existed between drivers of pack teams— rivalry that often led to serious clashes—the business was generally in the hands of a few wide-awake business men.

From 1763 on, these pack trains had the choice of two routes to reach Pittsburgh and the headwaters of the Ohio— via Lancaster and Chambersburg, Pennsylvania; and via Virginia by way of Winchester, Hagerstown, and Cumberland. Now and then itinerant traders travelled in strings, vending groceries and other necessary merchandise through the thinly populated country. They took country pay in return. Many of the tinware and other types of early peddlers joined these caravans for protection and company in the solitary stretches. And if they sought company, used as they were to lonely stretches of road, imagine how welcome along the forest trail were the pack trains to those in isolated clearings. They were their sole contact with the outside world.

As the frontiers crept farther and farther west, so did the pack trains. By 1822 we meet the first traders on the Santa Fé trail, crossing the prairie in detached bands, each man with a couple of hundred dollars' worth of stock and headed for the silver mines of what is now Nevada and the trade with Mexicans. Two years later, the business had grown to such proportions that eighty of these pack train traders set forth in a group. Some had pack mules, some stout wagons and carts. This great caravan carried goods valued at $30,000. Subsequent years saw much capital poured into this trade. The homeward trail brought back furs, buffalo rugs, animals, and sometimes specie from the silver mines. Farther north the pack trains trading with the Indians for furs brought back wares of aboriginal manufacture—moccasins, embroidered birch bark boxes and mats that the squaws made, together with corn, beans and wild rice the men gathered.

CONESTOGA WAGONS

In 1789 a venturesome wagon owner with four stout horses headed west for Pittsburgh with 2800 pounds of freight. He took the southern route through Virginia to Brownsville, Pennsylvania. And in doing so he initiated an itinerant industry that thrived for many years in Pennsylvania and was destined to play a major rôle in the prairie country of the West.

Again and again visitors to America in those early days— the thirty years between 1790 and 1820—speak of the great trafficking of these wagon trains—their numbers, their horses

and the vast quantity of goods they carried. Robert Sutcliffe, who travelled here from 1804 to 1806, says that a
thousand of these wagons came to the Philadelphia market.
An older diarist, Johan Schoepf, writing in 1784, puts the
figure at 700, some of them coming from as far as a hundred
miles. H. B. Fearson, who visited here in 1817-18 passed, on
a single stretch of road between Chambersburg and Pittsburgh, about 153 miles, no less than 103 of these wagons.
He also counted two hundred persons on horseback and about
twenty afoot. Quite a busy road for those times.

One would almost think it needed traffic officers. Indeed,
there were times when the traffic did get snarled. The stage
coach always had right of way, then the wagoners. People
afoot and on horseback could turn out into near-by woods
and meadows to avoid these early American traffic jams.

These Conestoga wagons, famed in song and story, first
appeared about 1760. A product of Pennsylvania Dutch
ingenuity they were named after Conestoga in that state.
The underbody was painted blue and the upper woodwork
bright red, and each wagon had a cover of cotton or linen
cloth stretched over big hoops and bleached white in the sun.
Sometimes they travelled in groups of ten or fifteen. The
driver rode one of the horses. On mountain roads a man went
ahead blowing a horn to keep the road clear. On the trip
west they carried woollen, linen, cotton, and silk goods, hardware and other manufactured articles that came from the
factories in Philadelphia or had been shipped down in coasting
steamers from the domestic factories of New England, or
were imported from the other side. On the eastbound trip
they brought back flour and other farm produce.

For passengers these Conestoga wagons offered very crude
transportation. Benches were placed from side to side, and the
fares clambered over them and sat facing the horses. The rear
seat, the only one having a back, was reserved for women.
The top cover offered sufficient protection, save in rainy
weather when leather curtains might be let down the sides.

At first the wagons could go only as far as Lancaster, the terminus of the first turnpike. There the goods were transferred to the backs of pack ponies, and off they would head for Pittsburgh. Later the road was pushed to Carlisle, which then served as transfer point, and finally it was cut all the way to Pittsburgh.

This progress in road building put the pack train men out of business. There was no little hard feeling between them and the Conestoga wagon drivers who usurped their work, and had grown so prosperous and influential that they referred to the Lancaster turnpike as the "Conestoga Road!"

Starting first as individual owners, the wagoners carried on the trade for some time. Then local capitalists amalgamated them, and soon the Line Wagon Company had almost a monopoly of this form of transportation. The company dreamed of making the drivers work in relays, new men going aboard at relief stations, but this failed, and each driver went the whole way with his load and was responsible for its safe delivery and the condition of his team.

And just as better roads made it possible for the Conestoga wagons to supersede the pack trains, so did further progress in transportation put the wagoners out of business. Their lament is contained in the lines quoted at the beginning of Chapter IV. The canals and increased river traffic also lessened the demand for their services. In the early 30's, tracks were laid between Philadelphia and Lancaster, and horses drew cars along them—an effeminate mode of travel. Finally, in 1834, the first locomotive-drawn train pulled out of Philadelphia for Lancaster—and that was the final blow at the noble trade of wagoning. Driven west, it found a second hour of glory when the pioneers crossed the prairies. More, it gave its name to a cigar—the "stogie" that the wagoners used to smoke. Truly, the Conestoga wagon created a noble epic.

It must not be surmised, from the foregoing paragraph that Pennsylvania was the only province that had good roads.

New England developed some passable roads quite early, roads down which the ox carts (or "bull teams" in charge of "bull whackers") of commerce and migration stumbled for many generations. Pennsylvania held the predominance because her turnpikes were the gateway to the West of those days. The South had nothing to compare with them; in fact, up to the Civil War the roads of the South were unspeakable. Robert Sutcliffe, having commented on the heavy traffic of the Lancaster Turnpike, makes an invidious comparison: "The appearance of things in the Slave States is quite the reverse of this. We sometimes meet a ragged black boy or girl driving a team consisting of a lean cow and a mule, sometimes a lean bull or an ox, and I have seen a bull and a cow, each miserable in its appearance, composing one team. . . . . The carriage or wagon appeared in as wretched a condition as the team and its driver." When F. L. Olmsted covered the same regions in 1853-4 he found precisely the same conditions.

TOBACCO ROLLERS

But for all her backwardness in transportation development, the South did offer one variant that had no counterpart in the North—the tobacco rollers of Virginia.

Since tobacco was the main crop of that State, and since the plantations on which it was grown were often located far from waterways, the owners cut through the forest paths that were called tobacco or rolling roads. After curing, the tobacco leaf was packed in huge casks. Into the centre of both heads of each cask was driven a spike that served for an axle. Then shafts were fitted and tied with hickory withes. To the shafts was nailed a box containing provisions and equipment for the journey. Thus accoutred, the tobacco rollers would start to trundle the cask along the crude paths. Sometimes they had to go as far as fifty miles, the journey taking two weeks. A rough, hard-fisted gang of men devoted themselves solely to this work. When darkness came, they made a bivouac, and at the roadside fire fried their bacon and cooked their hoe cake, and slept the sleep of the just.

There is something Titanic about this race of tobacco rollers—their huge and bulging muscles, their grunts, their curses and their constant sweat as they tumbled the casks around tree stumps and through sloughs and over unyielding rocks. They smack of Sisyphus rolling his stone everlastingly uphill. Perhaps one of these days some worthy poet, imbued with the romance of their story and inspired by their magnificent exertions, will give them place in a poetic hall of fame.

STAGE COACH DRIVERS

The stage coach and stage wagon era of America has recently come to life again in the appearance, all over the country, of motor buses. The huge charabanc thundering across country is merely the enlarged, speedier and improved descendant of the rattly and picturesque old stage coach that, once on a day, afforded the only swift means of road transportation. The peak of stage-coach traffic was reached just before the railroads came in. Out of Boston, in 1832, for example ran no fewer than 106 coach lines to all parts of the State and contiguous States. Equally abundant were they in other sections of the country wherever good roads existed.

Such a heavy traffic naturally employed a vast number of men, and they formed a class by themselves almost from the beginning of stage coach days. A rubicund, prosperous lot of fellows. Some of them owned their own coaches, some owned part, and others were merely employed as drivers.

At first the going was very bad and the coaches they drove lacked every semblance of comfort. Benches served for seats; then came in strips of leather for backs, then springs appeared and sometimes the body of the coach was swung on leather straps. Colourful and picturesque, they rumbled over the rough roads, and our ancestors, knowing no better means of conveyance, thought them quite smart.

In addition to his work as driver, the coachman served

also as bearer of messages and money, collector and payer of bills. He wore a large hat, and in it kept his messages. Later on he took to carrying small packages. Simultaneously with the passenger traffic arose lines of wagons that carried only freight and express goods. These coaches ran only on the turnpikes; once off the highway, the goods had to be transferred to a local and often poorer coach, or else packed on horseback or into carts.

When the railroads began to appear, the noble army of coach drivers saw their doom approach. Invariably the price of progress is that someone loses his job. Some of the drivers moved into the frontier areas, and some were employed by the railroad as conductors and brakesmen. In the far West the stage coach and its valiant driver continue up to within the memory of the present generation. And what the driver of the Eastern coaches may have lacked in adventure, was more than made up by the lurid and dangerous experiences that befell many of the men who drove through the Indian countries.

THE EXPRESS MAN

This custom of doing errands and carrying packages that had been the habit of stage coach drivers for fifty years was the inception of a great business. The express man and the various express companies that flourished at one time were the direct outgrowth of this accommodation.

While there is little or no romance about it, save from the commercial viewpoint, the beginning of the express business did have its amusing childhood. In the spring of 1834 the first passenger train ran in New England, and its conductor was one William F. Harnden. He had noticed that some of the erstwhile coach drivers had acquired passes from the railroads and were doing a tidy little business running errands. So, after five years of being a station agent and conductor, it occurred to him to make a regular business of this service. In 1839 he advertised himself as The Express Package Carrier and opened a small office in Boston and another in New York.

His New York office was part of the store in a basement that is now 20 Wall Street. You left your packages at the Boston office and collected them in the New York office. At first all he was asked to carry could be packed in a valise—letters mostly. As the business prospered, he extended his service to Philadelphia, Albany and other cities. At Buffalo he took on Henry Wells. His company activities extended even to England. It was called Harnden & Co.

At the same time Harnden was doing this, Alvin Adams started a rival concern. In 1850 he paid the New York and New Haven Railroad the lordly sum of $1000 a month for space in the car of an express train. Four years later he absorbed Harnden's concern and two other competing express companies and consolidated them into the Adams Express Company.

These were only two of numerous express companies—Wells, Fargo, and such—that sprang up in various parts of the country. One by one they were absorbed until the business was gathered into the hands of two concerns.

And that in barest outline, constitutes the short and simple annals of the express man.

EPILOGUE

HE rolling road moves on, and constantly is its speed changing.

We pass from wayfarers who trudge along labouriously to those who go by horse, and from those who go patiently by horse to those who rumble by in cart and wagon and gig, and, once more, from these to the swift transportation of railroads. Finally the automobile.

Into the weaving tides of the road is thrown this new and flashing colour. Once human endeavour took men whither they would be; to-day vagabondage is carried on by the endeavour of machines.

The articles the peddler sells, the Word the circuit rider preaches, the shows the early actors give, all are creations of human endeavour. These itinerants have scarcely any aid or support from mechanical devices as they follow their several callings along the road. Then the road dives into the dark forest of mechanical thraldom.

For a time these devices seem to dominate man. He is reduced to being merely a minder of machines. Years pass. Gradually he becomes their master. Gradually the rolling, unending road passes from beneath the sinister shadow. The same mechanical development that brings an end to romantic wayfaring returns it to us to-day in fuller measure.

Stand by the road and see this miracle at work.

The poor man takes his numerous and wearied family out of the miasmic tenement into the pure air and sunshine of the country. A rattly, battered automobile bears them there. To the sick afar from help the motor brings the physician quickly. The truck carries foodstuffs and raw goods with which men may work and clothe themselves and build their homes.

At first machines concentrate people into cities, clot them into

*noisome factories. Then other machines take them away from
cities—take them comfortably and with dispatch.*

*These machines are changing the face of the countryside.
The motor that affords means of swift passage along roads also
brings into being better roads. It makes country living not only
possible but eminently desirable. It revives the rich colour and
romance of the old road. The cross-country bus takes up the
work of the lumbering stage coach. The perambulating libraries
serve hungry readers as did once the wandering bookseller and
his tome-stocked cart. Motor theatrical companies bring delight
to country audiences, as the first troupes used to do. Grocery
stores on trucks and the motor wayfaring drygoods salesmen
carry on the necessary service of the Yankee notions peddler. To
a new race of isolated people, these modern itinerants come—
to families voluntarily isolated in country districts, men and
women seeking the solitude of green meadows and unbroken
hills as a surcease from the hectic trafficking of cities.*

*Through the hurrying tides of to-day's traffic weave not only
the ancient ghosts of all the vagrant past but the portendent,
darting shadows of future travel as well.*

*Till now vagabondage has been on one plane. Constantly it
has been in contact with earth. You stand by a road to watch it
pass. To-day the rolling road takes to the clouds. You must
watch the uncharted thoroughfares of the sky to see its wanderers.*

*From behind a cloud zooms the air mail plane carrying its
swift burden from city to city. Its shadow flashes along roads
where once the post boy rode, tooting his horn. Across the sky,
direct and unhindered by mountain pass or raging torrent or
mud-rutted road, sails the plane bearing travellers to whom time
is everything. Its hum drifts down across the lonely stretches
where once passed the early travellers, men and women to whom
time meant nothing.*

Peer ahead into the dawning of the future.

*Workmen fly from job to job. Peddlers go their rounds
awing. Parsons shepherd their scattered sheep from the heavens.*

.... *And into the meadows where once crazy old wanderers scratched figures on pumpkins, where pious crowds gathered for revivals, where peddlers flocked to Muster Days and fairs and vendues, these aerial itinerants come to rest, as a bird flutters down from the star-dusty avenues of the sky.*

In the research and writing of the text of this book and the assembling of its illustrations, I have been generously assisted by innumerable people in various walks of life. So numerous are they that it would be well nigh impossible to set down all their names in this limited space. I can only choose a few whose continued interest and suggestions have made the book possible. Mr. Samuel Hopkins Adams, Dr. James Truslow Adams, Dr. Arthur Adams of Trinity College, Mr. Elmer Adler, Professor Irving Brown of Columbia University, Mr. Albert C. Bates of the Hartford Athenaeum, Mr. George S. Bryant, Mr. Lucius B. Barber, Mrs. John P. Bainbridge, Mr. W. N. C. Carleton of Williams University, Mr. Walter Dyer, Mr. Fred Dayton, Miss Nellie Haskell, Mr. J. B. Kerfoot, Miss Nancy McClelland, Mr. Edmund Lester Pearson, Miss Gertrude Whiting, Mr. and Mrs. William Jay Robinson, Mr. Walker Lewis Stephen, Professor Odell Shepherd of Trinity College, Mr. John Spargo, Mr. Henry Shoemaker, and Miss Eola Willis. Since some parts of these pages have appeared in *House and Garden*, which it is my privilege to edit, I am indebted to Mr. Condé Nast for permission to reprint them. To Amory Brown & Co., I am indebted for permission to reproduce the *toile* that serves for end papers to this book. To Mr. Richard Ferris and Mr. Montrose J. Moses I am deeply indebted for advice on the research, and to Mr. Charles K. Bolton of the Boston Atheneum and the Rev. Glenn Tilley Morse, for permission to use old prints from their collections. And to many correspondents—descendants of peddlers and peddlers themselves —I owe deep gratitude for their quaint recollections.

R. W.

SILVER MINE
CONNECTICUT
1 OCTOBER, 1926

BIBLIOGRAPHY

NOTE: Roman numerals indicate the chapters containing material found in the following volumes:

A

Abbot, W. T.—"The Story of the Merchant Marine." 1919. XVI.

Adams, J. T.—"New England in the Republic." 1926. II.

Adams, J. T.—"Revolutionary New England." 1923. II.

Adams, J. T.—"The Founding of New England." 1920. II.

Allen, E. B.—"Early American Wall Paintings." 1926. IX.

"American Historical Record," Vol. I. 1872. XVI.

"American Antiquarian Society," Vol. XI. 1896. III.

American Tract Society—"General View of Colportage." N. d. X.

Anburey, F.—"Travels Through the Interior Parts of America." 1789. I.

Anderson, J.—"The Town and City of Waterbury, Connecticut." 3 vols. 1896. V, VII, VIII, XII, XIII.

Andrews, C. M.—"Colonial Commerce," in "American Historical Review." Vol. XX. 1915.

Andrews, C. M.—"Colonial Folkways." 1919. I, V, VII, IX.

Andrews, C. M.—"The Colonial Period." 1912. I.

Appleton's "Cyclopædia of American Biography."

Arfwedson, C. D.—"The United States and Canada in 1832, 1833 and 1834." 1834. XV.

Arnold, S. G.—"History of the State of Rhode Island." 1894. VI.

Asbury, F.—"The Journal of the Revolution." 3 vols. 1821. X.

Atwater, F.—"History of the Town of Plymouth." 1895. V.

Atwater, F.—"Memoirs of." 1922. III.

B

Babson, J. J.—"History of the Town of Gloucester, Etc." 1860. X, XVI.

Bailey, J. M.—"History of Danbury, Connecticut." 1896. II, XII.

Bailey, S. L.—"Historical Sketches of Andover, Massachusetts." 1889. XI, XVII.

Bailey, W. F.—"The Pony Express," in Century Magazine. Oct., 1898. XVII.

Bangs, N.—"The Life of the Rev. Freeborn Garrettson." 1852. X.

Barber, E. A.—"American Glassware, Old and New." 1900. IV.

Barber, J. W.—"Connecticut Historical Collections." 1838.

Barber, J. W.—"History and Antiquities of New Haven, Connecticut." 1856. XV.

Barnum, P. T.—"Struggles and Triumphs." 1876. XIII.

"Barnstead, History of." XIV.

Barry, J. S.—"Historical Sketch of the Town of Hanover, Massachusetts." 1853. VII, XI.

Bartram, W.—"Travels Through North and South Carolina, Georgia, East and West Florida, Etc." 1791.

Bayles, W. H.—"Old Taverns of New York." 1915. I.

Bidwell, P. W.—"Rural Economy in New England at the Beginning of the Nineteenth Century," in Transactions of the Connecticut Academy of Arts and Sciences. Vol. XX.

Bishop, J. L.—"History of American Manufacturers." 1864. II.

Blitz, Signor—"Fifty Years in the Magic Circle." 1872. XII.

Bogart, E. L.—"Economic History of the United States." 1912. II, VII.

Bolton, E. S.—"Wax Portraits and Silhouettes." 1914. IX.

Bolton, T.—"Early American Portrait Draughtsmen in Crayons." 1923. IX, XII.

Bourne, E. E.—"The History of Wells and Kennebunk." 1875. XI, XVII.

Bozman, J. L.—"History of Maryland." 1837. II.

Brace, C. L.—"The Dangerous Classes of New York." 1880. IV, XV.

Brearley, E. C.—"Time Telling Through the Ages." 1919. V.

Breckenridge, Mrs. F. A.—"Recollections of a New England Town." 1899.

Bronson, H.—"History of Waterbury, Connecticut." 1858. I, IV, V.

Brooks, E.—"My Schools and Schoolmasters," in Educational Review. Nov., 1901. XI.

Brooks, H. M.—"Olden Time Music." 1888. XI.

Brophy, T. W.—"Progress of Dentistry in America." The Making of America. Vol. VII. 1906. VIII.

Brown, I.—"Gypsy Fires in America." 1924. XIV.

Brown, W. H.—"The History of the First Locomotive in America." 1874. IX.

Brownson, M. G.—"Life of Demetrius Augustine Gallitzin." X.

Bruce, P. A.—"Economic History of Virginia in the 17th Century." 1896.

Bryant, G. S.—"Old Bet and the Origin of the American Circus," in Dearborn Independent. Feb. 25, 1922. XII.

Buckingham, J. S.—"America: Historical, Statistic and Descriptive," 3 vols. 1841. XIV.

Buckingham, J. T.—"Specimens of Newspaper Literature." 2 vols. 1850. IV, XVII.

Burroughs, S.—"Memoirs of the Notorious." 1926. XIV.

Burton, W.—"The District School as it Was." 1833. XI.

Byrne, M. St. C.—"Elizabethan Life in Town and Country." 1926. XIV.

C

Cable, S. H.—"Rise of Religious Liberty in America." 1902. X.

Camp, David N.—"History of New Britain, Connecticut, 1640-1889." 1889. II, IV.

Campbell, T. J.—"The Jesuits, 1534–1921." 1921. X.

Carroll, B. R.—"Historical Collections of South Carolina," 2 vols. 1836. IV, XI, XIII.

Cartright, P.—"Autobiography." 1857. X.

Carver, J.—"Travels Through the Interior Parts of North America in the Years 1766, 1767, and 1768." 1778.

Caulkins, F. M.—"History of New London, Connecticut." 1860. XVI.

Chase, G. W.—"History of Haverhill, Massachusetts." 1861. I, IV, VII, XVII.

Chastellux, Marquis de—"Travels in North America, 1780–81–82." 1827. I, III, IV, XIV.

" City Crier, or A Peep at Scenes in Town." 1850. XV.

Clark, V. S.—"History of Manufactures in the United States, 1607–1860." 1916. II, III.

Clayton, W. W.—"History of Onondaga County, New York." 1878.

Coad, O. S.—"William Dunlap." 1917. XIII.

Cobb, S. H.—"The Rise of Religious Liberty in America." 1902. X.

Cobbett, Wm.—"A Year's Residence in the United States of America." 1822.

Cogswell, L. W.—"History of the Town of Henniker, New Hampshire." 1880. III, XII.

Cogswell, W. T.—"History of Rockville, Connecticut, 1823–1871." 1872.

"Colonial Records of South Carolina." V.

Coman, K.—"Economic Beginnings of the Far West." 1912.

Commons, J. R.—"American Shoemakers, 1647–1895," in Quarterly Journal of Economics. Nov., 1909. VII.

Commons, J. R.—"History of Labor in the United States." 1918. VII.

Conklin, G.—"The Ways of the Circus." 1921. III, XIII.

"Connecticut, History of," edited by N. G. Osborn. 5 vols. 1925. III.

"Connecticut Courant."

"Connecticut Magazine, The."

Cook, J. F.—"Old Kentucky." 1908. I, VIII, XVII.

"Cries of New York." 1814. XV.

Crissey, J. W.—"History of Norfolk, Connecticut, 1744–1900." 1900.

Creswell, N.—"The Journal of Nicholas Creswell, 1774–1777." 1924. I.

Cushing, Wm.—"Yale Law Journal." Dec., 1920. VIII.

D

Daggett, J.—"History of Attleborough, Massachusetts." 1894. III.

Davis, C. H. S.—"History of Wallingford and Meriden, Connecticut." 1870. III.

Davis, James F.—"Tom Shows," in Scribner's Magazine. April, 1925. XIII.

Davis, John—"Travels of Four and a Half Years in the United States of America." 1803. II, XIII, XIV.

Dean, S.—"History of Scituate, Massachusetts." 1831. XI.

De Forest, J. R.—"Olden Times in New York." 1833. XV.

"Delaware Historical and Biographical Papers." Vol. III. XV.

Denison, F. D.—"Westerly (R. I.) and Its Witnesses, 1626–1876." 1878. VIII, XI, XII, XIV.

Depew, C. M.—"One Hundred Years of American Commerce." 1895. III.

De Roos, Lt. F. F.—"Personal Narrative of Travels in the United States and Canada in 1826." 1827.

Devol, G.—"Forty Years a Gambler on the Mississippi." 1926. XIV.

Dixon, W. H.—"New America." 1867. X.

Dow, L.—"History of Cosmopolite." 1857. X.

Drake, D.—"Pioneer Life in Kentucky." 1870. VII.

Drake, S. G.—"The History and Antiquities of the City of Boston." 1854.

Drinker, E.—"Extracts from the Diary of." 1889.

Dunbar, S.—"History of Travel in America." 4 vols. 1915. XVI.

Duncan, J. M.—"Travels Through Part of the United States and Canada in 1818 and 1819." 2 vols. 1825. II.

Dunlap, Wm.—"History of the American Theater." 1833. XIII.

Dunlap, Wm.—"History of the Art of Design in America." 1834. IX.

Dunton, J.—"Letters Written from New England." 1686. III.

Dwight, T.—"Travels in New England and New York." 4 vols. 1825. I, V.

Dyer, W.—"Early American Craftsmen." 1915. IX.

E

Eames, W.—"Early New England Catechism," American Antiquary Society Publications. Oct., 1897. IV.

Earle, A. M.—"Colonial Dames and Good Wives." 1900. IV, VII.

Earle, A. M.—"Costume of Colonial Times." 1894. III, IV, VII.

Earle, A. M.—"Home Life in Colonial Days." 1899. III, IV, V.

Earle, A. M.—"Stage Coach and Tavern Days." 1900. I, IV, XII.

Eberlein, H. D.—"Practical Book of Early American Arts and Crafts." 1916. IX.

Elliot, C. W.—"The New England History." 1858. X.

Elwood, G. M.—"Some Earlier Public Amusements of Rochester." 1894. XII.

Everest, C. W.—"The Poets of Connecticut." 1860. I, V.

F

Faris, J. T.—"Old Roads Out of Philadelphia." 1917. II, XVII.

Faris, J. T.—"When America Was Young." 1925. XVII.

Featherstonhaugh, J. W.—"Excursion Through the Slave States." 1844. V.

Felt, J. B.—"Annals of Salem." 1845. XII, XV, XVII.

Felt, J. B.—"History of Ipswich." 1834. XVI.

Ferris, B.—"History of the Original Settlements on the Delaware." 1845. IV, XV.

Field, E.—"The Colonial Tavern." 1897. I.

Fferth, J.—"The Experience and Gospel Labors of the Rev. Benjamin Abbott." 1825. X.

Fisher, S. G.—"Men, Women, and Manners in Colonial Times." 1898. XII.

Fisher, S. G.—"The Making of Pennsylvania." 1896. VII, VIII.

Fithian, P. V.—"Journal and Letters," edited by J. R. Williams. 1900. XI.

Flanders, H.—"The Lives and Times of the Chief Justices of the Supreme Court of the United States." 1858. VIII.

Flint, J.—"Letters from America." 1822. XVII.

Flynt, Josiah—"How Men Become Tramps," in Century Magazine. Oct., 1895. XIV.

Flynt, Josiah—"The American Tramp," in Contemporary Review. Aug., 1891. XIV.

Foerster, R. F.—"Italian Emigration of Our Times." 1919. XV.

Ford, H. J.—"The Scotch-Irish in America." 1915. XV.

Fowler, W. C.—"History of Durham, Connecticut." 1866.

Francis, J. W.—"New York During the Last Half Century." 1857. XIV.

Fraser, E. S.—"Pennsylvania German Painted Chests," in Philadelphia Museum Bulletin. Nov., 1925. IX.

Freeman, F.—"The History of Cape Cod." 1860. XV, XVI, XVII.

French, H. W.—"Art and Artists in Connecticut." 1879. IX.

Fuller, O. P.—"The History of Warwick, Rhode Island." 1875. XII.

Furman, G.—"Antiquities of Long Island." 1875. XVII.

G

Gaines, H.—"Journal," edited by P. L. Ford. 1902. VII.

Gold, T. S.—"Historical Records of the Town of Cornwall, Connecticut." 1877.

Goodrich, M.—"Historical Sketch of the Town of Pawtucket." 1878. XV.

Goodwin, M. M.—"The Colonial Cavalier." 1895. XVI, XVII.

Grafton, C. T.—"Civilized America." 1859.

Grant, Mrs. A.—"Memoirs of an American Lady." 1908. XV.

Greene, M. L.—"The Development of Religious Liberty in Connecticut." 1905. X.

Greenwood, I.—"The Circus: Its Origin and Growth Prior to 1835." 1909. XIII.

Griffith, R.—"Skilled Labor: The Puritan Heritage." 1924. VII.

Griffith, T. W.—"Annals of Baltimore." 1824. XVI.

Gross, J.—"Five Years in the Alleghanies." 1863.

Guilday, P.—"Life and Times of John Carroll." 1922. X.

H

Hadcock, G.—"Incidents in the Life of,—Ex-Professional Wood Sawyer." 1846. VII.

Halbeck, E. S.—"The American Circus," in Century Magazine. Aug., 1905. XIII.

Haliburton, T. C.—"The Clockmaker; or Sayings and Doings of Samuel Slick of Slickville." 1840. V.

Hall, A. N.—"The Old Wholesale Peddler," in New England Magazine. Aug., 1900. V.

Hall, Basil—"Forty Sketches." 1828.

Hall, A. O.—"A Manhattaner in New Orleans." 1851. XV.

Hamilton, A.—"Hamilton's Itinerarium," edited by A. B. Hart. 1907.

Hamilton, T.—"Men and Manners in America." 1833. I.

Hanna, C. A.—"The Wilderness Trail." 1911. I, XVII.

Hawthorne, N.—"Passages from the American Note Books." 2 vols. 1868. III, IV, VIII, XV.

Hazard, B. E.—"The Organization of the Boot and Shoe Industry in Massachusetts Before 1875," in Quarterly Journal of Economics. 1909. VII.

Hazard, T. R.—"The Jonny-Cake Papers." 1915.

Hazeltine, G. W.—"Early History of Ellicott, New York." 1887. IV, XIV.

Headley, J. T.—"The Chaplains and Clergy of the Revolution." 1864. X.

Heartman, C. T.—"The New England Primer Issued Prior to 1830." 1915. III.

Herbermann, C. G.—"The Sulpicians in the United States." 1916. X.

Hiltzheimer, J.—"Extracts from the Diary of Jacob Hiltzheimer." 1893. XII.

Hitchcock, Prof. R. D.—"An Address on Colportage." 1855. X.

Hodgson, A.—"Letters from North America." 1824.

Holliday, C.—"Woman's Life in Colonial Days." 1922. VII.

Houston, F.—"St. Memin," in House and Garden. Dec., 1924. IX.

Howe, H.—"Historical Collections of Virginia." 1845.

Hughes, S. E.—"History of East Haven." 1908. IX.

Hunt, T.—"Lives of American Merchants." 1855. V.

I

Iredell, J.—"University of Pennsylvania Law Review." Vol. 60. 1912. VIII.

J

Jacobson, A. C.—"The Earliest Manhattan Practitioners." VIII.

Jameson, J. F.—"The American Sancta Sanctorum in America," in Historical Review. Jan., 1908. X.

Jelliffe, S. E.—"Dutch Physicians in New Amsterdam." 1908. VIII.

Jerome, C.—"History of the American Clock Business." V.

Johnson, A.—"Connecticut." 1891. I.

Johnson, E. R.—"Ocean and Inland Water Transportation." 1906. XVI.

Jones, F. R.—"History of Taxation in Connecticut, 1636–1776." 1896. VI.

Judd, S.—"History of Hadley, Massachusetts." 1904. III, IV, VII.

K

Keir, R. M.—"The Tin Peddler," in Journal of Political Economy. Vol. 21. 1912. V.

Keir, R. M.—"The Unappreciated Tin Peddler," in Annals of American Academy of Political and Social Science. Vol. 46. 1912. V.

Kemble, F. A.—"Journal of a Residence on a Georgia Plantation in 1838–9." 1863. X.

Kemp, William—"Nine Daies Wonder." 1600. XI.

Kendall, E. A.—"Travels Through the Northern Part of the United States in the Years 1807–1808." 1809. II.

Kerfoot, J. B.—"American Pewter." 1924. VII.

King, J.—"Creole Families of New Orleans." 1921. III, XV.

King, J.—"New Orleans." 1895. XV.

Kinzie, Mrs. J. H.—"Wau-bun." 1856. XV.

Kittredge, G. H.—"The Old Farmer and His Almanac." 1904. IV.

Knight, Sarah Kemble—"Private Journal." 1704. III.

Kohler, M. J.—"The German-Jewish Migration to America." Pub. Amer. Jewish Historical Society. Vol. 1909–10. VI.

L

"Lancaster County, Pennsylvania, Historical Society, Proceedings." IX.

Lang, W.—"History of Seneca County, Ohio." 1880.

Lanman, C.—"Adventures in the Wilds of the United States." 1856.

Larned, E. D.—"History of Windham County, Connecticut." 1880. IX.

La Rochefoucauld—"Travels in North America." 1799. XI.

Lathrop, W. G.—"The Brass Industry in Connecticut." 1909. V.

Latrobe, C. J.—"The Rambler in North America." 1836. II.

"Laws of New Hampshire Enacted Since June 1, 1815." 1824. VI.

Leavitt, M. B.—"Fifty Years in Theatrical Management." 1912. XII.

Lee, J.—"A Short History of the Methodists in the United States of America." 1810. X.

Leeth, J.—"A Short Biography of." 1831.

Lewis, A.—"History of Lynn." 1829. XI.

Lincoln, C. H.—"The Revolutionary Movement in Pennsylvania." 1901. I, VI.

Lincoln, G.—"History of the Town of Hingham, Massachusetts." 1893. III.

Lippincott, H. M.—"Early Philadelphia." 1917. XII.

Little, W.—"History of Weare, New Hampshire, 1735–1865." 1888. I, III, V, IX.

Lyell, C.—"A Second Visit to the United States of North America." 1849. XII, XV, XVI.

M

Mackay, A.—"The Western World." 1850.

Macy, O.—"History of Nantucket." 1835.

Marcosson, I.—"The Autobiography of a Clown." 1910. XIII.

Marryat, Capt.—"Diary in America." 1839.

Martineau, H.—"Society in America." 1837.

Massachusetts Historical Collections, Vol. 69—"Commerce of Rhode Island." 1914. XVI.

Mavor, J.—"An Economic History of Russia." 1916. VI.

McCall, H.—"History of Georgia." 1909.

McDonald, J. J.—"Life in Old Virginia." 1907. XVII.

McRee, G. J.—"Life and Correspondence of James Iredell." 1858. VIII.

Mease, J.—"The Picture of Philadelphia." 1811.

Melish, J.—"Travels in the United States, 1806-07, 1809–11." 1812.

Mercer, H. C.—"The Survival of the Mediæval Art of Illuminating Writing Among the Pennsylvania Germans." 1897. IX.

Merrill, E. M. H.—"Cambridge Sketches." 1896. XI, XV.

Milham, W. J.—"Time and Timekeepers." 1923. V.

"Montgomery County, Pennsylvania, Historical Society, Proccedings." VII.

Montgomery, G.—"Recollections of Wilmington, Delaware." 1851. XV.

Moore, J. R. H. "An Industrial History of the American People." 1913. VII.

Moore, M. H.—"Old Clock Book." 1911. V.

Mumford, J. G.—"A Narrative of Medicine in America." 1903. VIII.

Murray, C. F.—"On the Road with the Big Show," in Cosmopolitan. June, 1900. XIII.

N

Nevin, A.—"American Social History as Recorded by British Travelers." 1923.

"New York Journal of Medicine." Vol. 49. VIII.

Niles, J. M. and J. C. Pease—"A Gazetteer of the States of Connecticut and Rhode Island." 1819. XVI.

North, C. M.—"History of Berlin, Connecticut." 1916. V.
Nutting, W.—"The Clock Book." 1924. VII.

O

O'Brien, F. M.—"The Story of the Sun." 1918. XVII.
O'Daniel, V. F.—"Life of Bishop Fenwick." 1920. X.
O'Fallon, J. M.—"The Work of the Birmingham Jewelers," in The Art Journal. 1894. III.
O'Reilly, H.—"Sketches of Rochester." 1838. XII.
Olmsted, F. L.—"A Journey in the Back Country." 1860. I, III.
Olmsted, F. L.—"A Journey in the Seaboard Slave States." 1863. IV, XVI.
Orcutt, S.—"History of the Old Town of Stratford, and the City of Bridgeport, Connecticut." 1856. XIII, XV, XVII.
Orcutt, S.—"History of Torrington, Connecticut." 1878.
Orcutt, S.—"History of the Town of Wolcott, Connecticut, From 1731–1874." 1874. I.

P

Packard—"History of Medicine in the United States." VIII.
Parkman, E.—"Diary of." 1899. III.
Parkman, F.—"Old Regime in Canada." 1874. I.
Pattee, W. S.—"A History of Old Braintree and Quincy." 1878. IV, V, VII.
"Pennsylvania Magazine." Vol. X. 1886. VII, XII.
"Pennsylvania Provincial Accounts." Folio 2014. VI.
"Penny Magazine." July 15, 1837. I.
"Pocumtuck Valley Memorial Association—History and Proceedings." Vol. IV. 1905. IV.
"Public Records of the Colony of Connecticut." 1872. VI.
"Push Cart Markets in New York City." 1925. VI, XV.
Pynchon, W.—"Diary of." 1890. XII, XV.

R

Ralph, J.—"A Trip with a Tin Peddler," in Harper's Magazine. Apr., 1905. I.
Religious Magazine, Jan., 1872—"A Singing School Fifty Years Ago." XI.

Religious Magazine, 1861—"History of the Oxford Singing School." XI.

"Report on Manufactures, 1810," American State Papers. V, VI.

Richards, C. C.—"Village Life in America." 1913. VII.

Rishel, C. D.—"The Life and Adventures of David Lewis." 1890. XIV.

Roads, S., Jr.—"History and Traditions of Marblehead." 1897. VII, XV.

Robin, A.—"New Travels Through North America." 1783.

Rogers, H. C.—"History of the Town of Paris and Valley of the Sauquoit." 1881. I, III, V, VIII, XVII.

Rowland, S. J.—"Street Cries of Philadelphia." 1922. XV.

Russell, C. E.—"These Shifting Scenes." 1914. VII.

Russell, G.—"Early Medicine and Early Medicine Men in Connecticut. 1893. VIII.

S

Sachse, J. F.—"The Religion and Social Conditions of Philadelphia." 1900. XII.

Sanborn, F. B., and W. T. Harris—"A. Bronson Alcott." 1903. I.

Scharf, J. F.—"History of Philadelphia." 1834.

Schlesinger, A. M.—"The Colonial Merchant and the American Revolution." 1917. I, IV.

Schoonmaker, M.—"History of Kingston, New York." 1888.

"Scotch-Irish Society, Proceedings of." XV.

Seabury, W. T.—"Memoirs of Bishop Seabury." 1908.

Shoemaker, H. W.—"Gypsies and Gypsy Lore in the Pennsylvania Mountains. 1924. XV.

Shoemaker, H. W.—"The Music and Musical Instruments of the Pennsylvania Mountaineers." 1924. XV.

Simms, J. R.—"History of Schoharie County, New York." 1845. XV.

Simson, Walter—"A History of the Gypsies." 1866. XIV.

Singleton, E.—"Social New York Under the Georges." 1902. XV.

Smith, E. R.—"Johnny Appleseed." 1916. XIV.

Smith, E. V.—"History of Newburyport, Massachusetts." 1854. I.

Smith, H. E.—"Colonial Days and Ways." 1900. VII.

Smith, S.—"Theatrical Management in the West and South for Thirty Years." 1868. XIII.

Sonneck, O. G.—"Early Opera in America." 1915. XI.

Sonneck, O. G.—"Francis Hopkins and James Lyon." 1905. XI.

Spaulding, M. T.—"Benedict Flaget." 1852. X.

Steiner, B. C.—"A History of the Plantation of Menunkatuck." 1897.

Steiner, W. R.—"First Physicians in America," American History. Vol. I. VIII.

Stiles, E.—"Literary Diary of," edited by F. B. Dexter. 3 vols. 1901.

Stiles, H. R.—"Bundling; Its Origin, Progress and Decline in America." 1871. X.

Stiles, H. R.—"History of Ancient Wethersfield, Connecticut." 1904.

Stimson, A. L.—"History of the Express Business." 1881. XVII.

Stone, W. L.—"Matthias and His Impostures." 1835. XIV.

Stout, W. W.—"Tonight at the River Landing," in Saturday Evening Post. Oct. 31, 1925. XVI.

Sutcliffe, R.—"Travels in Some Parts of America in the Years 1804–1805–1806." 1811. X, XVI.

Sweet, W. W.—"Circuit Rider Days in Indiana." 1916. X.

Sylvester, N. B.—"History of the Connecticut Valley in Massachusetts." 1879. XVI.

Sylvester, N. B.—"History of Saratoga County, New York." 1878.

T

Taylor, F. R.—"Life of William Savery." 1925. X.

Teall, G.—"Silhouettes, Old and New," in House and Garden. Aug., 1916. IX.

Thanet, O.—"The Tramp in Four Centuries," in Lippincott's Magazine. 1879. XV.

Thomas, A. C.—"History of Pennsylvania." 1913. XVII.

Thomas, G.—"An Account of Pennsylvania and West New Jersey." 1698. VII, X.

Thomas, I.—"History of Printing in America." 1874. VII.

Thwaites, R. G.—"Early Western Travels." 38 vols. 1904, 1905. XVI.

Thwaites, R. G.—"On the Storied Ohio." 1903. XVI.

Trollope, Mrs. F. M.—"Domestic Manners of the Americans." 1901. X, XV.

Tryon, R. M.—"Household Manufactures in the United States, 1840–1860." 1917. II, V.

Twain, Mark—"Life on the Mississippi." 1883. XVI.

U

Updike, W.—"Memoirs of the Rhode Island Bar." 1842. VIII.

V

Valentine, D. J.—"Manual of the Corporation of the City of New York." 1857.

Van Metre, T. W.—"History of Domestic and Foreign Commerce of the United States." 1915. II, XVI.

"Virginia Historical Magazine." Vol. 3. 1896. XVI.

Visscher, W. L.—"The Pony Express." 1908. XVII.

W

Walsh, J. J.—"Cures." 1925. VIII.

Walton, P.—"Comb Making in America." 1925. III.

Wansey, H.—"An Excursion to the United States of North America in the Summer of 1794." 1798.

Ward, E.—"A Trip to New England, 1682–1699." 1905. I.

Warren, C.—"A History of the American Bar." 1911. VIII.

Watson, E.—"Men and Times of the Revolution." 1856. XVI.

Watson, J. F.—"Annals of Philadelphia." 1830. VIII, XI, XII.

Watson, J. F.—"Historic Tales of Old Times." 1852. VIII, XI.

Watson, J. F.—"Annals of New York." 1846. XIV.

Weeden, W. B.—"Early Rhode Island." 1910. VII.

Weeden, W. B.—"Economic and Social History of New England." 1891. II, III, IV, V.

Westcott, T.—"Life of John Fitch." 1857. VII.

White, B.—"The Book of Daniel Drew." 1910. VII.

White's "Cyclopedia of American Biography." 1914. XIII.

Willard, J. W.—"A History of Simon Willard." 1911. V.

"William and Mary, History of the College of." 1874. VI.

Willis, E.—"The Charleston Stage in the XVIIIth Century." 1924. XII.

Willis, W.—"The History of Portland, Maine." 1865. XVII.

Winterbotham, W.—"An Historical, Geographical, Commercial and Philosophical View of the United States of America." 4 vols. 1796. XVI.

Woolman, John—"Journal of." 1922. X.

Worthington, E.—"History of Dedham, Massachusetts." 1827.

Wright, G. F.—"Charles Grandison Finney." 1891. X.

Wright, T. G.—"Literary Culture in Early New England, 1620–1730." 1920.

Wroth, L. C.—"Parson Weems." 1911. III.

Y

"Yankees"—"The New Monthly Magazine. 1826."

INDEX

Date Due

Feb 16 '37			
MY 1 5 '63			
JUN 4 '64			